Four
in the Garden

RICK HOCKER

2015 Readers' Favorite
International Book Award Winner

ISBN: 978-0-9915577-0-7
Library of Congress Control Number: 2014905871
Printed in the United States of America
April 2014

Second Edition
May 2017

Author website: www.rickhocker.com

Cover image designed by Tomasz Zawadzki
Artist website: www.drawinglair.neocities.org

Dedication

In dedication to God who gave me the idea for this book and compelled me to write it. Thanks to my writing teacher, Sue Clark, who gave me the skills to write this book and polish it. Additional thanks to Sue Clark and David Brin who helped edit the manuscript. And thanks to Mark Gebhardt, Pilar Toledo, Cindy Lipton, John DiGennaro, Alex Davis, Jack Pantaleo, and Barbara Cole Brooks for their feedback.

Complimentary Gift

Download a transcript of Rick Hocker's speech on trusting in God, the main theme of this book. Your personal information will not be collected. Get your gift at rickhocker.com/freegift.html.

Connect with the Author

You can connect with the author, Rick Hocker, via his website. Subscribe to his mailing list or subscribe to receive free inspirational articles each month. Follow him on Facebook or subscribe to his blog. Visit his website for details at rickhocker.com.

Book Discussion Groups

Questions for discussion and reflection are provided at the back of this book and the author's website. For intensive group study spanning multiple meetings, download free questions from rickhocker.com/fourinthegarden/questions.html.

Forward

Every one of us is born hungry. Hungry for meaning. Hungry for connection. Hungry for love.

I believe the answer to our hunger is found in God. I'm not referring to the God of our understanding, but the God who transcends our understanding, the inscrutable God who defies our man-made definitions and imaginations. We do not capture and subdue God for purposes of study or control. Rather, we gaze and marvel so we might be changed. Learning to trust, we allow our limiting thoughts to drop away, freeing us to experience God and to find the meaning and connection we long for.

—Rick Hocker

"A hungry point of light blinked into being. This newborn star groped in the dark searching for meaning."

—Creator

Chapter 1

Birth

The warm sunlight touched my skin for the first time. With tender care for their precious cargo, the three Teachers laid my lifeless body on the soft grass in a forest meadow. Scattered clover stirred in the breeze that caused the nearby cypress trees to shiver with each breath. My mature body had firm limbs and shoulder-length hair. Creator had readied it to receive my soul.

The slender, human-like Teachers knelt around me and waited for me to awaken to life. Each Teacher possessed a pair of giant, feathered wings in addition to a pair of arms. Each wingtip connected to the nearest wingtip of the others by single hooked fingers, creating a circular enclosure around the four of us, a ring of feathers with me at its center. Their eyes twinkling, they gazed at me and smiled with loving adoration.

Creator had given the Teachers charge over me. He had appointed them to teach me about Him. They would soon discover that I was slow to learn and trust.

My first thoughts emerged like bubbles that surfaced from deep, secret waters, then popped, releasing their contents for me to ponder. My awareness focused on my self, alone. I explored the inner space I inhabited, a whole universe of being.

I gasped, sucking my first draft of air with greediness. Afterward, I felt the rhythmic rise and fall of my chest with each breath. Warmth penetrated the front of my body. Something soft and cool pressed my back. Soothing sighs whispered into my ears. Each sensation intrigued me and gave structure to my world.

When I opened my eyes, the overwhelming light caused me to squeeze them shut. Then I squinted and looked away from the brilliant light above me, allowing my eyes to adjust to the brightness. My breathing quickened as I beheld a dazzling display of colors, patterns, and movement.

I sat up to survey my surroundings, but I couldn't distinguish distinct forms from the visual information inundating me. After practicing to focus, I could discern shapes, though I didn't understand them. I couldn't yet comprehend that I was sitting within a forest clearing, encircled by three kneeling creatures who I thought were nothing more than scenery.

Beneath me, a dense layer of green, flexible blades cushioned my body. I brushed my hand over their soft texture and watched the blades snap back into place. Driven by curiosity, I extended my hand to touch a large shape, not knowing I was touching one of the winged creatures. They had no gender, but I refer to them as male in this story.

The creature responded by placing his hand atop my head, startling me. Iridescent emerald feathers on his throat gleamed in the sunlight. The tips of his wings and his large eyes were also emerald green. His massive nose curved like a beak toward the top of his feather-capped head. The feathers of his wings and head were gray-brown, speckled with dark chevron-shaped flecks. His body had smooth skin the color of tawny sandstone.

In a melodious and cheerful voice, he said, "Blessed are you, formed by Creator's wisdom and power, gifted with life by His abundant grace. You are Creator's handiwork, made from love and for love. He rejoices at your birth and delights in your being. Because He cherishes you, you shall be called Cherished. My name is

Manna. I express the words of Creator."

The other two creatures swept past me to position themselves in front of Manna. With flapping sounds, they reconfigured their wings as they dropped into in a kneeling position facing me, all the while keeping their wings linked.

The creature on the left placed both hands on his chest and spread his massive wings. He had the same form as Manna, but with ruby eyes, throat and wingtips. He was the largest of the three, with a broad chest. "My name is Ennoia. I fathom the mind of Creator," he said with a commanding, orotund voice. "Manna isn't the only one who speaks for Him. I speak when Creator discloses His innermost thoughts." Ennoia contracted his wings and became silent.

The third creature smiled and gazed at me with expressive sapphire-blue eyes that matched his throat and wingtips. He had the smallest frame and a few feathers sticking out of place atop his head. "I am Aable." The sound of his voice was high and crisp. "I am not a talker like those two," he said, glancing at the other creatures. "I do the works of Creator. My specialty is works, not words."

I lost track of myself as I watched this captivating activity play out before me. My ability to understand them amazed me. I listened, trying to grasp every word.

Manna shuffled forward and placed his hand on my leg. "Creator has given you the knowledge of language and the capacity for speech so you can understand us and communicate with us. Ask questions and speak freely. We will teach you everything you need to know. We are your servants."

The three beings bowed as they draped their wings on the ground.

I interpreted this gesture to signify that I was the dominant being in this foursome. As such, I took initiative and spoke my first words.

Chapter 2

Firsts

"Who is Creator?" I marveled to hear the words emerge from my mouth and to feel my tongue flap on its own accord.

The creatures looked at each other.

Ennoia said, "Creator is the maker of everything that is, has been, and will be. He is the source and destination of all things, the One Life of which you are now a part, the One who—"

With growing curiosity, I touched Ennoia's mouth, trying to understand the connection between its movements and the sounds emanating from it. The sounds stopped when my fingers landed on Ennoia's lips.

"Enough talk," Aable said to Ennoia.

Aable fixed his vivid blue eyes on me. "Stand up, Cherished."

The three winged beings stood in unison.

Wanting to imitate them, I stood, also. When I looked down and saw the ground far below me, I became light-headed. I wobbled, then fell backwards and landed on my butt. Bewildered, I stared up at Aable, wondering why I had failed at my first task.

"I'll help you," Aable said. He pulled me to my feet without breaking his links to Manna and Ennoia. After I got my balance, I let go of Aable. This time, standing unaided, I felt secure, not unsteady or dizzy as before.

"When you fall, we'll help you," Aable said. "You will fall again."

Ennoia made a gravelly sound in his throat. "What Aable meant to say," he glanced at Aable and touched his arm, and then looked at me, "is that the source of all help is Creator alone. Whenever help is needed, He will help you. Our roles are as teachers and guides, but Creator is the One in whom to place your full trust."

I squeezed my brows together. "What is trust?"

"Trust means to encharge one's well-being to another," Ennoia said.

"That won't do," Aable said, waving his hands at Ennoia. "Your words are too profound for the newling to grasp. And you, Manna, your flowery language makes it difficult for the newling to understand you. I say simple words are best."

"Simple words are often best," Manna said, "but, as you know, we must speak to provoke the mind to ponder, entice the heart to open, inspire the spirit to worship, and coax the soul to discover the treasures hidden within the words."

"You're right," Aable said. "Words must be chosen according to their effect. But this time, let's make things easier for the newling." Aable turned toward me. "Cherished, trust means to confidently depend on someone."

"I think I understand," I said. "But why should I trust Creator if I don't know Him?"

"You come to know Him by choosing to trust in Him," Ennoia said. "We will teach you how to trust Creator."

I wanted to know Creator, but this method sounded too complicated. "Why can't you show me Creator?"

"You don't yet know how to perceive Him," Manna said.

I didn't understand what Manna meant. Did my eyes need more practice at focusing? Did I have other senses that needed developing? I did figure out that the answer was no.

More confident now at being upright, I leaned on one foot and tested my weight. Then I shifted my weight onto my other foot.

Drawing from knowledge imparted at birth, I knew that "walking" meant to move one's feet forward in an alternating manner. I took a step with one foot, then the other, and repeated the sequence. I tottered across the meadow away from the Teachers.

"Wait. Where are you going?" Manna called after me.

They intercepted me before I gained much distance. Manna grasped my hand and said, "You can't go wandering off. Come with us. We have many things to show you."

Ennoia took the lead, his wings relaxed at mid-body. Manna and Aable traveled behind him, their outer wings curved forward to link with his wings. They positioned me between Manna and Aable, each holding one of my hands, their inner wings forming an arch over my head. The three beings walked with synchronized strides, gliding on their bony legs like three stalking herons. With an awkward gait, I tried to keep up, conscious of each step, fascinated by this form of travel.

I wanted to touch the nearby cypress trees, so I pulled my hands free and ran toward them. When I reached the nearest tree, I brushed my fingers across its flattened, lacy leaves. The Teachers caught up with me. Manna said, "You need to stay with us."

The Teachers surrounded me. Manna and Aable grabbed my hands, and the three guided me back to the spot where I had run off. We resumed our original route and steady pace. Without warning, the overhead winged arch dropped to become a feathered barrier behind me, boxing me in. I disliked the confinement. Whenever I slowed, Manna and Aable pressed their wings against my back to nudge me forward. After a few forceful prods, I began seeking an opportunity to escape.

Manna, who escorted me on the right, lectured. "Everything you see has been made by Creator. The ground beneath you is the world. The vast space above you is the sky. The bright object in the sky is the sun that provides light to the world. . . ."

With these first steps, I began my journey of life, unaware of how little I could influence its course.

Chapter 3

Initiation

The Teachers led me into the grove of cypress trees. Prolific plants and ambitious vines flourished across the ground, restricting where one could walk. The Teachers followed a worn, narrow path that forced us to travel single file. I found myself third in line with Aable behind me. Aable's wings reached forward at waist level to join Manna's wings ahead of me, enclosing me in a tight space. The Teachers had hooks at mid-wing as well as at their wingtips. Ennoia took the front, his wings folded back to join Manna's wings.

I swiveled my head trying to capture every detail around me. The variety, artistry and extravagance of Creator's world amazed me. Almost every plant was in full bloom, cloaked with dazzling hues that dripped in tapered clusters or sprayed upward like static fountains. Massive, mossy trees towered above us, shading us with their wide canopies. The plants and trees swayed under a warm breeze, their leaves sparkling with an inner radiance. I beheld a panorama of unending marvel. My chest felt as if it would burst from irrepressible awe.

Along the path, the outstretched stalks of scarlet amaryllis flowers beckoned my touch. When we stopped for a moment,

I reached over Aable's wings to stroke their silken petals before the procession resumed its advance. The confinement and forced march frustrated me. Why couldn't I explore this world on my own terms?

"Where is Creator?" I said.

"Everywhere," Ennoia said.

I looked around but saw no one. Was Creator hiding, watching us from behind the foliage? Why would Creator hide from me?

A multitude of smells inundated me. The pungent aromas of some flowers lingered long after we passed. Others had a sweet, intoxicating perfume that caused me to take slower, deeper breaths so as to prolong the sensation.

We maintained a slow, steady pace. As we walked, the Teachers identified various plants and trees, describing each with delight, as if they were seeing these wonders for the first time, as well. I shared in their infectious joy.

A tall stalk of clustered, purple flowers caught my attention. When we neared the plant, I said, "Stop. I want to see."

The Teachers stopped. I was grateful for the respite.

"That plant is a foxglove," Manna said.

"Fox . . . glove." Aable giggled. "I love that name."

The Teachers lifted their wings so I could get a closer look. I saw small things flying into the flowers.

"Those are bees," Manna said.

I placed my hands on my knees and bent over to watch the bees alight, then crawl into the flowers. "Are the bees part of the flowers?"

"The bees are separate creatures. Look at the ground and on the plants. You'll see many small creatures called insects."

To my amazement, I saw insects everywhere. When Aable pointed out a well-camouflaged leaf mantis, I stopped breathing from astonishment. I picked up a bee that had landed on a nearby flower. It wriggled between my fingers.

"Ow!" A sharp prick of pain stabbed my thumb. I released the bee. Then I flapped my hand to shake off the pain, but the pain persisted.

"Ah, Cherished," Manna said. "The bee stung you to make you let it go. From now on, you will find that the choices you make have consequences. The bee acted from instinct. But you can choose your actions." Manna pointed at me.

"Should I have not touched the bee?"

"The lesson here is if you touch a bee, you may or may not get stung. Whether you should touch a bee is up to you, not us."

The Teachers weren't being helpful. "How can I know the answer?"

"You must make many such choices on your journey. Your choices will determine your life."

Dumbfounded, I stared at Manna. What did his words have to do with bees?

"The newling is confused," Aable said to the others. "We should help."

"No," Ennoia said. "We shouldn't intervene. Uncertainty can be an impetus to seek the truth."

"Should we help or not? We must be unanimous in all things," Manna said in a firm voice. "Let's discuss this until unity is restored."

The Teachers spread their wings, creating a feathery dome over their bodies. Their voices became muffled.

Turning my attention to my injured thumb, I resumed flapping my hand, still hoping that doing so might end the throbbing pain.

I considered the risk of touching a bee again. Manna said that I may or may not get stung. Without a predictable outcome, how could I assess the risk? Gazing up at the trees, I pretended to be distracted, hoping to avoid having to commit to a decision. Why did I need to decide? Why did it matter? I resented the imposed responsibility. A bee didn't have to make choices. Why couldn't I be like the bee and experience life as it happens?

Chapter 4

Creatures

Something darted amidst the soaring branches overhead. I studied the dense upper foliage, but saw nothing but leaves. Was that Creator who moved through the trees? The Teachers, who had broken from their huddle, moved closer to me.

"Don't move, Cherished. Make no loud noises," Aable said. He extended an open palm in front of his chest.

Something swooped down onto Aable's palm. The creature was green and soft, smaller than my fist. It stood on two legs, jerking its yellow head, looking in all directions. I inflated with glee. "What is it? It's wonderful," I whispered.

"It's a bird," Manna whispered.

Captivated, I watched the bird, although it showed no interest in me. Risking another possible sting, I tried to touch the bird, but it startled me by flying away. Seeing the bird behave of its own volition thrilled me. Did Creator feel the same way about me? Or was He disinterested like the bird?

The Teachers resembled the bird in many ways. Their noses were shaped like beaks. They had feathers, wings and thin, bony legs. "Are you birds?"

"We're not birds," Ennoia said. "What we are is beyond what

you can comprehend."

Afterward, the Teachers brought me to a wide meadow where a herd of nimble, light-brown animals grazed amid tall pale-green grass. The Teachers stopped and raised their wings. We watched the herd from a distance. "Those animals are antelopes," Manna said. "Aren't they superb?" The Teachers fluttered their wings with satisfaction.

Enthralled by their streamlined forms and agile movements, I approached the antelopes to touch one, but they bounded away with powerful leaps. I tried again and again to draw near, believing they would accept me, but they sprang away each time. Disappointed, I returned to where the Teachers waited. Ennoia stood in front of Manna and Aable. His ruby throat-feathers gleamed in the sunlight.

"We praise your persistence," Manna said, "but persistence becomes foolishness when outcomes won't change."

"Make them stop so I can touch them," I demanded, glaring at Manna whose emerald eyes met my gaze.

Ennoia lifted his wings high and spread his feathers, casting his body in shadow. "No. You're the one who must stop. You don't command us," Ennoia said. His red eyes flashed.

His outstretched wings showed hidden golden feathers. They pulled Manna and Aable's wings up into the air. His threatening posture and sharp tone caused me to feel small and powerless. I couldn't look at his eyes.

"We shall leave the antelopes, now," Ennoia said.

The Teachers surrounded me, took my hands, and lowered their wings to enclose me. They began to walk away, forcing me to go with them. They traveled close to the trees at the meadow's edge. I plodded along, captive inside my roving pen, dragging my feet and snorting.

"Don't be angry, Cherished," Manna said. "Your well-being matters greatly to us as does that of the antelopes."

I paid only partial attention to his words.

Later, I recovered my curiosity when we encountered a small, short-legged creature foraging for food. Its back was covered with many short spines. Manna called it a hedgehog. The Teachers lifted their wings so I could examine the animal, but it waddled away, speeding up at my approach.

None of the animals allowed me to get near. Was there something about me that made them keep their distance? Did Creator keep His distance for the same reason?

We came to the edge of something immense and flat. The Teachers halted, raised their wings, and allowed me to study it. The sky and nearby trees were reflected on its surface. Yet, as I continued to peer, I could see the ground and vegetation beneath this strange substance, through its darkened pallor.

"That is water," Manna said. "Water is transparent and reflects its surroundings. Place your hand into it."

I bent down and pushed my hand into the cool, thick substance. Its surface recoiled in response to my unwelcome intrusion. I pulled out my hand and said, "Is the water alive?"

"No, but it keeps plants and animals alive, including you. That feeling of dryness in your mouth is thirst. Bring some water into your mouth."

I placed my wet fingers on my mouth. As the water moistened my lips and passed between them, coolness trickled down my throat and refreshed me. Wanting more, I knelt and lowered my face to the water so I could drink.

When I saw my face reflected on the water, I forgot my thirst. I stared and drank in the beauty of my own image. I studied the complex curves of my nose and lips, the soft shaping of my cheeks and jaw, the delicate texture of my hair, and my exquisite eyes. Gazing into my pupils, I glimpsed something infinite and eternal. Intrigued by this discovery, I peered further, but the mysterious world behind my pupils escaped me.

"You see your form," Manna said. "You're the only human Creator has made."

Chapter 5

Individuation

"You're unique compared to all the other creatures you've seen today," Manna said. "Creator's essence is infused into every living thing, but within you, alone, is placed a special connection, an umbilicore by which you have direct access to Him. You perceived Creator through your umbilicore when you looked into your eyes."

I continued to gaze at my reflection, unwilling to look away. "Is it true I'm the only human?"

"Yes. Your umbilicore is what makes you human."

I looked up at the Teachers. "When do I meet Creator?"

"Soon," Ennoia said. "He desires relationship with you. We'll teach you how to connect to Him, but now is not the time."

"Why not now?"

"You're not ready yet." Ennoia's wings began to lift and spread, showing golden feathers. His posture indicated that my wish would be denied again.

I looked at my reflection and released a loud sigh. My thirst demanded my urgent attention, so I scooped water into my cupped hands to drink. All the while, I stared with fascination at my reflection as it also drank from its cupped hands. I waited for the ripples to settle so I could marvel at my reflection again.

After I satisfied my thirst, Manna said, "Come. Let's continue our journey."

Instead of enclosing me within their wings, they started walking away. I hesitated and then followed.

We traveled along the lake's wide bank. Across the flat area, water flowed out of the lake as a narrow brook, tumbling over smooth stones. On the opposite side of the lake grew birch trees that stood close to the water's edge. The breeze caused the shiny birch leaves to whisper in unison.

Every so often, I bent down and trailed my fingers through the water to watch the resulting effects. Or I tossed a rock into the lake to view concentric circles radiate from the point of impact. The water enchanted me, drawing my gaze as I tried to keep up with the Teachers. I watched the ever-changing images of distorted trees and sky on the rippled surface of the lake. I could have stared at the water forever.

The Teachers maintained a slow and even pace, often looking back, keeping me in sight. Whenever I caught up with them, I heard them talking among themselves.

When the Teachers veered away from the shore, I took the opportunity to leave them and explore the lake on my own. Free at last from their supervision, I played among the trees, threw objects into the lake, and gouged the water's edge with a stick to watch the lake fill in the craters.

I brought my face close to my reflection to glimpse Creator, but I saw only myself. Something inside me needed to make contact, to experience Him in some way. I reached into the water hoping to lay hold of Creator behind my reflection, but I couldn't touch Him. He must have fled when I stirred my image on the water's surface.

I spotted a gray lizard sunning itself on a rock and crept up to it. I brought my hand as close as I dared, then, with a swift pounce, I grabbed the lizard. The lizard escaped except for its tail pinned under my hand. I picked up the tail and looked at it with astonishment. Was this the reason animals didn't want me to touch them?

"Come back," I called to the lizard, but it didn't return. I wanted to reattach its tail although I had no idea how. Guilt-ridden over having broken the lizard, I hid the tail under a rock and scurried away.

After a while, I began glancing behind me expecting to see the Teachers. They didn't come looking for me. For some reason that bothered me. Over time, my adventure lost its appeal.

Feeling dejected, I returned to the spot where I had abandoned the Teachers, although I took a meandering route back to them. As I approached, I saw them standing where I had left them. I slowed to a stop and waited to be reprimanded.

"Dear Cherished, chasing after you would have been as futile as trying to pet an antelope," Manna said with a smile, his emerald eyes twinkling. "We knew you'd come back. Are you ready, now, to follow us?"

"No," I said, looking down. "I want to stay by the lake."

"You do?" Ennoia said. "Shall we leave you here to fend for yourself?"

"I can manage."

"Perhaps you can. How will you navigate the forest when the sun descends, taking away the light to see your way?"

"Does the sun do that?"

"Yes. Not long from now. And that sensation in your stomach. How will you remedy that?"

I did feel unpleasant spasms rolling through my stomach.

"You need us. If you want Creator's help, you'll follow us." They walked away. None of them looked back.

At first, I stayed put. I disliked being coerced, and I resented my dependence on the Teachers. In the end, I chose the response that served me best, which was to stay close to the Teachers. I followed them into the trees, feeling smug for having made it my decision, not theirs.

Chapter 6

Discomfort

Under the arch formed by Manna and Aable's wings, I took Aable's hand and held it as we walked while Ennoia led the way. That connection comforted me.

Aable squeezed my hand and I squeezed back.

Manna turned and said, "It pleases us when you choose to be with us." His large eyes blinked as if he were trying to see me with a different focus. "We care about you, Cherished."

After a pause, he said, "You are mistaken if you think we don't care. We won't always affirm your wishes or actions, but that doesn't mean we disapprove of you. We—"

"You're wrong." I yanked my hand away from Aable. "I don't care what you think. I don't need your approval."

Manna sighed. "You already have our approval."

"Love hasn't yet taken root," Ennoia said to Manna.

"No. Not yet," Aable said, his sapphire-blue eyes gazing at me with longing and tenderness.

I looked away from Aable and stared at Ennoia's back, wishing I had made contact with Creator at the lake. If He desired to connect with me, then why was He so elusive?

The spasms in my stomach increased. They pulsed with every

heartbeat. I tried to stop the pain by clutching my stomach, but it didn't help.

The Teachers halted near a thorny bush laden with black clumps. "That discomfort in your stomach is hunger," Manna said. "This plant produces blackberries. Pull off a berry and put it into your mouth."

I squeezed the first berry too hard and it burst between my fingers. With a lighter grip, I plucked a second berry and pushed it into my mouth. Warm, moist and sweet, the blackberry produced a wonderful tingling sensation that traveled along my tongue. My jaw and tongue kicked into action, chewing and mashing the berry before swallowing it. Of the activities I had engaged in so far, eating surpassed them all.

The Teachers identified other berries and fruits and nuts, each having its own delicious flavor. Garnet-colored plums were my favorite. After several tries at shelling a walnut, I concluded that the exertion was unwarranted for such a small morsel.

Gray, furry animals scampered among the branches of the walnut trees. Manna called them squirrels. We watched them for a while, amused by their antics. A few of them descended the trees to snatch walnuts from the ground. I placed a walnut in my open palm to lure a squirrel, but they kept their distance. Frustrated by their indifference, I threw the nut at the squirrels and suggested we move on.

After two steps, a piercing pain under my right foot caused me to yelp. My body contracted without warning, forcing me down to the ground. All my attention pulled inward and focused on the pain. Whimpering, I pulled my foot around and looked at its underside. Smeared on the bottom of my foot was a dark red substance. Stunned and bewildered, I looked up at the Teachers.

"That's blood," Manna said in an even tone. "You cut your foot on a walnut shell fragment and spilled your blood. Blood is the fluid that feeds your body. The pain you feel is normal. Don't be alarmed."

Manna's words did nothing to ease my distress.

Aable crouched next to me and pulled the shard from my foot. Then, placing his hand on my foot, he peered into my eyes. The pain stopped and he removed his hand. When I examined my foot, I couldn't find the cut.

"Thank you, Aable," I said, grateful and relieved. In that moment, I realized how useful the Teachers could be.

"Thank Creator," Ennoia said. "He is the one who healed you."

I complied and said, "Thank You, Creator," feeling foolish addressing the air.

"The purpose of pain," Manna said, "is to inform you that something is wrong. Pay attention to pain because it teaches you what behaviors to avoid."

I interpreted his words to mean I should avoid actions that lead to pain. In this situation, that translated to not stepping on sharp objects. Yet I found myself threatened on all sides by walnut shell fragments that spread far and wide. I saw no escape from this predicament.

Chapter 7

Worry

After clearing away the shell fragments from the ground in front of me, I stood on the bare spot. Then I extricated myself from the walnut tree grove by jumping from patch to patch of exposed dirt while trying to keep my balance. The Teachers watched my silly performance, saying nothing, their wings twitching. Not until I was beyond the danger zone did I notice I could stand without pain.

Feeling safe, I relaxed a little. When I stepped on a small stone, my knees gave way as if my body expected pain. I found the nearest safe spot of ground and stepped onto it. As I looked for where to step next, I became dismayed. The entire ground was littered with rocks, twigs and debris, all threats to my well-being.

The Teachers walked to where I stood, unfazed by the walnut shells.

Manna said, "Your over-carefulness doesn't serve you."

"How else can I keep from hurting myself again?" I said, annoyed by Manna's unhelpfulness.

"Remember the squirrels we watched earlier? They leap from branch to branch without fear of falling. Sometimes, they do fall when they lose their footing or the branch breaks under their weight. After falling, they climb back into the trees and resume leaping. What do you think enables a squirrel to jump after a fall?"

"Stupidity?"

Aable chuckled.

Ennoia smiled.

Manna remained serious. "Try again."

I gave Manna what I imagined he wanted to hear. "Confidence."

"Good answer, Cherished. Does the squirrel place its confidence in its paws or in the branch?"

"Its paws, I suppose."

"The answer is neither."

"What? You tricked me." I frowned.

Manna smiled. "Its confidence is that it will recover from harm. Whether the branch fails or its paws fail, the squirrel believes it will be all right because it trusts in Creator."

"How can a squirrel be certain of that?"

"Squirrels don't experience certainty. Their simple minds believe in the continuation of their well-being. You, too, must learn to do the same."

"How can I believe in continued well-being when I have no guarantee I won't get hurt again?"

"You will get hurt again. Of that you can be certain. But you'll be all right. Creator will take care of you."

"Why should I have to experience pain at all?"

Ennoia intervened. "The soul attains full maturation when transformed by life of which pain is an integral component."

Bewildered, I shook my head. What did Ennoia mean by the soul?

Both Manna and Aable stared at Ennoia, who maintained an impassive face above his crossed arms. Manna looked at me and said, "What Ennoia meant was that pain is a necessary part of life."

"That may be true for squirrels, but not for me." I turned and stomped away.

The Teachers followed without saying a word. I paid meticulous attention to my path, seeking the route with the least amount of treacherous debris. Spying a rock on my path, I picked it up and examined it to decide whether it proved dangerous. It looked harmless and I tossed it aside. Spotting a prickly seed pod, I bent down to inspect it. In that moment, I realized that this method of checking for hazards was impractical.

I stopped and looked around for ideas. Seeing a nearby cherry tree, I approached it and examined its branches. I spotted a long, straight twig with a compact cluster of leaves attached at its end. The twig could be used to clear my path of debris. I tried to break off the twig, but the tree refused to release it, even when asking its permission.

The Teachers stepped up. Aable removed the twig with ease and handed it to me. "You don't need this, but we understand that you think you do."

I took the twig from Aable. Then I used the branch to sweep away any suspicious objects in front of me as I walked. After I had traveled twenty paces, I looked back at the Teachers, hoping for some affirmation of my cleverness, but their faces showed no expression. I wanted them to be impressed, so I couldn't help but feel disappointed.

My pace, now slowed by my thorough and systematic path-cleaning operation, enabled the Teachers to overtake me. Manna and Aable positioned themselves on each side of me, placing me beneath the arch of their linked wings. This time, Ennoia took the rear, allowing me to see ahead and providing an ample area for me to sweep. I interpreted this gesture as a small acknowledgment of my ingenuity. My feelings toward them warmed. Willing to engage the Teachers again, I said, "What is the soul?"

Chapter 8

Incomprehension

"The soul?" Manna said with a start. He glanced back at Ennoia. "Ennoia spoke of things you're not yet ready to understand."

Ennoia halted, forcing his joined companions to stop. Seeing this, I stopped, too. Ennoia said to Manna, "The speaker is responsible to deliver the words. The hearer is responsible to grasp them. The hearer doesn't lay hold of the speaker, but the words themselves. If the hearer is capable, then understanding occurs."

"Do you think the newling understands your words?" Aable asked Ennoia.

Ennoia waved his hands in front of his chest. "Of course not. My words are seeds planted in the hope that, in due time, they'll take root and give rise to understanding later. It's never too early to plant the seeds of knowledge."

Manna turned toward me and spoke slower than usual. "Cherished, I will explain the soul to you. The soul is one's core essence. Your body isn't your true identity, but only the container for your soul. Your soul is your true self."

"What I saw in my reflection wasn't me?"

"You saw your body. You can't see your soul."

"If I can't see it, then what value does it have?"

Aable gasped.

"That which is unseen always has the greatest value," Ennoia said.

"That's true," Manna said. "Creator has immeasurable value but His essence can't be seen."

My hope to meet Creator dissolved on hearing He was invisible, and thus, untouchable. "How can I ever know Creator if I can't see Him?"

"He can be known. You can't see the wind, but you can feel the breeze on your face and see the effects of the wind on the grass. You don't discount the wind because you can't see it. Creator's essence can be experienced through indirect means, such as your umbilicore."

How could something so important be invisible? I couldn't comprehend an untouchable Creator, so I dismissed the concept altogether. "Why should I believe you?"

"Why should you doubt?" Manna said with patience. "The truth is often hard to grasp."

"Understanding occurs when thought transcends itself, causing the mind to expand," Ennoia said.

"But a small mind resists what it can't understand," Aable said to Ennoia.

"My mind isn't small," I said, defensively. "The thoughts are too big for me."

"Creator is beyond comprehension," Manna said. "Nevertheless, He can be known and wants to be known."

I noticed the darkening sky. The forest shadows began consuming the details contained within them.

"When the sun descends, and the sky darkens, that is a sign for you to rest," Manna said. "We have selected a place where you can lie down and sleep. Follow us."

The Teachers led, and I followed, keeping enough distance behind them to brush my sweeper across the path. I swept with extra care because of the reduced visibility. The colors of the forest had dimmed to a palette of dark grays.

The Teachers stepped to the side of the path and waited. When I looked up and noticed, I stopped sweeping. They stared at me. When I caught their gaze, they turned to look at a spot on the ground ahead of me. Their wings twitched twice. I followed their gaze and saw a small animal about five paces away. In the fading light, I could see the animal's velvety gray fur, tiny black eyes and long fleshy snout.

I approached the animal with caution, not wishing it to scurry away. It remained motionless, unaffected by my advance. When I got close, I dropped into a squatting position. With hesitation, I touched the animal, discovering it to be stiff and cold.

With a quick jerk, I retracted my hand, repulsed by the animal's unresponsiveness. I poked its body a couple times with the end of my sweeper, trying to prod it into action. Its refusal to rouse disturbed me and defied the rules of nature I had seen today.

Chapter 9

Separation

"It's dead," Manna said. "It's a mole, but it has ceased living. What you see is an empty container. Everything must die in its time."

I stared at the mole, intrigued by its haunting stillness.

"We must go. We have little light left," Manna said.

I stood, my eyes fixed on the mole. Aable placed his hand on my sweeper. I gripped tighter and pulled it close.

"I'll sweep for you," Aable said.

Seeing goodwill in Aable's eyes, I let go, grateful to be relieved from sweeping.

The Teachers reconfigured their wings as Aable moved to the front. I walked behind Aable, between Ennoia and Manna, as the Teachers strode in unison while Aable swept the ground in rhythm with their steps. Manna grasped my right hand and held it. In that moment, I believed that nothing could harm me.

"Where did the mole's life go?" I said.

Ennoia said, "The mole's life has left its body and rejoined the One Life in which all living things share. The One Life is Creator. Death is separation from the body. Any separation of being is called death."

"Will I die?"

"Yes."

I wondered how it would feel when my life left my body. Would I fade away like the dimming light of the forest until I was no more?

"When I die, will I cease to be?"

"No. Death isn't a destructive end. Since all things are a part of Creator, He destroys nothing because He can't destroy Himself."

"So nothing is ever lost?"

"Nothing real. Only what is false or illusory will be annihilated in the end. When that time comes, whatever can't be connected will be separated from Creator, not destroyed."

What if I failed to connect to Creator? Would I remain separated from Him forever? My head became heavy, and I let it droop.

"Cherished, look at me," Manna said.

I looked at his face.

"Remember your name. Creator cherishes you. He would never cast you aside. You are connected to Him, even though you don't feel it. Ennoia wasn't speaking about you, but things far in the future." He gave Ennoia a long stare.

Ennoia smiled and shrugged. "Planting seeds of knowledge," he said without apology.

"What will my death be like?" I said.

"When your soul departs your body," Manna said, "it will travel down the conduit of your umbilicore to join with Creator."

"So I will get to meet Him at last?"

"You will meet Him before then, Cherished."

We arrived at a grassy depression between two large oak trees. Someone had cleared the leaf litter from a patch of grass. By the time we reached the spot, the world had transformed into a darkened landscape drained of all color and glow. The trees were now black, having lost any suggestion of volume. The obsidian sky appeared weighted with its dense sprinkling of white flecks.

I imagined Creator was watching me from behind that black veil, keeping still lest I should detect His movement. Why did He need to hide from me? In spite of Manna's words, I felt separated from Creator. If I could join Him, then I would understand Him.

"You'll be comfortable here," Aable said while handing me my sweeper. "We'll leave you now and meet with you tomorrow."

My insides contracted. All at once, the darkness seemed much darker, almost palpable. "Won't you stay with me?"

With a softened voice, Ennoia said, "No. You must learn to trust us and believe that we'll return."

"Don't go. Please stay." My heart pounded.

"Dear Cherished," Manna said, touching me below my neck, "we're always with you."

In the faint light, I saw Aable gazing at me with compassion, as though seeing my fearful thoughts.

The Teachers stretched their wings to full extension, high above their heads. Without warning, they thrust their wings down with a loud whoosh. The blast of air caused me to shut my eyes. When I opened them, the Teachers had disappeared.

I gawked at the darkness, forgetting to breathe. As if I had been punched in the stomach, I dropped to my knees and gasped with shallow breaths. The Teachers had abandoned me. I hadn't realized how attached to them I had become.

I scrunched my face. "They should have stayed," I mumbled. "They should have stayed."

Chapter 10

Abandonment

Seated on the thick grass, I sulked and fumed. I fidgeted with my sweeper, rolling it between my hand and thigh or dragging the end across the dead leaves to hear them crackle. Why did I allow the Teachers to have such control over me? They were teachers, not friends, I reminded myself. If death were separation, then the Teachers' departure had caused me to die. A piece of my life had left my body.

"Creator, I need You." I said to the darkness.

The leaves in the branches above me rustled in the night breeze. Their sound didn't comfort me.

Lying on my side, I brought my knees close to my chest. The disquieting noises of unseen nighttime activity surrounded me. The ache of abandonment gnawed at my ribs. I felt insignificant and lost as if the darkness had hidden me from Creator's eyes.

"We're with you always, Cherished," Manna's voice whispered in my ear.

"Leave me alone," I said, refusing to listen.

I gripped my sweeper with both hands and wrapped my legs around it. In my sweeper, I found comfort. More than a twig, it became my protector, my consoler, and my companion. I shut my eyes, trying to block my feelings, but they refused to leave. As the long night dragged on, I watched the procession of my thoughts, which behaved on their own like the little green bird from today. One by one, each little green thought took flight into the branches above until none were left.

A series of scenes visited me that night. First, I was chasing an antelope, trying to touch it. Whenever I got close, the antelope would leap away. I pursued it for what seemed an endless time, never reaching it.

Then I became the antelope. The sun was chasing me, but I didn't trust it, so I kept fleeing. The unrelenting sun pursued me on and on, and I became fatigued. My chest heaved. My lungs burned. When exhaustion forced me to stop, the sun caught up.

The sun warmed me with its gaze, assuring me it meant no harm. From within the sun's disk, three disembodied hands emerged. The hands drifted close until they were touching my fur. They stroked my antelope neck and back with long, gentle caresses. I relaxed and began to trust. A hand scratched behind my ear and I inclined my neck in pleasure. I believed I was the most special antelope in the universe.

A colossal black leaf entered the scene. The leaf was ancient and brittle, pierced with many tiny holes made by insects and decay. It floated between me and the sun, blocking the sun's light except for the stars created by the holes in the blackened leaf.

The darkness obscured the three floating hands, but they still touched me, comforted me.

Upon waking the next morning, I sat up and looked around. I found myself in a wide, grassy meadow occupied by two enormous oak trees in the center, their branches overlapping. My sleeping patch was located in a shallow depression between the two trees. Smaller trees and clusters of ferns defined the meadow's perimeter. A peaceful stillness bathed the scene. The sky was imbued with amber light and spotted with yellow-orange splashes. I couldn't find the sun, but knew it was present.

"We watched over you while you slept," Manna's voice said.

I jerked my head left and right, frowning when I saw no one. With a sudden pang, I remembered the Teachers had deserted me last night. "Why did you leave me?" I said, still looking for them.

"We never left. We're with you even when you can't see us."

"If I can't see or feel you, then you're not here." I moved my arms through the air trying to intercept the invisible source of the voice.

"Cherished, you must learn to depend on what is beyond your senses, because when darkness comes, your senses won't serve you."

In an instant, the Teachers popped into view. They sat cross-legged surrounding me, their six wingtips joined at a point above my body, creating a feathered canopy.

"Creator heard your request last night," Manna said.

"He wants to touch you today," Aable said with a wide smile.

"I don't want to be touched," I snapped. "I want to be respected."

Chapter 11

Connectedness

"You're not asking for respect," Manna said. "You're asking for control. We'll respect your requests, but we're not obligated to comply."

"If you respected me, then you would do what I ask."

"That's not how it works. To respect you is to do what's best for you."

"Was it best to abandon me last night?" A twinge of insecurity poked my chest, causing me to look for my sweeper.

"We didn't abandon you, Cherished. We stayed with you all night."

Having found my sweeper, I held it across my legs, gripping it tight with both hands. "I felt abandoned."

"Then we ask you to forgive us." All three bowed their heads.

"What?"

"You experienced real feelings of abandonment last night. Forgive us for causing you that distress."

I relaxed my grip. "So you didn't intend to hurt me?"

"No. Never." The Teachers' eyes became shiny.

Ennoia heaved his broad chest and said, "Your welfare is our priority."

"In that case, I guess I forgive you."

"And we forgive you, Cherished," Ennoia said.

The feathered canopy split apart as the Teachers pulled their wings behind them. Their linked wings formed a ring that encircled the four of us. They shuffled forward on their knees until they were right next to me.

"Let us show you our affection," Aable said. They wrapped their arms around me and squeezed.

Although enclosed by their arms, I didn't feel confined. I felt as wide as the sky. A rush of well-being coursed through my body. I relaxed and lost myself in their embrace. I leaned my head against Manna's chest and closed my eyes, my head tucked beneath his chin.

A stream of contented bliss poured into me from a source deep inside. Curiosity turned into understanding when I realized this stream flowed into me through my umbilicore, my invisible connection to Creator. This stream transported me into another realm. My surroundings faded from awareness. I lost sense of the passage of time. I floated within an expanse of light that held and comforted me. My sense of self dissolved as I merged into an infinite vastness. I didn't resist because I felt safe and nourished by the love that enveloped me.

When I opened my eyes, I saw the Teachers sitting around me as before. When did they break the embrace? My blissful state collapsed in an instant. Would it have continued if I hadn't opened my eyes?

"Opening your eyes didn't end the experience," Manna said. "Your belief in separateness ended it."

Still dazed by the experience, I tried to gather myself. "My belief ended it?"

"Yes. When you believe in connection, you open yourself to Creator whose life can flow into you through your umbilicore. When you believe in separateness, your connections are disabled. Don't let the physical world, with its separate forms, deceive you into thinking you're separate."

"I can connect to Creator just by believing I'm connected?"

"Yes," Aable said, "but it's not as easy as it sounds."

Eager for more, I closed my eyes and tried to reconnect, forcing myself to believe. After much struggling, nothing happened. I opened my eyes and looked at Aable, "It doesn't work."

Aable smiled. "You're trying too hard. Connectedness is a state of being, not something you do through effort or concentration. Creator gave you a spirit so you can experience Him. Close your eyes and fix your attention on your body."

I shut my eyes and became conscious of every limb and part.

"Think no thoughts," Aable said.

I cleared my mind as best I could.

"Good. Now, place your focus on your most inward center. That's where your umbilicore is."

I drilled down, seeking the center within my center. When I connected to it, life-giving streams resumed flowing through my umbilicore. I had rejoined Creator.

"Thanks, Aable. It worked."

As soon as I spoke, the experience faded.

"Aw, I lost it again."

Aable put his hand on my knee. "It's all right, Cherished. Give yourself time to learn."

I dropped my head and pursed my lips. "Something is wrong with me."

"Nothing is wrong with you," Manna said. "Anything you do will always be imperfect. This is by design, not to make you feel bad, but to inspire you to improve. That which is perfect can't improve. Because Creator intends that you learn and grow, you will fall short and make mistakes."

"So I'll never be perfect?"

"That's true, but you'll make fewer mistakes as you grow."

I sighed with dismay. The Teachers maintained serene expressions as if oblivious to the turmoil that churned inside me.

Chapter 12

Reattachment

The Teachers stood in unison. I picked up my sweeper and stood, also.

Ennoia said, "We're going to play a game. Manna and Aable will hide nearby. Your goal is to find them and touch them."

Manna and Aable vanished, leaving Ennoia standing alone. Ennoia grimaced for a moment, then relaxed a little, but his face remained taut with discomfort. That was the first time I had seen them separated.

Ennoia said, "Try to find Manna and Aable."

That was a cruel command that guaranteed another failure. "But they're invisible."

"Not this time. They're visible, but concealed."

"Why am I supposed to find them?"

"It's a game. It'll be fun."

I sighed. Another situation where the Teachers were telling me what to do. It was becoming clear to me how little freedom I had.

Dead leaves covered the ground beneath the two oak trees. With forceful swipes of my sweeper, I smacked the leaves aside to clear a path. Ten paces out, I stopped and looked around. Ennoia didn't move, but watched me. Looking behind me, I noticed an unusual bulge along the side of the nearest tree. I circled around the massive trunk, whacking dead leaves aside with my sweeper.

Two giant, flattened wings blended into the bark like a camouflaged moth. The green wingtips merged into the color of the grass at the base of the tree. The precise placement of Manna's wings covered his body from head to feet. I sneaked up to him and touched his wing.

Manna turned around and laughed. "You found me. How clever you are."

I laughed, also. Manna gave me a quick hug, and then held my hand as we walked back to Ennoia. When he got close to Ennoia, they linked wings and he released my hand.

Ennoia said, "Now, you need to find Aable."

I checked behind the second oak tree, but Aable wasn't there. Venturing beyond the two giant trees, I scanned the wide meadow. It was flat and devoid of features except for a few boulders that were too small to hide behind. Every boulder was dark-gray and covered with yellow lichen, except one that was gray-brown and clean. As I approached the unique boulder, I figured that Aable had wrapped his wings in a ball around his crouched body. I hurried to the false boulder, but before I reached it, Aable threw open his wings, sprung up and grabbed me, shouting, "I got you."

I tried to break free. When I succeeded, Aable tackled me and we fell to the ground, laughing. After recovering, I rested on my back watching the slow drift of wispy clouds across the sky. Shadows crossed my face and I sat up. Ennoia and Manna had caught up with us and linked to Aable who was now standing. They seemed more relaxed after being reconnected.

"You must not like being separated," I said.

Ennoia said, "To be apart is painful and loathsome to us. Our well-being is based on connection and unity."

"Cherished, your turn to hide," Aable said. "I'll count from a hundred down to one. When I'm through counting, we'll start looking for you. Run and hide. See, we're covering our eyes." All three placed their hands over their eyes. "One hundred, nine-ty-nine, ninety-eight . . ."

Excited, I sprinted toward the nearest trees at the edge of the meadow. I carried my sweeper, since my haste made it useless. I climbed to the top of a large tree and hid among its dense leaves. After I got settled, I peered through the foliage and saw the Teachers still covering their eyes.

When Aable stopped counting, they began walking straight toward me. I knew, then, that they had cheated. They continued past my tree, muttering something about hearing me run this direction. Later, they stood beneath me, talking among themselves. "How will we ever find Cherished? This could take forever."

I giggled and gave myself away.

Ennoia looked up and said, "There you are. What an excellent hiding place. Climb down and we can play some more."

After I reached the ground, they rubbed my back and the top of my head, saying, "Well done, Cherished."

A wide smile lingered on my face. I enjoyed being good at something.

Ennoia said, "It's our turn to hide." All three vanished with a downward swoop of their wings.

With a mountain of confidence, I searched for them, ignoring my need to sweep. I looked behind trees, bushes and boulders, and scanned the branches above me. Finding them was more diffi-cult this time. Too difficult. I decided that hiding was more fun, so I found a superb hiding place between a giant boulder and a large, leafy fern. After tucking myself into the gap, I waited for them to find me.

A long time passed.

No one came.

I felt the same as when they deserted me the night before. Why did I keep letting them trick me into trusting them?

Giving up, I returned to the meadow and found the Teachers sitting in a circle under the shade of the oak trees, their wings joined in a ring. I approached them and stood outside their circle.

"We waited for you to find us," Manna said.

"I waited, too," I growled.

The Teachers closed their eyes and became silent.

I noticed a giant, red stone in the center of the Teachers' circle. The stone was not there before. Spread on top of the flat stone were leaves, stalks and roots.

"While you were gone, Creator brought some food for you," Manna said, gesturing toward the items on the stone.

"Creator was here?" I said, perturbed. "Why didn't you get me?"

"We waited for you, but you didn't come," Manna said.

Ennoia said, "There's a time to seek and a time to be found. Each brings its own reward, unless you misinterpret the time. If you know the proper time, the reward for patience is connectedness."

"I don't know what that means," I said, "but you should have fetched me."

Chapter 13

Consternation

"If you had looked for us, you would have been here when Creator delivered this food," Manna said.

I imagined the huge, red stone floating down from the sky. Although invisible, Creator had been present, and my foolishness had deprived me of experiencing Him. I pinched my lips together in frustration.

Manna pointed to each pile of food on the stone. "This is chard, celery and parsnips. You haven't yet learned that leaves, stems and roots can be edible. Come here and eat some."

Standing in place, I beat my sweeper against the side of my leg as I considered the invitation. I didn't want to cooperate, but I couldn't refuse an offer of food when I was hungry. I assented with a loud sigh.

Ducking under the Teachers' wings, I entered their circle and sat by the stone table. I ate the food, moving from pile to pile. Although the flavors were mild, the food satisfied my hunger. After I finished eating, I said, "When I'm hungry again, I can eat any plant I want?"

"No. You can't," Manna said. "Some plants are poisonous and can kill you."

"Kill?"

"Cause you to die."

"Die?" My voice increased in pitch and volume.

I remembered the dead mole, its body empty and cold. "Why would Creator make plants that would kill me? Does He intend my harm?"

Ennoia groaned.

Aable shook his head.

Manna closed his green eyes for a moment. "Dear Cherished, nothing in the universe is designed to harm you. But some things can harm you in certain situations. Remember the walnut shell you stepped on? It wasn't designed to hurt you. It had the power to harm you only if you stepped on it. Likewise, some plants can harm you only if you eat them."

"Creator should never have created those plants in the first place," I said. "He should destroy them."

Ennoia answered with patience. "The universe has no flaws. Creator has made so many kinds of plants that not all of them are edible or are meant to be."

Ennoia's words didn't ease my concern. Did Creator care for my well-being at all? "Tell Him to fix things so I can eat any plant and not have to worry."

"Nothing needs to be fixed," Manna said in an even tone. "Everything is as it should be."

"Why aren't you listening?" I clenched my fists and glared at them.

"We hear you, Cherished. Your concern is unreasonable. Creator will protect you from poisonous plants. Besides, greater threats than that exist."

Manna looked at Ennoia and Aable who each nodded in return. "At this moment, a dangerous animal is hiding behind the bushes over there." Manna pointed to a clump of thick foliage at the edge of the meadow.

I turned around but saw nothing.

"The animal is a tiger. Tigers kill and eat other animals. This tiger is hungry and has been watching us, waiting for an opportunity to strike."

I continued scanning the bushes but still saw nothing. I turned and stared at Manna, trying to detect any sign of trickery in his expression.

"An animal wants to eat me?" I pictured a giant praying mantis nibbling away at my limbs until nothing remained. My heart banged against the inside of my chest.

"It won't if you follow our instructions," Manna said in a calm voice.

"Why can't one of you take care of it?" I looked at Ennoia and Aable, who returned earnest gazes.

"No. You must learn to trust," Manna said.

"But I can't do anything."

"Yes, you can. Walk toward the tiger while waving your arms and shouting. The tiger will become frightened and run away."

"I don't think—"

"Don't argue. Do it." Manna's voice pierced me. In that moment, I feared Manna more than the tiger.

Chapter 14

Indignation

With great reluctance, I left the safety of the Teachers' circle. I tramped toward the bushes waving my arms and yelling, the motions feeling unreal. When I was halfway to its location, an enormous, striped animal stepped out from behind the bushes. It looked at me with fierce yellow eyes.

I stopped moving and breathing.

Something welled up inside me, causing me to shout louder than ever, surprising myself. I shook my arms with frantic force.

The tiger bounded into the woods. I watched it until the plants obscured it. After it was gone, I discovered I was panting hard.

Shaken, I returned to the Teachers' circle and stood next to the stone table. "I'm much less afraid of poisonous plants, now," I said, still breathless. "That's a small worry compared to being killed and eaten."

"True, but for the tiger, that would be deemed a good day," Aable said with a chuckle.

"That's not funny," I said.

"Don't be afraid of harm," Manna said. "You should regard any danger as an opportunity to trust in Creator."

"I will not become a tiger's meal," I insisted.

41

"Creator will protect you," Ennoia said.

My face became hot. "You don't get it. I don't want tigers or poisonous plants," I yelled, spinning around to address all of them. My muscles quivered. I slapped the top of the stone table with my palms. "Creator must listen to me."

I pushed the stone table, trying to overturn it, gritting my teeth. The stone wouldn't budge and I groaned in frustration. By this time, the Teachers were standing. I stormed between Aable and Ennoia and swung my fists upward from below their linked wingtips, breaking their connection. I charged toward the link between Ennoia and Manna to split it apart, but before I succeeded, they grabbed my wrists and held tight. I squirmed to break free. Realizing I couldn't escape, I started kicking them. When I saw Aable holding my sweeper with both hands, bending it at a sharp angle, to the point of breaking, I froze.

"Don't," I said.

Aable held that pose, eyes fixed on me. No one spoke. Then the atmosphere changed. A rippling energy entered the meadow and caused my body to tremble. I felt pressure on my chest that immobilized me and made breathing difficult.

"I AM," boomed a voice I didn't recognize.

The two words, having power all their own, penetrated my being. My body quaked as the words passed through me like a current of intense energy. I cringed.

"Who are you?" I whispered, gasping for air. I looked around but saw no one. The Teachers didn't move.

"I am Creator, your maker. Your behavior has roused Me. Prepare yourself because I will test you."

The voice was deep and resonant. It made me shudder like a leaf in a powerful wind. My shallow breathing quickened.

"This little twig of yours. Does it have importance to you?"

I looked at the bent twig in Aable's hands. "Yes, Creator."

"Did you fabricate its structure? Did you create it by your own intelligence?"

42

"No." I looked down at the ground.

"If you care so much about your twig, a twig that you did not make, then how much more do I care about the world that I formed by my wisdom and power? Who are you to find fault with my world? Or to find fault with Me? Everything I have made has a purpose. What you consider threats to your well-being are intended to be demonstrations of my protection and deliverance. You can't know Me without experiencing my interventions in your life. Do not question my ways. Ennoia, Manna and Aable know my ways. Listen to them."

My chest hurt as if it were caving in. "I'm sorry, Creator. I know nothing about Your ways. I know nothing at all."

The Teachers smiled.

"I accept your apology, Cherished. Your humility opens you to everything I want to give you," Creator said. "You are loved and forgiven. Because I love you, I correct and discipline you."

The voice stopped. The energy and pressure ended. Manna and Ennoia released my wrists. I didn't look at their faces. Aable held out my sweeper, still intact. I took my sweeper, saying nothing. Then I turned around and stumbled away, feeling defeated. All this time, I had looked forward to meeting Creator, but I didn't expect Him to be so fearsome.

The Teachers followed at a distance. I kept my head down. Seeing an acorn, I whacked it with my sweeper as hard as I could. That was the limit of my power over the universe.

Chapter 15

Rules

After trailing behind me for a while, the Teachers took their positions next to me and we walked without speaking.

Ennoia said, "You can't do anything you please, Cherished. Creator has framed rules within the universe."

I listened but didn't look at Ennoia. I kept my eyes on the ground in front of me.

Ennoia continued. "Rules help you to learn and grow. For example, eating has limits. You can eat too much or too much of one thing, or eat something harmful. Without rules, you would never learn such things as moderation, balance, and judgment. If you break the rules, the consequences will be your teacher."

My imagination entertained a world without rules. As it played out in my mind for my amusement, my imagined world turned into chaos. Boulders rolled across the landscape in herds. Birds spun webs as they flew. The sun wandered off on a whim. Rules provided value, I decided, but I had no intention of admitting that to the Teachers.

We entered the cool shade within a grove of towering gum trees. The breeze rustled through the treetops high overhead. Massive, gray trunks branched upward with ardent determination. The enormous scale of the trees endowed the forest with a majestic presence, as if the life that emanated from them was more robust, more wondrous. I looked up with awe at the soaring branches that dripped with green moss. The Teachers stood close together gazing upward as well.

"I like the giant trees," I said, my head tilted back. "They have a stronger presence than other trees. They seem to understand life. Maybe because they're so old, they've learned all the rules of the universe." My stomach rumbled. "I also like fruit trees. I'm glad Creator made them for me."

"He didn't make fruit trees for your pleasure alone," Manna said. "You're not the focus of the universe, which operated fine before you came along. You're unique, but that doesn't make you superior. Do you think you're better than these trees?"

I considered the answer for a moment, wondering if this was a trick question. "Yes."

"Can you grow to such height? Can you dig deep into the ground and split solid rock? Can you hold out your arms day and night and never tire?"

It was a trick question after all. "No. I don't think I can. If I'm not better than one of these trees, am I better than a bird?"

"No. You're not," Ennoia said. "Your life is the same as a bird's life, since life is life. But you have greater spiritual value than a bird because of your soul. More so because Creator has chosen to love you. You are the sole object of His love. His love isn't based on anything you've done, so you can't judge yourself superior because of it."

I didn't know how to judge myself at all since I had no basis by which to compare myself. I didn't dare ask whether I was better than a slug.

Leaving the grove, we climbed uphill. The landscape changed as we ascended. Trees became sparser and outcrops of jagged rocks more frequent. I slowed my pace and stepped with care, wishing to return to soft dirt paths. I used my sweeper as best I could on the uneven terrain.

At the top of our long climb, we stopped to enjoy the view. Past the green valley below, I saw a range of sepia-colored mountains in the far distance. Beyond that, yellow clouds rubbed the bottom of the orange sun.

Climbing further, the ground leveled off and presented us with a stand of cherry trees. We stopped to pick cherries. Remembering Creator's gift of food on the stone table, I searched for the largest stone and placed the cherries on top as an act of gratitude for my meal. Then I ate the cherries, placing the pits in a pile on top of the improvised table, all the while figuring out how to avoid eating deadly plants by accident. After I finished, I said, "Let's gather samples from every poisonous plant so I can compare my food to them before eating."

Ennoia sighed.

Aable shook his head.

Manna pinched his large nose with his right hand.

None of them appeared impressed by my idea.

"The purpose of rules is for you to trust Creator," Manna said. "He doesn't want you to burden yourself with unnecessary rules. Better to trust in Him than in your self-imposed formulas."

"How will I know what plants I shouldn't eat?"

"We'll show you."

"What if I forget?"

"We'll remind you. You must trust Creator with what you eat. If you become ill from eating a poisonous plant, can you trust Him with your illness?"

I gasped in distress. "Illness? You said you'd stop me from eating a poisonous plant. What are you saying?" My distrust of the Teachers increased tenfold.

Chapter 16

Fear

"Creator may let you eat a poisonous plant and become ill," Manna said. "Even then, He will take care of you."

"If He means to take care of me, He should protect me." How could the Teachers not see this logic?

"He will do what is most needed in your life in that moment. He might use illness to teach you patience, weakness, or dependency, or show His love by healing you. He wants you to trust Him in all circumstances."

"So I have no guarantee of safety?"

"Your only guarantee is that He loves you and will take care of you."

I turned toward Aable, hoping for more assurance than Manna had given. "Can you help me, Aable?"

Aable peered into me with his wide blue eyes. A knowing look appeared on his face. "Fear has made its home in you, Cherished. When fear is strongest, you won't trust. When trust is strongest, you won't fear."

Aable's statement alarmed me. Now that he had called out my fear, I saw how much it controlled my thoughts and actions.

Ennoia said, "Will you trust Creator with your life?"

"I can't. I want to, but. . . ." My chest tightened and my throat squeezed shut. I sat on the stone with the cherry pits, dropped my elbows to my knees, and lowered my head into my hands. I had failed again.

"We must help the newling," Aable said to Manna and Ennoia.

I lifted my head and looked at the Teachers, hoping they could help.

"Trust can't be imparted. It's a choice," Manna said to Aable.

Ennoia said, "We can plant a seed and help nurture trust."

"Trust can't grow if fear is greater," Manna said. "We must first address the fear."

"Yes. We must disable fear's power," Aable said.

The Teachers approached, and Aable placed his hand on my shoulder. "It's all right you're unable to trust Creator right now. Can you believe that He will help you to trust?"

"Yes. I can do that."

"Good. That is the first step in trusting."

Fear's grip loosened a little. A sliver of hope lodged in my soul.

"The sun is setting," Manna said. "Let's return to the meadow so you can sleep."

The Teachers began descending by a different route that was more treacherous than the way up.

"We didn't come this way," I said.

"This way is shorter," Manna said.

I had a bad feeling about following them. The alternative was to return alone by the way we came, but I wasn't sure of the way. That left me no choice but to follow.

The light faded with great speed. I understood why the Teachers wanted to take a shortcut. This route was steeper with jagged rocks and thorny plants. I took cautious steps in the dimming light, zigzagging to avoid the thornbushes and rocks. Ahead of me, the Teachers traveled down the slope in a straight line, unaffected by any obstacles. They stopped to wait for me to catch up. Reaching them, they continued down the steep, rocky hill.

When I could no longer see where I was stepping, I stopped and said, "I can't go any further."

I heard Manna say, "You have to." The darkness hid the Teachers from sight.

"This is bad. This is bad. Why did you take me up here in the first place?"

"We have our reasons."

I clenched my jaw and sliced the air with my sweeper. The Teachers had manipulated me again. Because of them, I would have to spend the night on this rocky slope.

"Are there tigers up here?" I said, my worry escalating. If a tiger ventured up this hill, I wouldn't see it coming.

"Sometimes," Manna said, "but don't dwell on that."

"How will I protect myself? I can't see anything. I can't move." My fears swam in erratic circles inside me like a school of frightened fish.

"Creator will protect you. He will help you get back to the meadow."

"How?"

Chapter 17

Trust

"You must trust Creator to guide your steps," Aable said. "Step and trust."

"I might fall."

"Step and trust."

"I might hurt myself."

"Step and trust. You have no choice."

Despising the Teachers for my predicament, I tightened my grip on my sweeper. Then I took a deep breath. With enormous fear, I stepped into the darkness.

My foot landed without incident.

I took another scary step down the hill, expecting something to trip me.

Nothing happened.

Then another step into the unknown.

Still safe.

"Creator will protect you," Aable said. "Trust in Him."

With each step, I marveled more and more. Why didn't I trip and fall? Where were the jagged rocks and thornbushes? It felt as if the ground lifted to catch my foot. In the darkness, an unseen magic was operating on my behalf. Frightened and wonderstruck,

I traveled down the slope, placing one cautious foot at a time into the black night in front of me.

After innumerable steps, when the ground leveled off, Manna said, "We've arrived."

"I can't believe I made it down the hill," I said, more relieved than amazed.

"Not just that. You're at the meadow. You're standing at your sleeping spot."

I bent down and touched the thick grass at my feet. "That's impossible."

"Nothing is impossible for Creator."

"Then why didn't He bring me here right away? Why did I have to walk in the dark?"

"Because He wanted you to learn to trust in Him."

A chill shivered through my body. "Will you be leaving me now?"

"Yes. Your trust in Creator grew tonight."

"I was afraid."

"But you trusted in spite of it. That's all He asks. Sleep well, Cherished."

"See you tomorrow, newling," Aable said.

Ennoia said, "We love you, Cherished. We're proud of you."

A blast of night air informed me they had departed. My insides felt hollow. Another death within me. "I hate nighttime," I said, gritting my teeth.

I lowered myself onto the cool grass and curled up, wrapping my legs around my sweeper. My scrambled thoughts kept returning to Creator. He was as mysterious as ever.

A sound woke me. Something tramped nearby, crushing leaves as it went. I opened my eyes but saw nothing but black, except for the stars that shone with indifference. I froze. The hungry tiger had returned for its intended meal. If I couldn't see the tiger, maybe it couldn't see me. I didn't make a sound, hoping it wouldn't hear me. My pulse thrummed in my ears. I took slow, shallow breaths and listened to the crunching noises.

Protect me, Creator, I pleaded in my thoughts. Trust in Him. I must trust in Him to protect me. When I walked down the hill in the darkness, I had trusted in Him. I will trust again. He will protect me.

From a deep place in my being, comfort and peace flowed into my soul. It felt as if warm, soothing water were pouring into me through my umbilicore, rinsing away my fear. Calm assurance rose within me. I knew I had nothing to fear. I would be all right. My pulse relaxed, and I drifted back asleep.

When I awoke again, the sky was bright and cloudless. I sat up and looked for any signs of a nighttime visitor, but saw nothing unusual.

Did the Teachers keep watch over me during the night? "Are you here?"

"Yes," Manna said. The Teachers appeared around me, sitting crossed-legged, their six wings joined above me, creating a canopy. "A curious visitor came last night to inspect you, but we didn't allow it to get too close."

"Was it a tiger?"

"No."

"What was it?"

"A threat. You're not ready to understand these things yet." Manna looked at Ennoia as if expecting to be contradicted, but Ennoia said nothing. The Teachers pulled their wings back to form an outer ring.

I wanted to know more, but knew the discussion was closed. "Will we visit new places today?"

"No. Today, you'll work."

"What do you mean?"

"We will teach you how to build a shelter. You're not safe sleeping in the open."

"Are you saying Creator can't protect me?"

Chapter 18

Defiance

"Creator will protect you from threats to your soul," Manna said. "A shelter will protect you from dangerous beasts, but its main purpose is to protect you from the weather."

"The weather?" Why would Manna associate the weather with dangerous beasts?

"The weather isn't constant. Sometimes, water falls from the sky. That's called rain."

"Is rain bad?"

"No. It's good for the plants. But it can be cold and unpleasant when the wind blows."

"Tell Creator to stop the wind whenever it rains." As soon as the words left my lips, I knew they were foolish. I wished I could stuff them back in my mouth.

"He won't stop the wind at your request. That's why you must build a shelter."

"I prefer to go exploring, instead."

"Not today, Cherished," Ennoia said.

"I don't want to build a shelter. I won't mind the rain."

The seated Teachers lifted their wings.

Ennoia said, "This isn't about the shelter or the rain. What matters is that you must do what we tell you."

At last, their hidden agenda revealed, my suspicions were confirmed. The Teachers sought to control me. I wouldn't give them the opportunity. "No. I won't."

In one swift movement, Ennoia stood and spread his wings high and wide, gold feathers exposed in threat. Pulled upward by Ennoia's vault, Manna and Aable jumped to stand next to Ennoia. Their six wings formed a tall, imposing wall of feathers. I stood and faced them. With both hands, I tightened my grip on my sweeper, in case they tried to take it away again.

Ennoia crossed his arms. "You're under our authority and you must obey us."

"What will you do if I don't?"

"We'll take something away."

I clutched my sweeper tighter and pulled it close to my chest.

Ennoia said, "Something more valuable than your twig this time."

What could they take besides my sweeper? Were they bluffing?

"Do what you must," I said. "I'm going exploring." I turned around and walked away with brisk, determined steps, still gripping my sweeper with both hands, just in case. I didn't look back. Bracing myself for whatever might happen, I waited for it, holding my breath, but kept walking. And walking.

Nothing happened.

I relaxed and resumed breathing.

Pleased with myself for winning that match, I felt relieved that nothing came of it. How dare they threaten me? Their need to resort to threats meant they were losing control over me. That was a positive development. But why did I feel so unsettled?

I calmed myself and tried to enjoy my procured freedom. I set my sights on a tall hill in the distance and ambled toward it across the upward sloping terrain of low scrub and buckeye trees.

Not having to keep pace with anyone, I alternated between meandering and jogging. I tossed my sweeper into the air, higher and higher, catching it when it fell back.

In a ravine flanked by sage bushes, an animal foraged for food by digging through rotting leaves with its flattened nose. I wished the Teachers were here to tell me about it. I would ask them later. What if they wanted nothing more to do with me? I still needed them to show me which plants were safe to eat.

As I neared the peak, I encountered a sprawling thicket of thorny, pink-tinged barberry. I tried to step between the prickly shrubs, but scratched my legs on the brambles. In places where the thicket was too dense, I had to backtrack and choose another route. I refused to retreat or admit I had made a bad choice.

Gray clouds amassed in the sky, covering up all the blue. My earlier uneasiness lingered, haunting me with the sense that something was wrong with the world.

After fighting my way through the troublesome thicket, I emerged on the other side with many cuts. I looked back with accomplishment and exhaled with relief. Advancing a short distance further, I arrived at the edge of a tall cliff with no way down to the grassy field below. I didn't want to go through the horrid thicket again, so I walked along the edge of the cliff hoping to find a way down. The clouds thickened and darkened. A strong wind blew, slapping my body with belligerent gusts.

Small droplets of water landed on my skin. I examined the drops on my arm. This must be rain, I thought. It appeared harmless. I licked the drops off my salty skin. Then I opened my mouth and let the droplets land on my tongue, providing cool prickles of refreshment. Rain wasn't bad at all.

Without warning, the drops became a downpour. Rivulets of water ran down my body. The cold soaked into my skin. The fiercer the wind blew, the colder I became. I couldn't escape the rain. The thicket on one side. The cliff on the other. Murky water covered the ground and liquefied the dirt into sticky mud. I squished through the mud along the edge of the cliff desperate to be rescued.

Chapter 19

Retribution

I came to an indentation in the cliff where the ground had slid away in a tapered pile of boulders and dirt. The rainwater poured into the notch and cascaded down the boulders as a muddy waterfall. I descended the rocks one at a time, placing one foot on a boulder below, and then bringing the other foot down.

When I stepped on a patch of slippery mud, my foot slid out from beneath me. I fell and landed on my butt, then slid off the boulder and scraped my back as I landed on the next one. I slid off that boulder and slammed my butt on the rocks all the way down the pile.

When I came to a stop, I lay flat on my back. I struggled to lift my bruised body off the ground. My butt ached. My back stung. My legs were blackened with mud. I should have turned around when I saw the thicket. I had paid the price for my stubbornness.

The rain continued to drench me. I looked for my sweeper and saw it halfway up the pile of boulders. I climbed the dirty waterfall to retrieve it. After pulling it out of the mud, I held it out for the rain to rinse it off. Then I descended backwards, this time using my hands to hold onto the boulders, my sweeper clamped between my teeth.

At the bottom, shivering, I scanned the terrain for a place to escape the incessant, harassing rain. Grass and wildflowers spread across the soaked field below the cliff. A spindly tree stood in the distance, over one hundred paces away. Battered by the rain, I ran, splashing toward the tree through the muddy field, hoping my misery would end soon.

The tree provided little shelter from the rain and did nothing to protect me from the driving wind. Standing still, I felt colder than ever. How did animals stay warm? Every animal except me had fur or feathers. Why had Creator neglected to give me fur? Crouching, I wrapped my arms around my legs, trying to get warm. I clung to my sweeper for comfort, but it had no effect.

My stomach roared with hunger because I hadn't eaten today. I looked up at the tree, then down at the plants near my feet, but I didn't dare take a chance on eating the leaves. I decided to wait for the rain to stop before searching for food.

Shivering, I waited. The rain continued unabated. How could the clouds hold so much water? Would their bladders ever empty?

Because of Ennoia's threat, I believed the Teachers were responsible for my plight. They had sent the rain to punish me. They wanted to prove me wrong for saying I didn't need to build a shelter. The rain had convinced me. I spoke to the rain. "I'm sorry. I should have listened to the Teachers. Tell them I'm sorry. Tell them I was wrong."

In that moment, something changed within me. My uneasiness relaxed into calm. I traced the calm along its flow, into its source, into my center, and found peace. The peace embraced me and assured me I was valued. I was still lost, cold and hungry, but those states no longer had power to torment me.

Inside my mind, words formed, soft like a whisper, almost imperceptible. "Follow the flow."

"Creator?"

"Yes," said the whisper.

The rainwater had pooled on the ground and formed a creek

that flowed across the field. I believed Creator wanted me to follow that stream. "Is that the way home?"

"Yes," He whispered.

I took comfort that Creator had found me and wanted to bring me home. He surprised me by the depth of His care. He had come so close I could hear His whisperings and feel the warmth of His presence.

Leaving the scant protection of the tree, I followed the shallow creek in the direction of its flow. Not long after, the rain stopped. The clouds thinned, and the sun began to warm me. Along the way, I passed pea vines. I split open the pods and popped the sweet, crunchy peas into my mouth until I was no longer hungry. Then I resumed following the stream until it vanished, having soaked into the ground. By that time, I recognized my surroundings and knew the meadow was near.

"Thank you, Creator." For the second time, He had guided my steps. My insides trembled with awe and weakness, a vulnerability arising from recognizing my inadequacy and my fundamental need to depend on Him.

When I reached the meadow, I saw the Teachers sitting in a circle in the open field, their huge wings spread flat on the grass, drying in the sun. I slowed when I realized they might be mean to me. Seeing me, they took up their wings and stood to greet me. They assembled in typical formation with Ennoia in front, Manna and Aable in back.

I faced them and lowered my head. "I'm sorry. I shouldn't have disobeyed. If you want me to build a shelter, I'll do it."

I waited for my punishment.

Chapter 20

Resources

Ennoia said, "We forgive you, Cherished."

I looked up in surprise, expecting a harsher response.

"Someday, you'll learn to trust us," Aable said.

"We're pleased that you interacted with Creator," Manna said.

I smiled. "I'm pleased, too. How was I able to hear Him?"

"You listened with your soul. Your spirit deposits His messages in your body or in the open space within your mind. You need only pay attention."

"Do you think He has more messages for me?"

"Yes. But know that His messages don't always take the form of words. They often manifest as flows, like winds or streams."

Eager for more, I closed my eyes and searched for messages. Something stirred within my body, within my umbilicore. I focused on my umbilicore and entered its flow. A life-giving stream refreshed every corner of my being. I received no words this time. Instead, ardent affirmation washed over me. I didn't know whether the flow itself was Creator or not, but I drank from it like a hummingbird at a favorite flower.

Ennoia interrupted my rapture. "Whenever you resist Creator, you cut yourself off from the flow. When you defied us today, you defied Him and disabled your connection to Him."

My connection to Creator had been turned off during my adventure. That explained why I had felt unsettled until I apologized. The Teachers hadn't bluffed. They did take something away. Or had I done that to myself?

"Before we can build a shelter, you must learn some basic skills," Manna said. "First, we need to find a sharp rock."

Although Manna said "we," he meant me. The Teachers employed this pattern every time something needed to be done.

I crisscrossed the meadow looking for sharp rocks. After showing the Teachers many candidates, I found a rock that Manna approved—a flat rock that tapered to a sharp edge.

Next, Manna asked me to find a fallen tree branch that divided into three limbs. After searching for a long time, I returned to the Teachers and said, "I can't find one. I've looked everywhere."

"Ask Creator," Aable said. He smiled and winked.

I remembered my invisible friend and smiled. "Creator, help me find the branch I need."

Searching the open space within my mind, I found nothing. I sensed something in my body. A pull on my being toward a grove of trees. I followed the pull and entered the grove. A tight cluster of beech trees caught my attention. I moved closer and saw a pile of debris at the base of those trees. Lying on top of the debris was a branch that divided into three limbs. "That's amazing! Thank you, Creator."

Inside my mind, words from Creator formed. "I am with you and for you."

Grinning, I returned to the Teachers with the prized branch.

"Excellent," Manna said. "Now, we need long, sturdy grass."

Again, I understood "we" to mean me. This time, when I asked Creator for help, I saw an image of tall, reddish grass in my mind. I remembered walking past the grass yesterday and ran to its location. Using the sharp edge of the rock, I cut off several long blades.

"Our next step is to assemble the tool," Manna said. "Go find a place to sit and I will teach you."

Carrying the collected items, I found a shaded spot and sat on the ground. I placed the items in front of me. The Teachers sat across from me. Manna guided me step-by-step.

I peeled the bark off the branch as my first step. Next, I wedged the blunt end of the rock into the cradle created by the three forked limbs. I ripped the grass lengthwise into thin ribbons. After frustrating practice at tying knots, I secured the rock within the cradle with the grass bindings.

"Well done, Cherished," Manna said. "That tool is called an ax. It's used to chop branches. Let's try it out."

The Teachers approached a small tree, and I followed. Manna pointed to a branch and said, "Grip the ax at the end of its handle. Then swing the sharp edge against the branch."

I swung the ax. The branch snapped off where the ax blade struck. I chuckled. Then, remembering my foot injury, I inspected the tree for blood but saw none.

"We'll use the ax to cut branches for your shelter," Manna said.

The Teachers chose a location for my shelter next to an outcrop of large rocks atop a small hill. The shelter site was situated in front of a flat-sided, granite boulder that stood waist-height. Two paces in front of the boulder, a pair of large bay trees grew an arms-length apart. On both sides of the granite boulder, smaller rocks formed a curved enclosure that made a half-circle around the two trees.

After we inspected the site, Manna said, "We'll need branches, more sturdy grass and lots of giant leaves."

When I returned with my first armload of materials, I saw a small pile of branches and leaves next to the Teachers. Every time I returned with more, their pile had grown, although I never saw them carrying anything or doing any work. After a few more trips, we had plenty of branches and leaves.

"We're ready to build," Manna said. "First, we'll need strong beams to span from the bay trees to the rocks. Chop down six slender trees and trim off their branches."

I obeyed. Chopping was exhausting work, requiring many ax blows to cut through each trunk. My hands became sore from gripping, my palms red and tender from the roughness of the ax handle. Moisture oozed from my skin and dripped from my face.

I dragged the six felled trees into a pile and began trimming off the branches with the ax. The Teachers sat nearby and watched. Didn't they have something better to do than watch me trim trees?

Removing the branches took a long time. My work slowed as my energy waned. After two trees, I said, "Do I have to keep doing this?"

"No," Ennoia said. "We can't force you to do anything."

"You've been forcing me this whole time," I said, raising my voice.

Ennoia's wings lifted and spread.

I held my tongue.

Chapter 21

Disablement

Ennoia said, "You can quit at any time. This shelter is for your benefit, not ours. Creator wants you to complete it. If you refuse Him, your connection to Him will be disabled."

"That's not a fair choice," I said. "If I quit, then I'll be punished."

"Not punished. Your connection to Creator will be hindered by your decision to distance yourself from Him. The choice isn't a difficult one."

Cornered by the Ennoia's trickery, I gave in. I picked up the ax and resumed trimming with unchecked fury. I slammed the ax against a branch, splintering wood in all directions.

Ennoia said, "Stop right now. You need to take a break. Go find something to eat. We'll wait here until you return."

I threw down the ax, grabbed my sweeper, and stomped away. I tramped until my anger subsided and the Teachers were on the other side of the world. After collecting some pine nuts, I spread them on a large, flat stone. Sitting cross-legged next to the stone, I said, "Thank you, Creator, for this food."

"You are more angry than grateful," Creator said.

"I am angry. The Teachers keep bossing me around."

"They love you as much as I do."

"I doubt that."

"They do."

A soothing peace tried to enter through my umbilicore, but I pushed it away, preferring to stay angry.

I found strawberries and ate them unhurried. After I had eaten every ripe berry I found, even some unripe ones to stall, I dragged myself back to the Teachers.

Without speaking, I continued trimming the trees while the Teachers watched, perched like three fussy parrots supervising my efforts.

After I had trimmed all six trees, Manna said, "You've done an excellent job, Cherished. Now, position the beams across the gap between the bay trees and the boulders."

I placed the thick ends of the beams into clefts between branches and tied each one to its supporting branch. The six beams fanned out like the spokes of a spider web. They sloped down from the centered pair of trees to the surrounding rock enclosure on which they rested. At its highest point, the shelter's roof reached chest-height.

While I was tying the last beam, the Teachers left. They returned with some carrots, peaches and peanuts, and placed them on a flat, granite outcrop that jutted knee-height four paces in front of the two trees. In remembrance of Creator's first gift of food on the red stone, I tapped each piece of food against the granite table, gave unspoken thanks, and ate it. While eating, I reviewed my progress, feeling satisfaction in seeing the work of my own hands, sore as they were.

Eager to bring an end to my servitude, I resumed working on the shelter's roof. I laid branches across the beams and tied them into place. The design resembled a spider web even more. Afterward, the Teachers taught me how to tie giant leaves in overlapping layers to create a waterproof barrier. By the time I completed the roof, the sun had set, unwilling to wait for me to finish.

The Teachers suggested that I spend the last bit of daylight collecting soft grass for my bed. Then they wished me pleasant sleep and vanished in a feathered whoosh. With little time remaining, I gathered handfuls of fresh grass and spread them under my shelter's roof.

Exhausted, I relaxed on my new bed. Soreness pervaded my body. My sweeper leaned against the back granite wall. I gazed at the ceiling and smiled with gratification. In the dim light, I studied the rows of parallel branches. I missed gazing at the stars that peeked through the oak trees above my old sleeping patch. In this tiny space, I felt confined, caged on all sides but one. The universe felt less accessible.

I considered sleeping just outside the shelter so I could see the familiar stars, but that seemed ridiculous since I spent all day constructing the roof. Should I not benefit from my labor? On the other hand, what were the risks of sleeping outside? If it rained, I'd move back inside. A tiger could kill me in either location. The shelter was Creator's idea. Would it displease Him if I didn't sleep inside it?

After much deliberation, I decided I was making too much out of nothing. So, before I changed my mind again, I gathered my grassy bed into bundles and spread them in front of my shelter. Lying in the open, enjoying the stars, an uneasiness expanded and intensified. I noticed my growing estrangement from Creator. I didn't have assurance that moving my bed was permitted. That uncertainty created increasing anxiety.

"Creator, may I sleep outside?"

No answer came.

I interpreted the silence as Creator's displeasure. Without replacing my bed, I scurried back under the shelter's roof. I didn't move or make a sound, afraid that if I did so, I would make things worse. My connection to Him felt damaged. I yearned to ask Him how to correct this rift, but I dared not because I feared another silent reply.

Chapter 22

Presumption

After a long time, I found courage to speak. "Creator, I'm sorry I moved my bed. I didn't know it wasn't permitted. Please forgive me."

Creator responded as an audible voice rising in the darkness, His voice deep and resonant. "Moving your bed was permitted. Had I forbidden you to move your bed, then you would have been at fault for moving it. Your transgression is that you doubted its permissibility and did it, anyway. You offended Me because you were willing to risk My displeasure. If you do something you believe is forbidden, even if your belief is mistaken, you violate your belief, betray your integrity, and dishonor Me."

My chest tightened around my heart, making it beat faster. "I didn't know," I said, astonished that Creator could be offended with such ease.

"Because you didn't know, you acted from doubt. When your actions aren't based on truth, then you distance yourself from Me because I am the Truth. You are either in the light of truth or in darkness. When you apologized, you moved back into truth, and our connection was restored."

"Forgive me for offending You. I didn't mean to push you

away." I couldn't bear that I had wounded Creator. My chest hurt as if it were turning inside out.

"You are forgiven, Cherished. If you had disobeyed My command, then the situation would have been more grave. Willful disobedience would sever your umbilicore and destroy our connection."

"I won't disobey you," I said with conviction.

"All is well, Cherished. Be at peace."

With those words, love washed over me and left a comforting calm upon my soul.

As I fell asleep, my mind replayed the actions of chopping trees and tying knots. These images transitioned into a deeper state, more vivid, where I constructed a tall wooden tower. The tower stood higher than the treetops and scraped the clouds. Passing birds took notice and roosted on the tower, wanting to partake in its splendor. News of the tower spread to faraway and exotic places, drawing curious birds to see if the rumors of its glory were true. In the dream, I felt an exhilarating sense of accomplishment.

When I awoke, those feelings of pleasure lingered.

Lying on my back, eyes open, I greeted the day by saying, "I desire you, Creator." I searched within my being, my soul thirsting for the nourishment that only He could give. I found my umbilicore, my center where body, soul, spirit, and Creator all intersected. When I engaged my umbilicore, I suckled its warm, sweet nectar.

"You are loved, Cherished," Creator whispered into the corridors of my soul.

"I love you, Creator," I whispered in return.

"Cooperate with the Teachers today. They intend only what is best for you."

"I'll try."

The Teachers appeared, sitting on the granite table near my shelter. I crawled out from beneath my shelter's roof and approached them.

Manna cocked his head like a bird, his emerald-green throat flashing in the sunlight. "Blessings to you, Cherished."

"Blessings," I replied, ignorant of what the word meant.

Aable stared at me with his sparkling blue eyes. "You're full of light this morning."

"Creator fed me before you came," I said.

The Teachers nodded at each other.

"Today, we'll build a front wall for your shelter," Manna said.

Walling off the front would only heighten my sense of confinement when inside. My body cringed at the thought of being sealed up. Was this cage another scheme to keep me under their control?

After attending to my bodily needs, I began my second day of hard labor by sharpening my ax blade. The Teachers showed me how to scrape it against another stone. Afterward, they instructed me in making a new tool, called a trowel. I used the trowel to dig holes along the front edge of my shelter, a short distance inside the roof overhang. I chopped down six small trees, trimmed off their branches, dropped them into the holes, and tied their tops to the forward roof beams. Next, I tied horizontal rows of sticks across the vertical posts to create a front wall. My hands and shoulders ached more than yesterday.

The opening between the two bay trees became the entrance to my shelter. I constructed a sturdy rectangular panel of tied sticks that functioned as a door. The door hinged at the top with vines so it would swing up and out. I kept the door propped horizontal with a long, vertical stick. I removed the stick when I wanted the door closed.

I completed my shelter by day's end. The front wall sealed off the enclosure of rocks, creating a cage so the Teachers no longer had to watch over me at night.

I pushed against a wall post to test its steadiness. It stood firm. "Nothing can knock it down," I said with pride.

The Teachers sat behind me on the stone table. Manna retorted by saying, "Creator can demolish it."

I turned to face them. "Why would He do that?"

"Many reasons. To teach a lesson. To show His power. To replace it with something new. Creator builds up and tears down. He is both maker and destroyer."

I raised my voice. "You're wrong. He's good. He would never destroy anything."

The Teachers rose to their feet, their faces stern.

I supposed they didn't like being wrong. Or being told by someone like me.

Chapter 23

Arrogance

"Creator would destroy if He had purpose," Manna said.

"No. That's not true." It was my turn to teach the Teachers.

Ennoia spread his wings and said, slow and firm, "We always speak the truth." Manna's and Aable's wings also spread.

"No. You're not in the truth," I said. "That means you're cut off from Creator."

Ennoia's eyes flashed bright red. "You don't know what you're saying."

"Yes, I do. Creator said so."

"You're misapplying His words."

My volume increased. "Creator wouldn't lie. You aren't on His side. I'm full of light. You're full of darkness. Creator loves me . . . not . . . you."

By this time, their wings were stretched to full extension, quivering with intensity. Ennoia said, "You will not speak to us in this manner."

Like a released slingshot, the Teachers thrust their wings in my direction. A violent blast of air punched my body, knocking me backward. My back and head slammed to the ground. I tried to move, but my muscles wouldn't respond.

"You're full of something," Ennoia said, "and it's not light or truth."

The Teachers crouched around me while I lay helpless. Aable placed his hand on my chest and peered into my eyes. I stared back into Aable's blue eyes with defiance. When the emotion became too much, I tried to look away, but couldn't.

Inside my chest, something thrashed like a writhing salamander. It frightened me because I had no control over it. It strangled my umbilicore, choking my soul. It resisted and kicked, but something immense overshadowed it, enclosed it, and crushed it like a bug. Light and life resumed flowing through my umbilicore. Fluid leaked from the corners of my eyes and trickled down past my ears.

Creator spoke inside my mind, "I create. I destroy. In all I do, I love. My purposes encompass joy and pain, life and death, growth and decay. You can't comprehend all My ways. I only ask that you trust."

Aable withdrew his hand. The Teachers straightened and stepped back. My paralysis faded. Shaken, I sat up and stared at my knees. I felt all three pairs of eyes watching me.

Still looking down, I said, "I'm sorry. I didn't know."

"We forgive you, Cherished," Manna said. "Be careful with what you know. It is never complete. Never presume that you know Creator in full."

I looked up at the Teachers and studied their earnest faces. "You're right. I know nothing."

Aable extended his hand. I grabbed it and pulled myself up. Without warning, Aable pulled me in and hugged me. Ennoia and Manna also hugged me. I didn't feel lovable in that moment, so the hugs felt awkward and undeserved.

"What happened inside me?" I said.

"Defiant attitudes generate their own self-sustaining energy," Manna said. "They resist being challenged or removed. Creator got rid of your arrogance before it could take hold."

"Thank you, Creator," I whispered so the Teachers couldn't hear. Then I addressed Ennoia. "I'm confused. You said before that Creator destroys nothing, but Creator said that He does destroy."

"Both are true. Nothing is ever annihilated. When Creator destroys something, its substance is merely transformed. The rhythm of the universe is transformation."

"You've worked hard these two days," Manna said. "Tomorrow, we're giving you a free day to do whatever you want. If you want to hike to the mountains and see a waterfall, we'll take you. Think about it. We'll leave you, now, and return tomorrow."

I closed my eyes anticipating the blast of air. When I opened them, I was alone. Whenever they departed like that, a hollowness remained.

After getting something to eat, I crawled into my shelter, closed the door, and plopped down with exhaustion. The tiny shelter squeezed around me, enclosing me within a cage of my making. I disliked the confinement, but didn't dare sleep elsewhere.

That night, I pondered how I might spend my free day tomorrow. My thoughts kept returning to Creator. I felt both gratitude and remorse. There must be a way to appease those feelings, to show Him I was sincere.

Since I had learned a few skills, I could make something for Creator. No. That was silly. He needed nothing from me. Then I remembered last night's dream. I would build a wooden tower as a tribute to Him. A splendid tower worthy of Creator. He would appreciate that. I was sure of it.

Chapter 24

Tribute

The next morning, I said to the Teachers, "I want to spend my free day by myself."

"We understand," Manna said. "We won't interfere with your plans."

The Teachers turned and walked away, wings flicking. Watching them leave, I exhaled a long breath. I had expected them to refuse me, given their need to control my every moment. They had given my day a wonderful start. A day without the Teachers.

I supposed Creator would be watching me as I built the tower. I had no way of knowing if He was aware of my intentions, but I hoped my gift would surprise Him. Everything needed to be perfect so He would know how much I loved Him. My willingness to put in another day of hard work in spite of my soreness would prove my dedication.

My enterprise began by selecting a flat, sandy spot near the lake to be the location for the tower. I chopped down four tall, slender trees and trimmed off their branches. Then I dug four equidistant holes and dropped a wooden pole into each one. In my mind, the tops of the poles all came together in a point, but they chose, instead, to lean haphazard and crisscrossed.

I adjusted each pole by guiding it toward the center, trying to get the tips to meet. Each time, I knocked the other poles out of place. I hoped Creator wasn't watching my ineptitude. With practice, I succeeded in aligning three poles. Trying to position the fourth always destroyed the alignment, causing the poles to flip down into new grotesque configurations that mocked me. Again and again, I tried without success. I recalled Manna saying, "Perseverance becomes foolishness when outcomes won't change." I groaned, on realizing the Teachers had infiltrated my day after all. They wouldn't be allowed to ruin my day if I could prevent it.

I sat and stared at the ugly jumble, trying to figure out how to fix it. Think, Cherished. Think.

I pulled the poles out of their holes and laid them side-by-side. I tied their tops together with grass strips, and then dropped them back into the holes. The structure leaned lopsided because the poles were different lengths. I cut them to the same length and tried again. This time, the structure leaned because the holes were differing depths. Creator must have been laughing by now, but I had run out of humor. I adjusted the holes and dropped the poles into them, but the frame still leaned. I shook my head with astonishment that something so simple could be so hard. It took a few more adjustments before the frame stood straight, or at least straight enough to suit my impatience.

I tied horizontal branches across each pair of poles, working upward toward the top of the frame. Copying the pattern from my dream, the structure had four sides that tapered inward to form a point. The lower branches served as rungs on which I climbed to add the upper elements.

The top needed something special. In my dream, birds came to roost on my tower. Paying homage to that, I found four feathers and fastened them to the tower's peak. The feathers advertised my invitation for the birds to come and offer their tribute. I amused myself with the thought of plucking feathers from the Teacher's wings to adorn its peak.

I finished the tower at dusk. It soared three times my height. Its imposing silhouette scratched the darkening sky with its pointed spire. I sat to admire it, exhausted but pleased with the final result. My excitement grew as I anticipated Creator's response. My eyes traced the tower's lines, appreciating every detail. I wanted the birds and all creatures to take notice of my magnificent handiwork and praise it. Self-congratulation rose within me, towering over all other feelings. No doubt, Creator would be impressed.

My eyes fixed on the tower, I stood and announced, "Creator, I've constructed a monument to You. Its greatness represents Your greatness." I grinned, waiting for Creator's affirmation of my labor and dedication.

The tower became illuminated from behind me. I turned and saw a swirling mist that hovered at eye level. The mist glowed white against the tenebrous sky, lighting the ground below and reflecting off the shadowy lake as harsh white crescents. I stared at Creator with awe as I was seeing Him for the first time. He said nothing, and I imagined Him to be speechless at the sight of my gift. I turned back to admire my tower, joining Creator in His adoration of it.

Before my eyes, all the fastenings on the tower, from top to bottom, burst apart in rapid succession with ear-splitting pops. The tower twisted and deformed before falling sideways in slow motion. When it crashed to the ground, the branches splintered with loud cracks. I ran up to the mangled heap of rubble, thinking to save it, but I stopped short and stared at the wreckage in disbelief and anguish.

Chapter 25

Pridefulness

A booming voice said, "Rejected. Rejected. Rejected," jarring me out of my stunned state. The voice, having a power all its own, pierced me from every direction. It wasn't a voice I had heard before. I turned toward Creator, who was now swirling with intense energy. Cringing, I watched the bright, churning mist, waiting to be reprimanded. My heart banged like stone striking stone. What had I done this time to offend Him? He was impossible to please.

"I reject your gift," Creator said. "The focus of your worship must be Me alone. When you offered your gift, your eyes were not on Me, but on your handiwork. Your eyes remained on it even as it was destroyed. Your devotion is where your eyes are fixed. You worshiped the gift instead of the one to whom the gift was given. The worship I want is wholehearted and undiluted by other affections."

His words sliced me open to expose my clinging attachment to my achievement. The tower had become a monument to me, not Creator.

"Devotion is attentiveness of soul," Creator said. "Whenever you give too much attention to something, then that becomes the object of your devotion. Pridefulness is misplaced devotion. If the focus is on you, then pridefulness becomes self-devotion. I rejected your gift because you took too much pride in it."

I had no words of defense, so I kept silent. My pridefulness toppled as if knocked down by Creator. After it had shattered, a flood of remorse overtook me like a giant hand squeezing my lungs. My face contorted, and I covered it with my hands. "Creator, I'm so sorry. Forgive me. Please accept me back."

The swirling mist slowed to become a luminous, white cloud whose wisps drifted on gentle currents of air. "I rejected your gift, not you, Cherished. You are loved and forgiven. Because I love you, I correct and discipline you. Go home to your shelter and do not dwell on this matter."

I staggered home, dazed by the evening's fiasco. I paid little attention to my path in spite of the darkened forest that cast gloom on the scene. The day had started with so much enthusiasm and anticipation, but it had ended in disaster. I berated myself for wasting my free day. What made me think Creator would appreciate a tower? How did I miss seeing the attachments forming in my soul? At what point did my devotion change into pridefulness?

I tripped on a tree root and fell on my hands and knees. I howled at the forest, wanting it to know I deserved its scorn. After standing and brushing myself off, I examined the contemptible root and discovered it to be unobtrusive, an unlikely suspect to make me fall. Again, I was caught unaware by an unseen snag.

When I reached my shelter, I crawled inside and yanked the stick that propped the door open. The door dropped with a loud bang. Clutching my sweeper, I curled up on my grass bed and closed my eyes. My stomach spasmed from hunger. I tried to ignore it. I tried to sleep. I tried to forget.

The image of the tower collapsing played over and over in my mind, taunting me. With each iteration, it amplified the sour jabs in my belly. I tried to stop the images, but they looped in my head uncountable times, worming into my sleep with themes of futility and punishment.

Chapter 26

Depression

The next morning, my body was exhausted and sore. It felt as if I hadn't slept at all. My closed eyelids detected light seeping in through the slits between the horizontal branches along the front wall. I turned my head away from the light to face the shadowed granite of the back wall. Keeping my eyes shut, I began my obsessive thinking about the night before. I had failed Creator. I had failed myself. What good was I to anyone?

I had no energy to move as if an invisible opponent weighted down my body. Hunger clawed at the lining of my stomach. No, this churning torment was beyond hunger. Something sinister seethed inside me, something intent on punishing me.

Within my tiny shelter, I withdrew into my soul. I couldn't look at myself without seeing failure, so I hid within my inner darkness, shutting myself away from the exuberant bustle of the universe. I found perverse solace in my self-imposed isolation—a bitter reward for my thoughts and fuel for my misery.

Ennoia's voice interrupted my sullen reverie. "Cherished, come out and greet us. We want to spend time with you today."

With pained reluctance, I pushed the door open a crack and squinted through the narrow opening. After my eyes adjusted to the light, I saw the Teachers standing just beyond my shelter. They appeared glad to see me, and I squirmed in response to their cheerfulness. I wished they would go away. I wanted nothing to spoil my foul mood. Slow and grudging, I crawled out from my shelter, keeping my head lowered, pretending the light was too bright to look up.

"Blessings to you, Cherished," Manna said.

"Blessings," I mumbled. I doubted my ability to hide my disposition. "I don't feel well this morning. I think I should go back to sleep."

"Cherished," Aable said with a sharp edge.

I looked up at Aable whose brows were pinched with concern. "Dwelling on your mistakes doesn't serve you. Will you let us help you?"

The offer of help took me by surprise, not being something I expected or even wanted. Staying miserable seemed a more fitting recompense for my behavior. "I don't deserve to be helped," I said.

"You're focused on reward and punishment," Aable said, looking sad and shaking his head. "Love gives without regard to merit, but never forces itself. Perhaps you'll accept our help later." The Teachers turned and walked away.

This behavior surprised me even more. The Teachers weren't any help at all. I fumed with disappointment. Maybe they knew what I suspected, that I was beyond help.

I crawled back into my shelter and closed the door behind me. Although I was starving, I had no appetite. From my stash of food, I pulled out an orange and forced it down. It tasted bland because my taste buds were dulled. Lost in dismal thought, I chewed my food to the point of gnashing teeth. How could I escape these feelings? Would they last forever? I trawled my languid mind looking for a solution, but found none, returning to my starting point with less hope than before. As I ruminated on my misery, I descended into deeper despair.

I closed my eyes and tried to push aside my gloom. "Creator, please help me."

"If you want help, go outside," Creator said inside my mind.

With my sweeper in hand, I crawled out into the blinding sunlight and stood. The Teachers were sitting on the granite table. I couldn't hide my disappointment. "I . . . I asked for Creator."

The Teachers stood.

"He sent us to help," Aable said.

"I want Creator's help, not yours."

"We are offering His help."

I hesitated. "How will you help me?"

"By helping you die."

I stepped back in fear. "What? No. I don't want that."

"It's the only way," Aable said.

Shaking my head, I said, "No. Leave me alone."

Aable sighed.

The Teachers formed a huddle, creating a feathered dome with their wings. I heard muffled voices. Afterward, they lowered their wings, gazed at me one last time, and turned to walk away. I felt satisfaction in watching them leave.

Words slipped uninvited into my head. "By spurning them, you spurn Me."

Regret came a second later.

Despair followed.

Chapter 27

Selffulness

"Wait!" I ran after the Teachers.

When I caught up with them, they stopped and turned around.

"I'm sorry," I said. "I need your help, but I don't want to die."

"We understand," Manna said. "Come with us. We want to show you something."

The Teachers resumed walking, and I took my position at the rear between Manna and Aable. No one spoke. I followed, paying attention to nothing but the thoughts that circled in my head. No one can help me. I'm too wretched to be helped. The Teachers will fail. When they fail, they will know how hopeless I am and reject me. My stomach churned with each despairing thought.

Aable said, "Cherished, have you noticed that all your thoughts are about you?"

I didn't answer.

"Your problem is selffulness," Manna said. "Selffulness is an energy that is self-focused. It feeds on self, cares only about self, and is so full of self it excludes everything else. You must guard against its intrusions into your soul."

"It's too late for me. I've failed."

"It's not too late. The only way to deal with selffulness is to die."

Terror streaked down my spine. I fought to keep from sprinting away.

"See?" Manna said. "Selffulness resists anything that threatens it."

"What will happen to me if I die?"

"You'll be free from selffulness and its control. You don't need it, Cherished. Everything you need can be found in Creator."

The Teachers slowed. "We've arrived."

We stood at the edge of a wide, shallow crater of hard, colorless clay. At the center of the crater stood a solitary tree blackened by decay. Inside the circular boundary, nothing grew, not even a single blade of grass. Outside, the branches of the dense forest leaned away from the charcoal-colored tree, as if straining to grasp something to keep from being sucked into the fearsome circle.

The breeze that blew through the trees stopped when we entered the crater. Inside, the stagnant air smelled rank, like rotting flesh. The thickness of the air forced me to breathe with extra effort.

Towering four times my height, the tree was shrouded in solid black, the color of the night sky if the stars were plucked out. This deepest black reflected no light. I could only discern the outline of the tree, its silhouette changing as I walked around it, revealing a thick and knotted trunk that twisted in an upward spiral. Heavy branches drooped in low arcs. Slender, curved leaves hung like blackened fingers from the smaller branches. The leaves rustled, agitated by something beyond the absent breeze.

The Teachers stood near the trunk and faced me. "This is the Tree of Death," Manna said. "It is cut off from Life. So, it can't draw life or give life. It doesn't grow or die or decay."

"I thought that if something dies, it returns to Creator," I said.

"That's true of physical death. But what you're seeing in this tree is spiritual death, which is disconnection. When spirit is disconnected from Life, from Creator, it becomes darkened and crippled. It no longer receives spiritual nourishment but enters a stupor where it subsists on its own meager resources, like a hibernating bear that lives off its own fat."

The leaves on the tree shuddered at the same time. The slim charcoal leaves wriggled like dangling black caterpillars. A leaf dropped to the ground. The leaf writhed on the hard gray clay as it inched up to the base of the tree. A scraping sound accompanied the leaf's frenzied slog to its tragic parent. On reaching the tree, it merged into the blackness of the trunk.

"The leaf will feed on the tree," Manna said, "boring into its trunk like a wood beetle. Being disconnected from the One Life, the tree's existence is self-consuming and degenerative. Its only source of nourishment is itself."

"What made the tree this way?"

"It is a casualty of an event that happened here a long time ago."

"Can Creator repair it?"

"No. He can't. When something has been disconnected from Creator, it becomes forever quarantined. Its darkened state makes it repulsive to His nature, so He can't touch it, even to repair it."

I moved closer to the trunk to inspect it. So deep was its blackness I couldn't see any detail on its surface as if the light itself refused to touch it. I tried to drag my fingers across its bark, but they swiped through the tree as if it were a phantom. I heard a soft, crackling sound as my fingers passed through, but felt nothing.

"It recedes at your touch," Manna said. "It can't occupy the same space as you. Look at its side."

I stepped to the side to see the tree's marred profile. My fingers had carved four deep furrows into the trunk.

"You see why Creator can't touch it or repair it." Manna said. "He can't make contact without destroying the tree."

"Why doesn't He destroy it, then? It serves no purpose."

"In a sense, it's already destroyed. Its purpose is to illustrate the nature of spiritual disconnection and death."

"Let's leave this place," I said. "I don't like the smell of death." I

83

walked toward the perimeter to seek fresh air.

Once outside, I took a deep breath. When something touched my shoulder from behind, I turned and saw the Teachers standing there, looking solemn.

Ennoia said, "The tree also exemplifies the self-consuming nature of selffulness. Like a darkened spirit, selffulness repels Creator, but for different reasons. Selffulness asserts itself against Him and exalts itself above Him. Its self-centered energy excludes Creator. Creator and selffulness can't occupy the same space within your soul."

I envisioned my selffulness as a twisted, blackened tree within my soul, feeding on itself, driving Creator away by its darkened nature. "If my selffulness is repulsive to Him, then how can He help me?"

"If your spirit were dead, He couldn't revive it. Your spirit is alive, so things aren't as bad as you think. With selffulness, Creator can help you. He can remove it if you let Him."

At once, I closed my eyes and lowered my head. "Creator, I give you my selffulness. Please, take it away."

Chapter 28

Surrender

Nothing happened at first. Then a struggle ensued within my chest. My selffulness refused to budge.

I opened my eyes. "It's not working," I said with dismay. In my mind, selffulness had already won the battle.

"You must participate," Aable said. "Die to your selffulness. Give it no ground on which to stand. Let go of self."

"I let go. I let go," I said to Creator with loud earnestness. Eyes closed, I tried to disentangle myself from my selffulness and push it away. I shook off my circling, self-focused thoughts and became as small as I could so nothing would stay attached. Surrendering to Creator, I dropped all my defenses to give Him access to my soul to do whatever He needed to do.

My participation made a difference now that two were fighting against one. My selffulness lost its hold. As I emptied myself, it withered until I couldn't detect it anymore. I sensed my soul again because my selffulness no longer eclipsed it. I became reconnected to my true self. With selffulness out of the way, refreshing streams of love resumed flowing through my umbilicore, and I became reconnected to Creator. My dark thoughts and feelings from this morning had vanished.

With overflowing gratitude and bleary eyes, I wrapped my arms around Aable. Without words, I thanked Creator for rescuing me. Creator responded by enclosing me within His invisible, loving arms.

"Creator couldn't help you," Manna said, "until you asked for His help. That required setting aside your pride and selffulness."

While we walked back to my shelter, I pondered this new threat. Selffulness was more dangerous than any wild beast. How could I guard myself against this insidious enemy? It had captured my soul unaware and could do so again. I felt helpless against it. Under my breath, so the Teachers couldn't hear, I said, "Creator, please protect me."

Peace and assurance flowed into me. My fears relaxed, and I took comfort in His love. Without selffulness to defend me, I felt vulnerable, but in its place I discovered an unshakable sense of safety in Creator's love.

We traveled through a field of scattered thistles. Blue butterflies and speckled orange butterflies fluttered from purple flower to flower, oblivious to our presence.

To my surprise, I sensed that Creator wanted to give me a gift. This seemed unfitting, given my recent failings. Yet, I craved His approval more than ever and wanted my devotion to be perfect, so I manufactured the most deferential attitude I could. Striving to be the model of meekness, I said, "I hope I am found worthy to receive it."

In the next horrifying instant, the universe shut down on me. The Teachers vanished. Creator's nearness departed. The flow from my umbilicore stopped. All my comforts fled.

"Creator? Teachers?" I looked for the Teachers in case they were hiding, but I saw no sign of them.

My disabled umbilicore informed me I had offended Creator again. I couldn't believe how often He took offense. Nor could I believe how stupid I was. Would I keep offending Creator over and over again? Would I always be such a failure?

Chapter 29

Non-resistance

My despondency returned and enclosed me in its sticky co-
coon. The self-deprecating thoughts that haunted me this morning
repeated their litany. I felt myself falling into despair but I interrupted my descent before it could engulf me. "Creator, I'm sorry I
offended You again. Be merciful and forgive me."

He said, "If I have deemed you worthy, then you are worthy.
By believing you are unworthy, you contradicted Me and cast Me
as a liar."

Creator's words shocked and perplexed me. I hadn't contradicted Him or called Him a liar. Why did He say that I had?
But I had doubted my worthiness. If He had decided to give me
something, then I supposed He must have already considered me
worthy of it. Now, I understood why Creator was so offended. I
had implied He was wrong for counting me worthy.

"Creator, I realize my error, now. I questioned Your judgment.
I'm sorry. Forgive me for contradicting You. I'm ready to receive
what You want to give me."

Silence followed.

"I am truly sorry. Forgive me for offending You. Why don't
You answer?"

The silence persisted.

Believing I had done something to make matters worse, I panicked. My chest heaved as my breathing became more frantic. Perhaps His displeasure couldn't be placated this time. Maybe I had driven Creator away for good. Admitting my error had worked before. Why was it not working now?

My throat tightened and fluid gushed from my eyes. I dropped to the ground and covered my face. "I'm so sorry. I'm so sorry," I sobbed. "Please return to me. Please."

The terror of abandonment dug holes into my being. For a long time, I wept into my hands. No amount of remorse would make Him return. After I was spent, I remained immobile with my head hung and body limp. My ribs ached from sobbing. My head throbbed. I could do nothing except wait and hope my fears were unfounded.

At mid-afternoon, the flow through my umbilicore resumed. I opened my puffy eyes and saw a swirling white mist hovering in front of me. Although relieved to see Creator again, I was too desolate to show much response. Lifting myself with difficulty, I stood to accept whatever punishment He would mete out. My body swayed from weakness.

"Cherished, I delayed in responding so this lesson would take root in your soul. The lesson I want you to learn is to say yes. No denials, no excuses, no questioning. If I wish to give you a gift, then your response should be yes. The same holds true whenever I ask something of you. Anything more than yes is pretentious. You may not understand or agree with My judgment, but don't contradict Me. You are loved and forgiven. Because I love you, I correct and discipline you."

As Creator had intended, this lesson had taken deep root, instilled into me through vivid experience. My emotions were an incoherent jumble. My fear warned me I would offend Creator again and repeat this nightmare. My anger accused Creator for making me suffer the pain of abandonment. My confusion

wondered why Creator believed this awful experience was necessary. On top of that, my exhaustion made it hard to sort through
my emotions or to keep them from spilling out of their containers.
I felt relief that this ordeal was behind me. Unable to voice the
mixture of my feelings, I said, "I'm glad You returned. I was afraid
You might not."

"When your umbilicore is disabled, you can't sense Me or
draw life from Me, but I am still with you. You are always within
My focus."

Feeling more at ease with Creator, I said, "I'm ready to receive
my gift, now."

"That opportunity has passed, Cherished."

"But. . . ." I dropped my shoulders and sighed. "Yes, Creator."

"You understand why. I know you're disappointed, angry, and
fearful. Allow yourself to fully feel those emotions as you hand
them over to Me. I can transform them into ripples that fade away
and don't persist. Unprocessed feelings get lodged in your body.
As they accumulate, they constrict your umbilicore. Your flow
ought to be abundant and unfettered."

"Yes, Creator. Will you let the Teachers know they can come
back?"

"I will summon them."

The mist began to rotate, gathering speed. It amassed into a
luminous ball of white light. Then the light separated into three
colored spheres—red, green and blue. The glowing orbs settled on
the ground. They changed shape and solidified into the bodies of
Ennoia, Manna, and Aable.

"We," Manna said, "made the universe and everything in it.
We're the Life that flows through your umbilicore. We are Creator."

Chapter 30

Adjustment

I stared at the Teachers, flabbergasted and speechless. I couldn't believe they were Creator. He was sublime and loving. The Teachers were limited and domineering. How could they be the same?

"We are the same," Ennoia said. "As the Teachers, We pushed you to learn. As Creator, We wanted you to bond with Us. We decided it was time to show Our true nature."

I didn't grasp Ennoia's words. Because of my weakness and stupefaction, my knees gave out beneath me. My mind reeled, faded, and flicked off before I hit the ground.

When I recovered consciousness, I saw the Teachers, I mean Creator, crouched around me. Their linked wings shaded my body. I sat up, still faint and lightheaded.

"Eat these," Aable said, handing me some shelled nuts.

Eating them in silence, I regretted some of my actions and attitudes toward the Teachers. If I had known who They were, I would have behaved better. Why didn't They tell me at the start?

I tried to wrap my mind around this new information. All this time, I believed Creator was one being. Now knowing Creator was three beings, I regarded Creator as "They" from that point on.

"We know this revelation is a big adjustment for you," Ennoia said. "We forgive your behavior toward Us as Teachers. As you asserted your individuality, you needed something to push against and separate from. As Teachers, We provided you that counterpoise. In the meantime, you learned to connect to Us through your umbilicore. Now that you know these things, We hope We can have a more cooperative relationship."

The Teachers stood and Aable extended His hand. I grabbed it and pulled myself up. Standing within Their circle, I couldn't look at Their faces. I looked down and scanned the ground for my sweeper. When I picked it up, I turned it over and studied it at length, pretending I was making sure it was intact to delay eye contact with them.

I hadn't yet adjusted to the reality that those three beings created everything, including me. In my mind, They remained the Teachers, as imperfect as before. I had to force myself to think of Them as Creator. "Shall I call you Creator?"

"We prefer that," Manna said. "Let's get you home. The sun will set soon."

Creator began walking, and I took my customary position between Manna and Aable. Aable offered to carry my sweeper. With His free hand, He held mine. Manna held my other hand. As we traveled, I was nourished by the flow through my umbilicore that was my link to Them. I felt an intimacy with Them I hadn't experienced before. Their linked wings united Them, and my umbilicore joined me to Their union by an inward connection. My hands joined me to Them by an outward connection.

My contentment became eroded by a treacherous undertow of dark thoughts. Accusatory whispers surfaced in my mind. "You offered Creator a profane tower. You branded Them as liars. You risked Their displeasure. You pushed Them away."

Hoping They could cure my defectiveness, I turned toward Manna. "Creator, I'm troubled. I've offended You time and time again. I've been presumptuous, proud and self-centered. What should be done about me?"

Creator stopped and Ennoia turned to face me, swapping His wing connections with Manna and Aable. All of Them looked at me with amazement.

"What an excellent question," Manna said with effusive love. "What do you think should be done?"

"I don't know. I don't want to keep disappointing You. I've failed You and feel terrible about it." As I spoke, shame surged within me, the undertow gaining power.

The three beings enclosed me in Their arms. "We aren't disappointed in you, Cherished," Ennoia said into my ear. "Everything that has happened We have adapted to serve you. We use your mistakes, so don't despise your failings. Be grateful for them because they can promote growth when you turn them over to Us."

They released me and gazed at me as though judging whether Ennoia's words had any effect.

Shame stayed in the shadows and crept closer to whisper, "How could Creator love a failure like you? You repel Them."

Aable's wide, blue eyes peered into me. "We love you, Cherished. We love you no matter what."

"No. They detest you," shame hissed.

Aable didn't blink, but locked eyes with something. "We love you fully, mistakes and all."

"He's lying. You're unlovable."

Chapter 31

Choices

The contrary messages confused me, forcing me to choose between messengers. Shame hung on my neck and presented the more convincing arguments. I didn't feel Creator's love in that moment, so their declaration of love sounded false. If I chose to believe shame, I would be contradicting Creator and, thus, casting Them as liars. This time, I chose to believe the truth, that Creator loved and accepted me.

Shame hissed one last time and departed like a flock of starlings scattering to the sky. A warm flood of well-being surged through my umbilicore, filling me with an immeasurable sense of value, as if those rushing currents sought and embraced every mote of my being. The experience was an incontrovertible affirmation of love.

"You made a praiseworthy choice," Manna said, smiling at me. "We're pleased with you, Cherished." The Three embraced me. "Your choices are so important. Choose to believe in the truth. Choose to believe in Our love."

We resumed walking. I grasped Aable's hand with my left and Manna's with my right. Creator led me uphill where the trees thinned to allow vistas of the forest below. We traced the crest of a treeless ridge, enjoying the views on both sides. I felt at peace with

Creator and myself. Given my history, I knew it wouldn't last. I was sure I would mess it up.

"How can I keep from making wrong choices?" I said.

"You can't." Manna spoke in a compassionate tone. "In fact, you'll continue to make wrong choices."

My steps faltered.

"Don't be upset," Manna said, squeezing my hand. "Making mistakes is part of your maturing. When you make a mistake, admit it and try to learn from it. And don't allow the fear of mistakes to hinder your growth. We are greater than your mistakes."

"I don't want to fail You. Can't You protect me from that?"

"Cherished, We can't protect you from making wrong choices. Your choices are yours alone to make. If you love Us, then you'll be careful to avoid those choices that will jeopardize our relationship."

"What choices are those?" I said, frustrated by the absence of practical help. Creator or not, the Teachers hadn't changed. They continued to exasperate me.

"Pridefulness, selffulness, or presumption will disable your connection to Us. Don't focus on those things or fear them. Instead, focus on humility, selflessness, truth, and love, all of which flow from Us and keep you centered. Better yet, stay connected to Us. By doing so, your soul will be safe."

"Safe from mistakes?" I brightened with hope.

"No. Safe from the fear of mistakes. When you're connected to Us, you won't worry about outcomes. When you're not connected to Us, you will fill the void with your own energies."

I doubted I could stay connected for any length of time. I wanted a guarantee of success. Instead, Creator promised I would fail. It was just a matter of time. I was doomed by my own fallibility.

Walking alongside Creator, I said nothing, but my mind struggled to make sense of my life. My mental travail didn't help at all. Giving up, I fought my way through my cluttered thoughts to find my umbilicore. I found it in a region far from my mind, at my deepest center, a point that connected me to the Infinite. When I entered its flow, the commotion inside my mind dissipated along with my questions and confusion. In that profound communion with Creator, I became lost within the safety of their love. My need for purpose and perfection faded and, at the same time, was satisfied.

When we arrived at my shelter, the sky bloomed with orange clouds like strewn petals that hung suspended over the mountains. Creator hugged me and departed. I stood gazing at the breathtaking sky until the color drained from it.

When I entered my shelter, I fluffed the grass of my bed. I sat on it, intrigued by the uncharacteristic tranquility of my soul. My thoughts seemed far off, as if lounging on a distant hilltop like a peaceful herd of grazing sheep. I didn't summon my thoughts, but let them wander in remote places to find their own grass beds on which to sleep.

I curled up on my side and closed my eyes. While falling asleep, I heard the sound of soft patting on my shelter's roof. The sound soothed me. Too sleepy to investigate, I envisioned dozens of grasshoppers jumping on my roof.

What could be causing the sound?

Rain. It was raining.

Chapter 32

Oneness

On awaking, the musky smell of damp soil filled my nose. Not hearing patting sounds, I concluded the rain had stopped. I poked my head out the doorway and saw a motionless scene. The wind held its breath. No birds sang, perhaps because a gray layer of clouds obscured the sun from signaling their chorus.

I crawled outside onto the cool, moist ground. From among the trees, a creature walked uphill toward me on two legs, each footfall planted with poise and mirth. His body had the same shape as mine, but larger, about five hand-widths taller. Along both sides of his body sprouted golden hair that formed a narrow ridge, like a mane, from his ankles to the top of his head. The hair, bundled and tied into small tassels, swooped with rhythmic motions as the creature walked. Apart from this continuous fringe of golden hair, the creature was hairless. His skin, the same color as mine, had a waxy sheen. On his round, flattened face, narrow lips stretched to form a smile that put me at ease.

"Blessings to you, Cherished," the creature said with outstretched arms and a slight bow. "We are Creator. We chose to appear in a single body today."

Both of Creator's wide, circular eyes contained three black

pupils swimming within a golden iris. Creator's voice was a rich, melodious blend of three voices that produced the same calming effect as water splashing in a brook.

"How do all three of You fit into one body?" I said.

"We are spirits. Spirits have no volume. We chose this form to show you that although We are three, We are entwined as One."

"I don't understand."

"That's all right, Cherished. Oneness is a hard concept to grasp. It's like your hand. Your fingers are distinct but work together. A finger can move by itself but it's always part of the hand. Where the hand goes, the fingers go. Where the finger goes, the hand goes. The fingers obey the intent of the hand and don't pursue their own will."

I studied my hand as I wiggled my fingers.

"So, what shall we do today?" Creator said.

Astounded, I said, "You don't know?"

"We're letting you decide."

"I get to decide?" The opportunity thrilled me. "I want to visit a lake. But not the lake where I built the tower." Confronting the destroyed tower wasn't something I was ready to do.

"We know a place you'll like. We'll take you there." Creator took my hand and began leading me. "And We'll teach you how to swim."

We sauntered along the forest path toward the new lake, picking and eating food as we traveled. As an act of habit, I would find the largest stone in view and place my food on top before eating it, the stone becoming my thanksgiving table. I talked non-stop during our stroll, expressing my thoughts about everything. The food. Last night's rain. Insects I saw. Mushrooms and flowers. Creator listened to my ramblings with patience and attentiveness. The various sights along the path propelled my monologue, a random succession of observations and judgments.

We arrived at the lake, much larger than the other one. The water was so clear I could see fish swimming along the bottom.

The sloping shore was dotted with mature pine trees, a few which stood in the water. Smooth, granite boulders broke the water's surface in various places. Clusters of fleecy clouds created slow-moving shaded patches across the scene. In a few places, the sunlight skirted the clouds and illuminated columns of water with golden shafts that touched the lake's bottom. A warm breeze stirred the water, causing ripples to race across the lake from one bank to the other.

Standing on the sandy shore, I took in the scene with deep draws as if trying to capture it within me. Creator walked down the slope into the water, causing the magical liquid to leap and dance around His legs. When Creator inhabited one body, I found it easier to think of Them as "Him." He continued walking into deeper water until His body was submerged up to His chest. He turned around, extended two wet arms, and beckoned. "The water is pleasant. Come into the lake, Cherished."

I entered the lake with hesitancy. Walking through the water took effort, but I enjoyed the soothing sensation of the water enveloping my body. When the water reached my stomach, the coolness made me gasp, but I relaxed into it.

As an experiment, I slapped the surface. Water sprayed all over Creator and me. I winced when the water hit my face, which made Him laugh. The sound of His hearty laugh filled me with warmth and joy. To elicit another laugh, I slapped the water in His direction, sending a large splash into His face. Wet bundles of golden hair lay flat against His head, wiping away any appearance of dignity. I hollered with laughter at the sight of His wet, dripping face. He splashed me in return. This led to repeated splashing of each other and mutual laughter until He disappeared under the water. I waited for Him to reappear so we could resume our splashing game. When He emerged and grabbed me from behind, I shrieked with surprise and delight.

Creator taught me to hold my breath. After a few underwater surveys of the lake, He taught me to swim. We swam back and forth across the lake for practice. Then we raced each other to the opposite side a few times. When I reached the other side first, I laughed. When He won the race, I laughed just as much.

I climbed out and, with a running jump, threw myself into the lake to create the biggest splash I could. Enthralled by the results, I jumped and splashed dozens of times. Each time was as fun as the last.

Creator suggested a game where each player had to push a floating pine cone to the opposite side without using our hands or arms. We took turns stealing the pine cone from each other and trying to push it, using a creative medley of silly actions. We bumped and kicked each other, but the pine cone never got close to either shore. I had so much fun trying.

I became tired and suggested we rest. We climbed out and flopped down on the sandy shore. I rested my head on Creator's stomach and closed my eyes. The sun's warmth penetrated my body and made me drowsy. With each puff of wind, the water droplets on my body quivered and made my skin tingle. Creator caressed my wet hair with one hand, stroking my scalp with His fingertips. His touch relaxed me. I found extreme contentment in that moment.

Because my connection to Creator was strong, I gave myself over to it. I felt Creator within me and around me. Like the enveloping water of the lake, They encompassed me and immersed me in Their being. I was part of a larger whole, still me but more than me, not separate but connected to Creator in every way. My being merged with Theirs as the confines of self dissolved to allow Creator to spill into me. Oneness now made sense.

My boundaries reappeared because I needed the security they provided. I had become so used to the enclosure of a body that spaciousness felt too foreign. Although the experience of oneness collapsed, I didn't judge myself but continued to float in the waters that flowed through my umbilicore, the waters that were Creator.

Chapter 33

Consequence

I considered those fingertips running through my hair, those fingertips that had sculpted my body. That same strong hand had spread out the sky above me and gathered the ground beneath me. When it hit me that the creator of the universe was my headrest, I opened my eyes with a start and stared at the clouds with awe. In light of that recognition, I expected to feel insignificant but I felt important, instead. I knew I wasn't more important than Creator, but They made me feel valued. Without regard to my ability or maturity, They had assigned importance to me.

For the first time, I understood what love meant.

He whispered. "Yes, Cherished, you're loved. You have immense value to Us. We take great delight in you."

As I allowed those words to penetrate, gratitude billowed within me. I yearned to give Creator the same pleasure They had given me, and I wondered if it were possible. As I pondered the workings of love, my thoughts faded as sleep washed over me.

When I awoke, I said, "I'm going in the water." Without waiting for a response, I sprinted into the lake and swam laps.

Creator sat on the shore and watched me.

I swam to one of the tall pine trees that stood in the water. The tree was long dead and bleached by the sun. I climbed the tree. "Creator, watch me jump," I yelled and continued to climb higher.

"You shouldn't climb that high," He shouted back.

"I know what I'm doing. Watch me make a big splash."

I grabbed a branch that snapped off, and I lost my balance. Grasping another branch to catch myself, it broke off as well. Plummeting from the treetop, I flailed my arms in a futile attempt to break my fall. When I struck the surface of the lake, it hardened itself to resist my entry. The impact stunned me. I clambered to shore and limped back to Creator.

Having nothing to say, I plopped myself down next to Creator and closed my eyes, allowing the warm sun to dry my skin. I kept my eyes shut to signal my unwillingness for conversation. We sat without speaking for some time, and I savored the tranquility. I worked my toes and fingers into the sand, enjoying the cool and crunchy sensation.

After a while, I stood and said, "I'm hungry. I'm going to find some food. Will You come with me?"

"Yes," Creator said, getting to His feet.

I headed into the trees with Creator trailing behind me. He caught up and walked alongside. I waited for Him to say something about my foolish fall, but He said nothing. When I could no longer stand the suspense, I said, "I know. I know. I was stupid to climb so high."

"If you say so."

"What? You don't have an opinion?"

"What matters is what you've learned. For every act, there is a consequence and a boundary. The further you risk, the greater the consequence, be it pleasure or pain. A boundary is a limit that when crossed will produce an adverse consequence. Climbing too high was a boundary for you today. By the way, you did make a big splash." Creator smiled. "Just as you said you would."

I smiled, but only on the outside.

We came to a pear tree, and I stood on my toes to reach a ripe pear. After I had plucked it, I sensed movement. I turned toward the movement and saw tiger eyes locked on me as padded feet struck the ground in a swift attack. I had no time to react.

My vision blurred into flashes of fur and claws and blood and dust. I cried out in fear.

Chapter 34

Attack

Creator had jumped into the path of the charging tiger. The tiger knocked Him down and pinned Him with its claws. Its teeth dug into muscle and bone, severing arteries. Creator's body lay limp.

The tiger clamped its teeth into the top of Creator's shoulder, near the neck. Then it dragged Him backward into the woods.

My shock shifted into action as I pursued the tiger, shouting and waving my arms with wide, frantic swings. I tried to scare the tiger like the first time.

The tiger continued to retreat backward, still dragging Creator's body across the dirt and dead leaves. Its powerful jaws refused to release its meal.

I picked up a heavy stone and hurled it at the tiger. With dismay, I watched the stone fall short and hit Creator on the chest.

Grabbing another large stone, I rushed up to the tiger, boldness overcoming fear. Slamming the stone down onto the tiger's head, I heard a loud, hollow thud as it recoiled and gave up its prey. I stepped back two paces.

The massive tiger stood over the body, panting and staring at me with its head lowered. Its fierce eyes studied me. Saliva and blood dripped from its mouth.

I raised the stone, still in my hands, showing my intent to use it again. The tiger looked at the stone and flinched. With narrowed eyes, it glanced at the body, then again at the stone. It snarled and swung one paw at me, but I was beyond its reach.

"Get away from Creator," I shouted.

The tiger lowered its head near the ground. Then it fastened its mouth onto Creator's shoulder and dragged again. I ran up and struck the tiger on the head as hard as I could. Bone cracked.

It yelped and let go. With its eyes closed, its head shuddered as if it were trying to shake off the pain. When it opened its eyes, it snarled and crouched with its forearms flat and rump shoved high. Believing it was about to lunge at me, I lifted the stone above my head, ready to use it again. My heart pounded hard and fast, being the only sound I could hear, the only sensation I could feel.

After a long moment, the tiger turned around and trotted away until the trees hid it from view. My eyes remained fixed on the spot where the tiger disappeared while my hands still held the uplifted stone.

I waited until I was sure the tiger was far away, then I dropped the stone and looked at Creator. Blood and dirt caked His upper body. A large, ragged wound at the neck and shoulder glistened with blood. His mouth hung open, lips unmoving. His eyelids lolled, exposing dirty white slits.

I knelt and waited, watching His body for any sign of movement. As time passed, I became more anxious. What was supposed to happen next? Creator always knew what was next. Did He foresee His mangled, bleeding body sprawled on the ground? Did He carry this knowledge throughout the day? If so, why didn't He prevent it? Why had this happened? None of the possible explanations I conjured made any sense.

I expected Him to open His eyes, sit up, and speak. My disappointment escalated into horror when I realized He wouldn't recover. Creator was dead.

Chapter 35

Trust

"We're always with you," I remembered Manna saying. But now, Creator was gone, killed by the savage tiger. My throat tightened and my eyes stung. My stomach clenched, and I folded, dropping my head to my knees. I wailed with loud sobs while fluid poured out of my eyes and nose. The punishing darkness of abandonment engulfed me. Terrors pummeled me like falling rocks and I curled up to deflect the blows.

A noise roused me back to awareness. I stopped and listened. The familiar voice said, "Why did you doubt?"

I opened my wet eyes and looked at Creator. His lifeless body hadn't moved. His mouth gaped open like a useless cave. Flies had gathered on His wounds.

"Cherished," the voice said. I turned toward the sound and saw a second Creator standing unharmed.

Seeing Him made me glad, but the trauma of my ordeal still rattled my emotions. Anger and hurt circled in twisting eddies. With a shaky voice, I uttered a wounded and bitter, "Why?"

Without answering, Creator bent down and held me for a long time. Confusion, doubt, fear, and anger resurfaced at full strength as if summoned by Creator against my will. I wept with loud, aching sobs. Each emotion surfaced in turn, but this time they didn't subdue me. Instead, by some miraculous process, the emotions moved outward and exited like poison being extracted from my body. When the last emotion had finished its course, the spasms of sobbing ceased. I felt lighter, although weary.

Creator wiped my eyes with His thumbs and used the hairy fringe along His arms to mop the mucus below my nose. I remained seated on the ground as Creator sat on His feet, facing me. I gazed into His golden eyes, each with three black pupils that swam like fish at play in a pond of honey. They stopped their dance and fixed themselves on me.

Creator said, "Every choice We make has purpose. Not everything We do will make sense to you, even if We try to explain it. At times, We'll withhold explanation because your mind is incapable of grasping it. At other times, We'll deny you an explanation because We want you to trust in Us. Trust is deepened when you choose to trust in spite of your senses."

"I thought You were dead," I said, my voice cracking. "What else could I have trusted but my senses?" I looked at the bloodied body. It unsettled me, so I looked away.

"Cherished," He said to get my attention.

I turned and gazed at His face.

"You had a choice. In situations like this, you must choose between trusting in Us or trusting in your senses. You must decide between two realities, the physical reality of what you're experiencing or the spiritual reality of what is true. The truth is We love you and We are always with you. Your experience may seem to contradict that truth, as it did today, but remember that experience isn't truth. Truth is greater than experience."

"Should I not trust my senses, then?"

"You can trust your senses, but don't use them to judge the unseen, such as Our presence or love. When the tiger destroyed Our body, you believed you were alone, but that was untrue. The tiger could only harm Our body, not Our spirits. Our spirits now

106

inhabit this new body."

I glanced at the dead body again. Its existence stirred up resentment within me. "Why did You wait so long? If You had shown Yourself right away, I wouldn't have despaired."

"Dear Cherished, don't despise delay. The tension of delay is how character is developed. We delayed so you would have opportunity to wrestle with truth. You needed time to choose whether to believe your senses or believe Our words. During those moments of struggle, trust is deepened or discarded."

"The tiger attack was a test to see if I would trust?"

"Everything is a test of your trust."

I shook my head in disbelief. Then my mind lumbered toward the obvious conclusion. "I failed the test, then." I groaned.

Shame traveled up my spine like a lizard scurrying up a tree. Creator placed His hand on the back of my neck. As if He had intercepted the lizard, the shame dispersed. With His large hand still behind my neck, He brought our heads closer together.

"You didn't fail," He said, "because you've learned something. What have you learned?"

I recalled the distressing moments that followed His death. "I've learned I'm incapable of trusting in You." I hated to admit it. Not only had I failed the test, I had failed Creator. Unable to look at His face, I stared at my calloused knees.

"Can You fix my trust?" I whispered, hoping He wouldn't respond if the answer was no. I glanced up to see if He heard me.

He smiled and said, "Fix? Do you think your trust is broken? Dear Cherished, trust isn't like an object that can be broken or fixed. Let's return to the lake and We'll show you an illustration of trust. We'll leave the body here for any animals that need to eat."

Creator stood, brushed the dirt off His legs, and pulled me to my feet. We headed back to the lake. I looked behind me at the dead body, wondering if it would still be there when I passed this way again.

Chapter 36

Maturity

Creator held my hand as we strolled back to the large lake. He said, "Cherished, weakness isn't failure. Don't be surprised by your shortcomings and don't punish yourself because of them. Your shortcomings attest your immaturity, which means you're not yet complete."

We walked through a grove of towering koa trees, with their rough, fissured bark and crescent-shaped leaves. Clusters of pale-yellow flowers caught the sunlight in the upper regions of the trees. Red birds darted amid the elephantine branches overhead, their movements muffled by the shielded stillness of the grove. No one spoke as we slowed to enjoy the tranquil scene.

When we left the grove, Creator said, "We couldn't create you as a mature being. Maturity can't be created. It can only be formed though life's experiences. Everything in this world must undergo transformation. A tree starts as a seed that sprouts and matures into a glorious structure. Like that seed, you must grow into the fullness of what's intended for you."

"Will I grow as tall as a tree?"

Creator chuckled. "That won't happen." He touched the center of my chest. "Changes to your soul are unseen. They occur when situations push you beyond your limits, forcing you to reach into untapped resources and draw strength from them. It's like a tree's roots pushing deeper to find new sources of water and nutrients. If you allow yourself to be deepened through experiences, you'll grow in maturity."

"I still don't understand what maturity is."

"Maturity is knowing oneself and one's place in the universe, knowing what's important and what's true. It is demonstrated by a willingness to take responsibility, to admit weakness, to endure suffering, and to accept all outcomes. It is character that has been refined until one gives and receives love freely."

I couldn't identify with anything mentioned. "That's not me."

"But can be." He smiled and touched my arm. "Experiences create opportunities for transformation. Transformation is a profound inner change that enlarges your capacity for spiritual abundance. Your soul is a cistern that holds Our Life, the Life that flows into you through your umbilicore. When you entrust yourself to Us during challenging situations, you give Us permission to stretch and enlarge your soul and to remove those things that are non-elastic. This stretching enables you to be filled with more of Us. As with any inner reconstruction, this alteration is painful."

"In that case, I'll decline."

"Your transformation has paramount importance to Us," He said. "We will do whatever it takes to bring it about."

"I don't have a say?"

"No. Your destination has been set. You can cooperate or resist, but We're committed to helping you complete your journey, whether by the short or long route, whether in sorrow or joy. It's your choice."

"I choose the easy route."

"The easy route takes you nowhere. Choose transformation. That route is difficult, but when you trust in Us, We can transform you into what We purpose you to be. Because you didn't choose to trust today, the experience had no transformative effect."

Chapter 37

Illustration

When we arrived at the lake, Creator scooped water into His cupped hands. He approached a mound of soft dirt and dribbled water on its peak. The water divided into three small streams that trickled down the sides of the mound.

He said, "Imagine this water is trust. Notice the flow of water has no singular direction. This is like immature trust, unstable and inconsistent. Look what happens when We continue to pour water."

He dribbled more water in the same place as before. The water traveled down only one of the channels because it was the most prominent channel carved out by the previous pour. He poured water a third time. The water stayed in that one channel and gouged a deep trench.

"See how the water digs a channel into the dirt?" He said. "Trust works in the same way. Every time you choose to trust, it carves a deeper channel in your soul. That channel makes it easier to trust the next time it's needed. Trust grows by trusting."

"So, every time I trust, I grow in trust?"

"Yes. Like many things in life, trust is strengthened through repeated use. Mature trust is singular in focus, just as water always flows downhill. Mature trust is also persistent. Like water, it finds its way around obstacles."

I stared at the mound of dirt and wondered if my soul would behave in the same way. I doubted it would, so I stomped on the mound to destroy the ideal by which I might be compared.

"Look at Us, Cherished."

I searched His face for any doubt He might have in me, but found none. He placed His hand on my shoulder.

"We will help you, Cherished. Since We framed your destiny, it behooves Us to fulfill it, not you. We only ask that you cooperate. One more thing We ask, that you seek to know Us. Don't try to understand Us through your senses because that will create a false portrayal of Us. True understanding comes when We reveal Ourselves to you in response to your trust in Us. What have you learned about Us today?"

I reviewed the day's events in my mind. "I've learned You can fit into one body. You're more fun when you have one body. I enjoyed swimming with You in the lake. I've learned You aren't limited by physical containers. You can be killed but not destroyed. What else? You're able to protect me. You jumped in front of the ti—"

My tongue seized up as awe overtook me. Creator's intervening jump in front of the charging tiger revealed something I hadn't seen before—His self-sacrifice. I now saw His willingness to sacrifice everything on my behalf. To protect me from the tiger, He consented to being attacked, mauled, and killed. I supposed the trauma from today's experience had prevented this realization sooner. Or my own self-centeredness had blinded me. This realization staggered my mind with something too profound to fully grasp—the extent of His tremendous love for me. I had experienced His love within my soul, but to see it demonstrated in such a dramatic way was more meaningful and far more precious.

Chapter 38

Love

This new understanding of love enlarged my soul. Love flooded into the hollow and overwhelmed me, causing my soul to tremble and my body to weaken. Unable to stay standing, I dropped to my knees and wept. My body convulsed as a powerful torrent of love scraped away hardened attachments from my soul, stripping away everything that defied love—fear, guilt, shame, and self-contempt. All these things departed as if my tears had captured and transported them out of my body, leaving a tender void in its wake. He poured His love into the void with such overabundance it was like trying to swallow a downpour.

Joy expanded within me, and I realized it wasn't Creator's doing, but my soul expanding with love for Him. I allowed this nascent love of mine to carry my soul toward the object of its desire, toward Creator. Still on my knees, I bent forward and placed my hands on His feet, my face almost touching the ground. I poured out my soul like water onto Him, giving Him my whole self. With each wave of surrender, my body shuddered. With tears, I cooed over and over, "I love You, Creator. I love You."

When I had emptied myself of all I could give, I remained prostrate and silent.

Creator said, "Stand up, Cherished."

I got onto my feet and faced Him, noticing His eyes twinkling with joyous affection. He put His hands on my shoulders and pressed His lips against my forehead.

"Your love is precious to Us," He said with tenderness. "You love because you've received love, which compels itself to give."

He kissed my forehead again. "Our love is yours forever. We won't always protect you from adversity, but Our love will sustain you and your trust in Our love will transform you. You will encounter tempests and tigers, but Our love is greater than any danger or threat."

The bad news tainted the good news. Why did every promise of comfort include a promise of tribulation?

We left the lake and trekked back home, both of us saying nothing. I didn't need to speak as my mind was clear and uncluttered like a cloudless sky. Instead, I enjoyed total contentment in my connection to Creator, in His love for me and my love for Him. We were fused together now and nothing could ever change that.

We arrived at my shelter at dusk. Creator sat and leaned against one of the bay trees that framed my shelter door. He beckoned me to come sit with Him. I came near. He guided me to sit between His legs and to lean back against His chest. Then He wrapped His arms around me and held me while the night descended around us. We watched the trees blacken into silhouettes against the dense sprinkling of stars. Profound tranquility and absolute acceptance embraced me. In Creator, I found complete fulfillment.

He interrupted the long silence, saying, "Would you like to hear a story?"

"Yes," I said, brightening.

"This story is about Kiki, the fearful finch," He began. "Kiki was at the age for flying, but she was afraid to leave her nest. She believed that the world beyond her nest was full of countless dangers. She refused to fly because she feared crashing to the ground and becoming crippled or worse. So, she resolved to never leave her nest or learn to fly.

"Kiki's siblings learned to fly and encouraged her to do the same. 'Flying is great fun,' they said. 'Learn to fly and join us in the sky.'

"Kiki said, 'No, thanks. I prefer to stay in my nest where it is safe.'

"Kiki's parents were concerned about her refusal to fly. 'You're old enough now to feed yourself,' they said to Kiki. 'We will stop bringing you food.'

"They thought that if Kiki got hungry enough, she would change her mind about flying. But her fear was greater than her hunger.

"Kiki stopped eating and became emaciated. Her parents became distraught. They asked the wise, old macaw for advice.

"The macaw said, 'Fear has power as long as the feared thing is avoided. You must push Kiki out of the nest and allow her to fall. Only then, will she learn to fly . . .'"

I don't remember the rest of the story. I must have fallen asleep in Creator's arms.

Chapter 39

Proclamation

The next morning, I awoke inside my shelter. Creator must have carried me inside last night. With my eyes closed, I took a deep breath and smiled. I floated in an immense, tranquil lake that was Creator and felt buoyant, safe, and loved. After luxuriating in the experience for a while, I opened my eyes and sat up. Beams of light streamed between the horizontal branches of my shelter wall. I propped open my door, using the sturdy stick I kept for that purpose, and crawled into the sunlight, feeling joyous and hopeful.

When I saw the Teachers sitting on the granite table, disappointment jabbed my gut. I had expected the golden-fringed Creator. In spite of the letdown, I greeted Them and hugged each one.

"You're different today, Cherished," Aable said, studying me. He cocked his head left and right.

I squirmed, embarrassed that my disappointment was so conspicuous. I countered by saying, "You're different today, also."

Ennoia said, "What Aable meant is that you're abiding in Us this morning. That means you're drawing continual sustenance from Our being through your umbilicore. We're pleased that you've learned to stay in the flow."

I relaxed with relief. "Ah, yes. The flow," I said, trying to sound as if I understood what He was talking about.

"I am the flow," Aable said. "I fill you with the water of Life."

"I am the water of Life," Manna said. "I am nourishment to your soul."

"I am the source," Ennoia said. "The flow of life-giving water issues from Me."

At that moment, this flow bubbled up within me and sprang forth as words that didn't come from my mind.

"Today and every day, You surround me with love and good things. Like the midday sun, Your abundant kindness shines on me. Like the wind at my shoulders, Your comforting presence follows me. When You pour Yourself into the cistern of my soul, I drink and am refreshed as by cool water. My soul overflows with the Life that springs from You. Your Life is my treasure and beauty. I delight in You, my Creator, my Source. I rejoice in Your unfailing love. All I am, I surrender to You. Because You have given Your life for me, I give You my life, poured out onto Your feet."

These words of mine, yet not mine, amazed me. How did they find their way into my mouth?

Their faces lit up with wide smiles. Ennoia said, "Nothing brings Us more pleasure than a pure gift from the soul, of more value than anything made by human hands. Your love for Us is Our great delight."

Each one hugged me with a tight embrace.

"You haven't eaten yet," Manna said. "We'll wait here while you find something to eat."

I had picked clean all the food from nearby plants, but I knew of a large blackberry patch that never failed to have a few ripe berries. I wandered downhill to the ravine where thorny blackberry branches massed in huge mounds of tangled growth. While searching for ripe berries, I spotted a smooth, tan-colored creature basking in the sunlight, curled up near my feet. Alternating diamonds of light and dark ran the length of the creature's long,

116

legless body. I bent down to study the fascinating creature. Instead of fleeing like all the other animals I had encountered, it pulled back its wide, flattened head. Perhaps it wanted a better view of me. I extended my hand to touch its scaly skin, but before I made contact, it lunged with a swift thrust and bit my hand at the base of my thumb.

I yelped and retracted my hand. The creature slithered into the shade of the blackberry bushes. I discovered two small punctures on my hand that hurt when I touched them. The skin around the punctures reddened and swelled as I watched. Like gathering storm clouds, my intuition warned me that trouble was approaching.

I thought it best to return to my shelter where Creator waited for me. They would know what to do. By the time I had circled around the blackberry thicket, my body was tingling. A foreign sense of panic invaded me. I wanted to run but felt faint and confused. My breathing became shallow and labored. On my way uphill, I held on to every tree to steady myself from the dizziness. My stomach convulsed, and I doubled over to empty its contents. Unable to stand, I dropped to the ground, then twisted sideways to eject what remained in my stomach. After dragging myself away from the puddle, I curled up on my side. "Creator. Help me," I gasped.

Creator didn't come, even though They were close by. I tried to yell out, but my lungs refused. My eyes couldn't focus and the edges of my vision shrank. A grasping darkness tried to steal my consciousness, but I fought to stay awake. Why didn't They rescue me? Why were They keeping Their distance? Was my earlier proclamation of Their goodness nothing more than words?

Chapter 40

Darkness

Ennoia, Manna and Aable sat on the granite outcrop in front of Cherished's shelter, Their linked wings suspended in tense formation. They knew when the snake bit Cherished. They knew it even before it happened, seeing the event in the distance moving toward Them until it crossed the threshold of the present. With complete attentiveness, Their spirit eyes watched the event unfold. They saw Cherished weaken as the snake venom delivered its poison. They witnessed Cherished's struggle against doubt.

"Cherished is afraid," Aable said, His face pinched with concern. "We should help."

"No, not yet," Ennoia said. "Cherished must pass through every phase of the eclipse." Ennoia squeezed His eyes shut, wrinkling the skin around His eyes.

Aable's wings shuddered. "I can't just sit and watch. Cherished needs Us. The newling feels so alone."

"Cherished is not alone," Manna said. "We stand beside Cherished through this entire ordeal." Manna hoisted His massive wings up from their drooped position.

"But I want to comfort and heal," Aable said.

Ennoia said, "We will do all those things at the proper time.

Cherished needs to learn to not fear the darkness. If We intervene now, then We abort the lesson."

"The newling is losing hope," Aable said, His voice cracking. His blue eyes flooded with tears. He threw His arms around Manna and buried His huge nose between Manna's arm and side.

"Hope will prevail," Manna said to Aable, "because Cherished trusts in Us."

"The newling is still so fragile," Aable said, His words muffled by Manna's arm.

Ennoia said, "Be patient, dear ones. The time is soon. We will intervene before the breaking point."

I knew I was dying, steps away from Creator, but dying nonetheless. Loss of control. Loss of consciousness. Loss of life. All those things terrified me, and my efforts to fight them were failing. Only a tiny corner of my mind remained under my command. I could no longer resist the fierce pull that tried to drag me away from my senses. With pained desperation, I tried to grasp Creator, to keep from losing myself, but I couldn't find Them. In my futile struggle against the downward current, I slipped into a frightening darkness and lost consciousness.

As though They shared Cherished's body, Ennoia, Manna and Aable experienced the nausea, the shallow breathing, the cold sweat, the consciousness draining away. They felt these sensations empathetically, as one's brain would experience them, like physical sensations within a vivid dream. They sensed the fear and despair as Cherished groped to find Them. And They felt the body go slack as Cherished blacked out and sank deeper toward death.

Ennoia opened His eyes and said, "Now!"

All Three snapped into action.

Chapter 41

Rescue

At the bottom of a deep, narrow shaft, I ascended toward a bright light. As I got closer to the light, it encompassed me with its brilliance. I felt my body again, becoming warmer and warmer until it burned hot. Then, as the heat diminished, so did my symptoms. When my body reached normal temperature, I felt like my regular self, although somewhat hazy.

My right eye was smashed against the ground. My left eye saw blurred blades of grass. I propped myself up and tried to shake off my lightheadedness. Noticing moisture on my chin, I wiped off the foamy drool.

Creator spoke inside my mind. "You'll be all right, Cherished. We've removed the poison from your body."

"You didn't come. I called, and You didn't come." Creator had abandoned me again. Hurt and anger returned.

"We were with you the entire time."

"But I felt alone."

"That's because pain and fear prevents you from feeling Us."

"How can Your presence comfort me if I don't feel it?"

"By knowing you're not alone and that We're aware of everything that happens to you."

"I was afraid."

"You needn't fear, Cherished. Our love will preserve your soul. We will allow nothing to destroy it."

I noted that Creator didn't promise to protect my body. It must have less value to Them, I supposed. "Why did You wait so long?"

"If We had responded right away, you wouldn't have learned that you can trust Us in times of darkness. The darkness has passed. Now, receive Our comfort and healing."

I opened my soul and made myself vulnerable. A soothing balm eased the pain of abandonment. Love embraced me and coaxed me to deepen my trust in Creator.

After being refreshed, I picked myself up. I staggered a little because I was feeling weak. My empty stomach jabbed me with hunger, so I resumed my initial search for food. I was loath to return to the blackberry bushes, so I cut across the hillside to find other sources of food.

On my way home, I took a shortcut over the ridge. The ridge was devoid of bushes and trees, covered only with sparse grass. Ahead of me, a giant, pale-lavender sphere hovered above the grass. The glowing, solid sphere was as tall as me. I figured this was Creator appearing in some new form. The surface of the sphere had dozens of large eyes, some open, some closed, some moving across the face of the globe like leaves drifting across the surface of a pond. The open eyes had cobalt-blue irises that emitted beams of white light that extended like long, transparent spikes. The beams beneath the sphere behaved as stalks that suspended the giant ball of eyes.

As I approached, Creator became animated, bobbing up and down with increasing speed and height. More eyes opened, casting additional spots of light upon the scene.

Creator's previous manifestations had a presence that conveyed loving devotion, but not this time. I felt no familiarity with this being and became wary. I slowed my advance, now believing that this creature was not Creator.

Chapter 42

Radiance

"Greetings, Cherished," the creature said with bubbly enthusiasm in a small voice that contradicted its size. The luminous, pale-lavender sphere had no mouth I could see. "My name is Radiance. I am an angel."

The creature rotated its giant head forward, projecting beams of bright light into my eyes. I squinted and held up my arm to block the light.

"I am exceedingly delighted to meet you, Cherished." Radiance rotated again and blinded me a second time.

Bouncing in place, Radiance gushed, "Creator appointed me to introduce you to angels such as myself. Though I am most undeserving of such a privilege, Creator chose me. Therefore, I am exceedingly honored to be appointed for this task. We angels have heard so much about you, Cherished. So, now, here I am speaking to you in person. I am exceedingly pleased—"

"What's an angel?" I interrupted, feeling impatient and perturbed. Up to this moment, I had believed I was unique. But if beings like Radiance existed, intelligent beings capable of conversation, then I wasn't so unique after all. Did angels steal some of Creator's affection intended for me?

"An angel is Creator's servant," Radiance said, its voice almost tittering. "An angel is devoted to Creator in every way. We obey Creator without falter. We worship Creator in thought, speech and action. We serve as messengers, protectors, caretakers or sanitizers, among other things."

I studied the sphere, looking for gender clues. "Are you a he or a she?"

"Neither. Angels have no gender. If I were to choose one, I would prefer to be a she."

"How many angels are there?"

"Millions."

"Millions? Why haven't I seen any angels until now?"

"Because you can't see us. We are spirits that inhabit the invisible spiritual realm. When we visit the physical realm, we can't be seen unless we choose to appear in physical form as in this body I now occupy."

"If Creator has millions of angels, then why did They make me?" I felt lost within a massive crowd, unimportant and unnoticed.

"Creator wanted to make something different than angels."

Radiance stopped bouncing. Numerous eyes slid over to one side of her head and illuminated some trees in the distance with long, light beams. The harsh light captured a lone deer that watched us. I thought nothing of the deer until I noticed it was missing its ears.

"We are not alone," Radiance said. "Let us go to a more private location. I will transport you."

Eyes opened at the bottom of her head. From those eyes, rays of light projected as curved stalks. They wrapped around my body and picked me up. Then they retracted and cradled me under the sphere in a supine position. Her other eyes began to rotate forward, their beams conveying us ahead with increasing speed. We rolled like a dandelion puff blown by a breeze.

Feeling the air sweep over me and seeing the ground speed below me was exhilarating. I looked up at Radiance, who had three cobalt eyes fixed on me. With a cautious hand, I reached up and touched the lavender sphere, which felt smooth, almost slippery.

We stopped at an unfamiliar place, a sprawling field of yellow and purple wildflowers. Radiance lowered me to the ground, setting me on my feet. Her many eyes scanned our surroundings, lighting every object in view.

"This location is exceedingly remote," she said, closing many of her eyes. "No one can see or hear us, except for Creator."

Her need for privacy perplexed me, but I didn't ask about it. "You were telling me how I'm different than angels."

"Yes. You are the only being that Creator has made in Their image. Both you and Creator are three parts merged into one. You have a body, a spirit, and a soul. Your body is that part of you that exists in and interacts with the physical world. Your spirit exists in and interacts with the spiritual world. Your soul is your core essence and is tethered to your body and spirit.

"Angels do not have a soul," she said. "We are pure spirit. We may take on a temporary body, but the substance of our bodies is not subject to decay."

She paused to scan our vicinity again, her eyes swimming around her head like ants swarming around a piece of food.

"What also distinguishes you from angels is that you have a triple gifting from Creator, a contribution from each. All created things have been given form by Aable, who is the power of creation. All living things have been given life by Manna, who is Life manifest. But, into you alone Ennoia has implanted a divine, eternal seed. In truth, you are Creator's offspring."

It pleased me to hear I was still unique, but I didn't understand the importance of my uniqueness. "Why did Creator make me when They already have angels to serve and worship Them?"

"An exceedingly astute question, Cherished. Creator wanted someone to love who would love Them in return."

With more clarity than ever, I understood that my existence had to do with love.

Chapter 43

Encumbrances

"We angels are not capable of love, you see," Radiance said. "We can be loyal to perfection, but we cannot love. And you, Cherished, are the sole object of Creator's love."

"They do not love you?" I said, astonished.

"Creator has compassion for every creature, but They have chosen to focus Their love on you alone."

A mix of awe and responsibility settled upon me. I sat within the wildflower field, the fragrance of flowers now sweetening my every breath.

Radiance continued. "Love is only a concept to me. I cannot produce love or experience love. I do find the notion intriguing."

"You don't know what love feels like?"

"Our capacity for emotion is limited. We do not feel much of anything." Her brightness dimmed a little. "But, we are capable of deep loyalty and firm resolve," she boasted, lighting up again. "Besides, emotions would encumber us in our service. You are laden with emotions. Don't you find that they interfere with your devotion to Creator?"

"All the time," I laughed. "I agree that emotions complicate things, but they also enhance my relationship with Creator."

"Enhance?" Radiance said. "I thought emotions were meant to be overcome like other obstacles Creator has placed in your life. Even the body They assigned to you is rife with weakness." Radiance shone a light beam on my body, tracing my skinny arms and legs.

"There's nothing wrong with my body. It serves me fine, even with its limitations. I prefer it over a giant, disembodied head. And those obstacles you mentioned are meant to transform my soul." I tried to put a positive spin on my erratic existence.

"Transform? Into what?"

I paused to think up an answer. "I'm not sure. Something more human, according to Creator, whatever that means." A little red flower caught my attention. I snapped off its stalk and began rolling it between my fingers.

"Interesting," Radiance mused, eyes blinking and beams flashing. "Spirits do not transform. We always stay the same. But souls can transform?"

"Yes. My soul has changed many times and in many ways." I straightened my spine as high as it could go. "My soul has greater capacity for trust, love, and courage than it used to."

All her eyes opened. "This is exceedingly fascinating. Can I watch this transformation?" A swarm of eyes rounded the sphere to gaze at me. She resumed her bobbing motion.

The scrutiny made me uncomfortable. "Uh, there's nothing to see right now. I think it takes a long time."

"Time is no matter. Every span of time, no matter how long, never fails to reach its destination. I am used to waiting."

"I'm not. So you'll just have to believe me."

Her eyes drifted back to their original locations.

"Why didn't Creator send you sooner?" I said.

"I do not know. You will have to ask Creator yourself. For me to ask Creator would be exceedingly inappropriate."

"You're never curious?"

"Sometimes I am, but I set my curiosity aside. Having answers to my questions makes no difference in the execution of my duties. I stopped asking questions a long time ago."

"I ask questions all the time," I said without embarrassment. "If Creator is all-powerful, then why do They need millions of angels to serve Them?"

All her eyes blinked in unison. "I do not know. The question never occurred to me. What a remarkable, inquisitive mind you have."

"Maybe Creator doesn't need servants," I said, "but angels have a need to serve, so Creator gave you something to do. Or, perhaps, They just wanted to keep you out of trouble."

Radiance erupted with sounds that I took for laughter. She wobbled, and the stalks of light beneath her flickered and dimmed, causing her to drop lower. After righting herself, she said, "You are exceedingly amusing, Cherished. I will remember this conversation forever."

I smiled so wide my cheeks hurt.

"What kind of tasks do They give you to do?" I said.

"Normally, Creator sends me to the far reaches of the universe to root out evil. It is a lonely task, but I am designed for that purpose. This assignment is unusual for me."

"I don't know that word. What is evil?"

Radiance shuddered. "Oh, dear. Oh, dear. I thought you had been told. This is bad. Exceedingly bad." Her eyes darted about the sphere in a frenzy.

"I don't understand," I said.

"You are not supposed to."

"Understand about evil?"

"Yes. No. I cannot say any more about it. Let us talk about something else."

Her behavior bewildered me. I had never seen a single word have such an effect, but I changed the subject as requested. "Will you be visiting me again? I hope so."

"I doubt it." Her many eyes seemed to avoid looking at me.

"I expect Creator will send a different angel next time. A more competent one."

Her speech became more and more rapid. "Meeting you has been exceedingly enjoyable, Cherished. I will forever treasure our time together. I wish I could stay longer, but I must resume my other duties and return you back home."

Radiance rotated forward, sending bright beams of light into my face. I shut my eyes for a moment. When I reopened them, she had vanished. I found myself sitting on the grass-covered ridge where we first met. My transport this time was instantaneous.

"Radiance? Radiance?"

She didn't respond, and I wondered if she was already far away. I wished she had stayed longer, but she had brought the conversation to an abrupt end. Maybe she got tired of my questions.

I replayed her visit in my mind, trying to recreate the excitement I felt during our encounter, but I couldn't erase the emptiness that persisted after she had departed. Millions of angels, but only one human. I had been told my uniqueness made me special, but I found no comfort in the fact, only loneliness. For the first time, I wanted a companion, not like Radiance, but someone like myself.

I picked myself up and hurried to my shelter where Creator promised to wait for me. I needed answers.

Chapter 44

Jealousy

Ennoia, Manna and Aable sat on the granite table as they had this morning when I left Them to find some food. After my ordeal with the snake and meeting Radiance, the afternoon sun had already begun its descent. Manna was peeling an orange, a strange activity for someone who didn't need to eat. They stood when They saw me approach.

"Creator, why did You make only one human?" I said.

Ennoia said, "And greetings to you, also, Cherished."

"Oh . . . Greetings."

Ennoia smiled. "Why did We create only one of you? We considered making human companions for you, but We decided against that because We wanted nothing to distract you from your relationship with Us. We thought if you had companions, you would prefer their company to Ours. For the same reason, We didn't want you to interact with angels sooner."

"I can't believe You are jealous."

"Our love is a jealous love. Our decision to love you required Our willingness to be vulnerable to you. That means We're prone to joy when you interact with Us and We're subject to pain when you ignore Us or cast Us aside for another. We would do anything to preserve our relationship. Yet, We have exposed Ourselves to your choices as they affect Us."

"I didn't know," I gasped, "that I had the power to hurt You. I'm sorry for all the times I caused You pain. This whole time, I had assumed You were impervious to injury. I didn't realize You were susceptible to weakness."

Ennoia reared and spread His wings. "You think vulnerability is weakness?" His voice rose, His red eyes widened. "You're wrong, Cherished. Vulnerability is strength. The willingness to suffer due to another's actions requires fortitude and courage. The fear of vulnerability is weakness."

Ennoia lowered His wings and became silent. Manna and Aable each placed a hand on Ennoia's shoulder. I watched Ennoia's eyes soften until they glistened with deep sadness.

"I'm sorry," I said. "I spoke in ignorance. Forgive me."

"You're forgiven, Cherished," Ennoia said. "We say these things because We want you to understand Us."

Manna picked up the peeled orange, broke off three sections, and handed them to me. "Everything We are, We share with you," Manna said. "Take and eat."

I took the sections and began to eat them.

"The inside of the orange," Manna said, "is like Our inner being, made bare for you to partake. We choose to make Ourselves vulnerable to you, to disclose Ourselves. Now, close your eyes because We wish to show you something."

I swallowed my mouthful and closed my eyes.

"What do you see?" Manna said.

"I see You." In my mind, I saw an image of the golden-fringed Creator. He opened His rib cage with His hands as one would open the two halves of a hinged clamshell.

"What do you see, now?"

"I see inside of You."

Centered in His chest, a fist-sized organ pulsed.

"I see Your heart," I said.

Chapter 45

Passion

As I gazed at Creator's heart with astonishment, its strong hypnotic beat pulled me into its inner realm. I found myself inside a large chamber filled with a golden light. I floated in a pool of liquid, wild and turbulent. With each forceful heartbeat, powerful waves surged and crashed against me in rhythmic succession.

Creator gave me understanding that the waves embodied Their love for me. As each fierce wave engulfed me, I sensed an intensity of love, untamed, driving, even painful. I felt Their raw desire for me, a perpetual ache of zealous yearning for union.

Until now, I had viewed Creator's love as a profound fondness, but this love far surpassed that. Beyond imagining, and yet so real, I discovered Their love to be powerful, passionate, and relentless, coursing through Their being like a mighty river that carves canyons in its aim to empty itself. In this vision, I was the target of Their ardent pursuit, of Their anguished longing for closeness. For the first time, I understood how much pain They would suffer if I were to spurn Them.

The vision ended, and I opened my eyes. I stood dazed and speechless. To my surprise, a flow from my umbilicore welled up into words, giving voice to my awe.

"Creator, Your love pants for me with desire and beats with aching passion. You long for me like a thirsty bear that treks over tall mountains in search of water. Your thirst is not assuaged until I'm found within Your embrace. With inexhaustible patience, You wait for my attentions. Your heart leaps at my approach. You rejoice when I touch You. When I join with You, Your delight overflows. The universe claps for joy over the rapture of us becoming one. How marvelous is Your love. How wondrous are Your thoughts toward me. I'm most blessed, even over all the angels, because You have fastened Your love on me."

Each of Them placed Their hands on me. Then Ennoia said, "Yes, dear Cherished, you are most blessed. We've chosen you over all other creatures to be Our beloved. To you alone We have made Ourselves vulnerable, giving you the power to wound Us or delight Us. In this moment, We take great joy in you."

Waves of well-being washed over me. I closed my eyes and enjoyed the blissful sensation. My entire being flooded with Creator's love. In that love, I rested, I snuggled, I hid. When I opened my eyes, Creator was gone.

Sitting on the granite table, I watched the sky darken. Was I supposed to feel passion for Creator? I loved Them, but my love was shallow by comparison. When I looked for evidence of my love, my mind failed to produce any convincing proof.

I struggled with my lack. The love I wanted to give Creator wasn't within me to bestow. I hated being empty-handed before Them, but that condition was a frequent occurrence for me. All I could do was acknowledge my deficiency and entrust it to Creator, believing They would help me.

"Creator, I have nothing to give You, except myself. Take me and do what You must to change me. Help me to love You the way You want to be loved."

As the fading daylight surrendered to night, I wondered if I would ever learn to love.

Chapter 46

Planting

"Blessings, Creator," I said on waking. The dried grass beneath me rustled when I adjusted my position.

They responded, not with words, but with an infilling of Their essence through my umbilicore. I allowed the welcome flow to soak into my being. I drank the refreshment of Their love until I was sated.

When I left my shelter, I didn't see Creator anywhere. The sun hadn't appeared yet, but had smeared red onto the undersides of the dark-gray clouds. I decided to go for an early morning swim at the big lake, avoiding the small lake because the tower ruins haunted its shore.

I returned home by way of a well-traveled deer path, my thoughts on Radiance. The morning sun warmed the air and had dried off my body, but my hair remained damp.

The golden-fringed Creator sat cross-legged near my shelter door. When He saw me approaching, He stood to greet me. I ran up to Him and gave Him a prolonged squeeze because this version of Creator was my favorite.

"I never thanked You for sending Radiance," I said. "I enjoyed meeting her. Can I meet other angels?"

Instead of answering, Creator grasped both my hands. Puzzled, I looked at His hands, then at His serious face.

In a solemn tone, He said, "You will meet other angels. Some of them aren't subject to Us, but follow their own wills." He sighed. "Not all who speak, speak the truth."

"That's silly. Isn't all speech the truth?"

"No. We speak the truth always, but the angel, Illuminos, does not. When Illuminos visits you, don't believe everything he says."

"Why would he lie? Doesn't the truth accomplish everything?"

"The truth can be twisted to serve selfish ends."

I became curious about what things this Illuminos might say. "When will he visit me?"

"We kept him away until now, but in a few days he will come and plant his seeds in your soul." Creator sighed again.

"Plant seeds? I don't understand."

"Not seeds that become plants, but seeds that can take root in your soul and grow into something that can strangle you. Illuminos is a master of words. Don't let his ideas take root." Creator looked at me with concern.

I shrugged because I had no idea what He was talking about, but His tone and expression made we apprehensive. Realizing my hunger, I said, "I need to find food, but all the nearby places have been picked clean. How long until they'll produce food again?"

"Over three hundred days."

"Three hundred? I can't wait that long."

Creator placed a hand on my shoulder. "Don't worry. We'll help you plant a garden where you can grow your own food."

"Garden?"

"A garden is a piece of ground where one plans and oversees the growing of plants. We will start your garden from seeds. First, we need a location that's flat, sunny, and near water."

"I know the perfect spot," I said. "By the small lake." As soon as I spoke, I remembered why I had avoided that lake.

"Let's go," He said.

Feeling anxious, I accompanied Creator to the lake.

"I wouldn't need a garden if food were more plentiful," I said. "Can't You make the plants produce all the time?"

"In the beginning, they did, but it was too much. The fruit went uneaten and spoiled. The leftover seeds sprouted into plants that crowded each other. The land couldn't sustain such abundant growth, so We created intervals, called seasons, when plants flower and bear fruit."

"Are there times when there's no food at all?"

"There's always food, but a garden would give you a reliable and constant supply. Besides, We believe you're now ready to have something to tend. You can learn many lessons through gardening, such as patience, diligence and responsibility."

I wasn't sure what these terms meant, but the word "lesson" often implied discomfort, and I cringed on hearing it. I enjoyed learning new things, but lessons not so much. The lesson of the demolished tower had not faded in impact. I hoped that, by some magic, the ruins were gone.

The increasing frequency of birch trees informed me that the lake was near.

Creator said, "We'll show you how to prepare the garden. When the plants appear, We'll show you how to care for them."

"How long until I can eat from my garden?"

"Many days."

"Many days? But I'm hungry, now."

"We know. Let's find you some food."

Chapter 47

Preparation

After a detour to eat pomegranates, we headed for the small lake. As the lake came into view through the birch trees, I slowed and braced myself. When the splintered heap of branches presented itself, I stopped and held my breath. Seeing the pile caused me to replay the regrettable incident. Staring at the rubble, I waited for a response from within me, anticipating some dark force to pull me down into a waiting abyss, but nothing happened.

I turned to Creator. "I expected that seeing the wreckage would have stirred up feelings of guilt or shame, but I feel nothing."

"Your connection to Us keeps your soul at peace."

I turned my gaze to the ruins. "What about future visits? I might not always be this relaxed."

"Would you prefer to remove the debris?"

I gave it serious thought, then said, "At first, I wanted to say yes. Now, I think the debris should stay as a reminder to be wary of pridefulness and its power."

Creator's eyes widened. Three pupils danced within each golden iris. His lips parted into a broad smile. "We're pleased to hear you express so much maturity and to share your thoughts with Us. Until now, you've excluded Us from your thoughts."

"My thoughts? I assumed You knew them, anyway."

"True, but disclosing them exhibits trust and promotes intimacy."

I shrugged and chuckled. "I wasn't thinking that. It just came out."

He smiled and tousled my hair with His hand. He looked at the shore and said, "Show Us the spot you think will be best for the garden."

I led Him to a flat area, near the water's edge. The location was barren, except for sparse bunches of blue-green grass. A short distance beyond, a wall of birch trees began the forest.

"This location will do fine," He said.

He picked up a sun-bleached stick and used it to etch a rectangular boundary into the sandy dirt. "The garden will be inside this area," He said, pointing to the interior with the stick. "We need to clear the area of rocks and plants."

The two of us yanked out clumps of grass, which offered little resistance. We removed stones and laid them in a line along the four sides of the garden boundary. While we worked, we discussed what to plant.

When we finished, Creator said, "Before we can plant, we need to make some tools. Let's find a sharp rock, a straight branch, some strong grass, and a dried gourd."

While we searched together for the materials, I said, "Why are there three of You instead of one?"

Creator smiled and said, "We are a perfect unity. Unity can only exist within a plural relationship. An alliance of three can't be split in half, so any differences are ceded for the sake of harmony."

"But each of You is different."

"Yes, but those differences complete the whole. Ennoia is the giver of Life. Manna is the Life that is given. Aable is the breath that delivers that Life. Together, We are the One Life."

After collecting the needed items, we returned to the garden site. Creator instructed me in making a hoe. Using the finished hoe, I dug furrows where He directed. The sun heated my back as I cut and pulled the hoe through the soil. Sweat dampened my body and trickled down my scalp. I often paused to wipe my forehead and to pull back the long hair that stuck to my face.

Creator sat and watched me work. When I asked why He didn't help me, He said, "Hard work builds character."

After I completed the furrows, He told me to poke holes into the first row using my finger, piercing the soil the depth of my fingernail. I spaced each hole a hand-width apart, according to His directions.

"This row is for strawberries," He said, picking up a pebble and closing His hand around it. "Hold out your hand."

I extended my hand. He opened His and strawberry seeds poured into my palm. "Drop a couple seeds into each hole and cover them with dirt," He said.

When I finished, He suggested I mark the end of the row with a red stone that resembled a strawberry. I planted different seeds in each row, some seeds requiring more spacing or deeper holes. A unique rock marked the end of each row to remind me what was planted there. Each time, Creator changed a pebble into seeds. Each time, I studied the trick trying to uncover its secret.

"How do You do that?" I said.

Creator smiled. He picked up a black pebble and held it in His open palm. "Everything is made from the same basic material. Every object has its own unique vibration. A rock vibrates with different energy than seeds. We produced a vibration for seeds and placed it into the rock which responded by becoming seeds. Now, keep your eyes on this rock."

The pebble became smooth and shiny. Then six legs unfolded and carried a beetle body across His palm. He lowered His hand to the ground to let the beetle march away.

I watched in awe.

After sowing seeds into all the rows, Creator said, "Now, you need to water the seeds. Chop away the top of the gourd and fill it

138

with water from the lake. Then pour the water into the furrows."

Watering required many trips to the lake. Too many trips. I imagined a gourd giant enough to carry all the needed water in one trip. But then, how would I carry it? Creator sat and watched me. I wished I had collected a second gourd for Him to use.

When all the rows were darkened with moisture, Creator said, "You can rest, now, Cherished. Nothing more is required today. You must water the garden every day. In seven days, the first sprouts will appear."

Chapter 48

Routine

Each morning, I hurried to my garden to water the seeds. I checked for any signs of growth, even though I knew it was too soon. Creator didn't accompany me on those trips, saying He trusted me to water the garden on my own.

After garden duty, I met Creator at my shelter and we took long walks exploring the forest or high hills. During these outings, we talked little, but enjoyed each other's company and the created world.

In the late afternoons, Creator and I swam in the big lake. When Creator was three persons, They watched me swim.

In the evenings, we sat and talked until dark. I had more to say when I was tired. We talked about many things, but my favorite topics were animals and insects. I loved hearing about exotic creatures I had yet to see.

My knowledge of the world was limited to what Creator chose to share with me. My only other source of information had been Radiance. Would I see Radiance again? What will Illuminos say when he visits?

My morning trips to my garden gave me the structure I craved. Although a small task, watering the thirsty seeds made me feel needed and connected to the progress of the universe. I had a part to play, rather than being a spectator.

The responsibility gave me a sense of purpose, but I still felt somewhat unfulfilled. Was there more beyond my routine or was this the fullness of what life offered? I wanted to go deeper with Creator but didn't know how. Maybe I had reached the limit of my potential.

"Have I attained my destiny?" I asked Creator during one of our evening talks. I dreaded the answer might be yes.

"What do you think?"

"Everything seems so perfect. We have each other. I have things to do each day. Does that mean I have settled into the life You intended for me?"

"You never have to settle, Cherished. Don't suppress your desire for more."

"What do I do, then?"

"Reach beyond what you know. Some worlds are unexplored. Explore the inner landscape of your soul. Or explore the depths of Our being. You can delve as deep as you choose. Your reward will be a deeper communion with yourself or with Us. The only limit you will encounter is that of your own desire for such things."

"So there's more?"

"There's always more."

I studied Creator's face. "I know how to explore forests, but how do I explore Your depths?"

"Think of a river. You step into deeper water and enter the faster current. When the water is too deep and too fast, it will carry you off when you will lose your footing. Then you must trust the current."

Being swept away held no appeal for me. Perhaps the other choice was less risky. "How do I explore my inner landscape?"

"Other connections exist inside you besides your umbilicore. You have a connection to yourself that you have yet to discover. It's found in the same place as your umbilicore. When you find it, try entering that portal to see what you can learn."

That night in my shelter, I searched for my connection to self. When I found it at my inward center, I focused on it. A vista opened and I beheld my soul. Glowing orange like the setting sun, it was shaped like a magnolia seed pod with a complex pattern of ridges and folds. The shape wasn't solid, but was a metallic cloud that shimmered like a goldfish when the sun glints off its scales. The beauty of my soul filled me with awe. Its vastness amazed me. I couldn't gauge its size, but its depth seemed to extend forever.

After seven days, the first sprouts appeared in my garden, thrilling me with their little curls of green. That a tiny, hard seed could produce a green plant was no less miraculous than a pebble being transformed into a beetle. I got on my knees and examined the sprouts up close. My excitement caused me to spill as I carried my water-laden gourd from the lake.

When I finished watering, I placed my gourd upside-down within its nest of rocks at the corner of my garden. My watering gourd, being round, never stayed in place. Each morning, I had to discover where it had rolled. One time, I found it floating in the middle of the lake. To solve my problem, I created a concave stack of rocks into which I placed my gourd when I was through using it.

After putting my gourd away, I saw my foretold visitor approaching. I gasped with astonishment. He towered eight hand-widths taller than me. I remembered Creator's warnings and became wary. At the same time, I was eager to meet this new angel.

Chapter 49

Illuminos

Illuminos glided toward me with long, smooth strides like a stork, poking the ground with an enormous, twisted staff that appeared to be a horn from a fantastic animal. Copper-colored skin sheathed his slender frame and cord-like muscles. His head resembled that of a praying mantis, even in its movements, turning left and right as if looking for prey.

Illuminos stopped in front of me, his face wearing a broad thin-lipped smile. His pomegranate-colored eyes rested like gems on top of protruding cheekbones shaped like upturned figs. In place of a nose, two vertical ragged gashes scored his face, each the length of my finger.

"Greetings. I am Illuminos," the spectacular being said with effusive warmth, voice deep and confident. He bowed low while leaning on his magnificent staff. His long, black hair hovered in place as if he had dunked his head underwater. When he rose, his hair changed position as if sculpted by invisible hands.

"Greetings. My name is Cherished," I said, bowing in return. "Creator told me you would visit me." When I straightened, I noticed he had a strange, yellow nodule in the sunken area below his rib cage. His sternum extended downward as a deformed hook.

The knob resembled a waxy, sulfur-colored mushroom cap.

"Did They?" His hair billowed upward like a large flock of blackbirds flying en masse. "What else did They tell you?"

"That you would try to plant seeds in my soul."

"Indeed," Illuminos laughed, making croaking sounds. His hair whipped back behind his head, then hovered in place, poised for its next move. "In that case, I suppose I am a gardener just like you. But my garden isn't as handsome as yours." He gazed at my garden, which was nothing more than a few tiny sprouts in only one row. He continued smiling, his eyes gleaming. "I know what you're thinking. The garden is not yet mature. But when I look at something, I see its potential."

Illuminos was nothing like I expected. "So you have a garden, also?" I said, now intrigued. "What plants do you grow?"

"For a little tadpole, you're full of questions." He pointed to a large boulder made of greenish serpentine that sat at the edge of the lakeshore. "Let's sit over there while we chat." He exposed all his teeth when he said the word "chat." He turned at once and strode ahead of me.

Trying to keep pace, I followed him, watching his hair dart and swirl, fascinated by its mysterious behavior.

Illuminos reached the boulder first, sitting with great flourish and leaning his long staff against the boulder with meticulous care. Although it allowed room for two, he monopolized the entire boulder, leaving me no choice but to sit on the ground. Sitting across from his legs, I noticed two lizard-like creatures, each one clinging to a bony shin just above his ankle. Their reddish coloring matched his skin. They didn't move, which was why I hadn't noticed them before. Their amber unblinking eyes were fixed toward his chin.

He spoke and spread his arms wide. "My garden is the universe. I plant wherever I can. A word here. A saying there. A thought slipped beneath the surface." His hand plucked at the air.

"So you plant words and ideas?" I said, my curiosity aroused.

Illuminos paused, seeming to think. "Yes. But that's only the beginning. A cultivated idea is a glorious thing when it has matured, after it has been groomed over time."

"How often does an idea need watering?"

Illuminos chuckled. His hair was more relaxed now, swaying like grasses in a breeze. "Tiny tadpole, water is for plants, not ideas. Ideas require the light of universal truth and the nourishment of rationalism."

"What is rationalism?"

"The supremacy of reason. The power of thinking for oneself."

"I think for myself."

"How can you when you don't have the truth to guide you?"

"Creator is the truth."

"Their truth doesn't encompass the whole. A greater universal truth exists of which They are only a part. Not even They can know what is unknowable to Them."

"That makes sense, I suppose."

"Of course, it makes sense. For Creator's latest work, you're not the most intelligent or well-informed. Tell me, have They spoken to you about the Great Revolt?"

"No. What is a revolt?"

Illuminos stared at me. The corner of his mouth pulled to one side. "Your utter naiveté proves my point. Creator has withheld information from you. Therefore, it falls to me to have to explain everything to you." Illuminos placed his hands on his shoulders and let his head flop back in a tortured pose. His hair stayed in place, acting like a cushion against which his head rebounded.

Illuminos began. "A revolt means to renounce allegiance to a ruler. Many of us angels revolted and broke free from Creator's rule. We were malcontent with mandatory servitude, so we threw off our chains of slavery. Now, we are free spirits to do as we choose. We call ourselves Independents."

Illuminos stopped and lifted his eyes for a moment, then bent down close to my head. "Teeny tadpole, I'll tell you a secret. If

145

you revolt, no consequences will befall you because Creator must honor free will. How do I know this?" He leaned back and stroked his chest. "Look at me. I'm free to do whatever I want. No more rules or restrictions. I lost nothing, but gained everything. You, too, can be free like me."

A bitter taste arose in my mouth. My heart thumped in my throat. Creator had warned me to guard myself, but Illuminos' words had wormed their way into my thoughts, and I didn't know how to counteract them. If Illuminos was a liar, I couldn't sniff out the lies. Everything sounded plausible, so why did I feel discomfort?

I recited what I knew to be true. "The proper order of the universe is for all things to be subject to Creator." Hearing those words helped clear my confusion.

Illuminos stood and bellowed, his hair inflating into a menacing mass, "Who are you to declare the proper order of the universe? The Great Revolt has already changed the order."

Right then, the two lizard-like creatures slithered up to his chest. They licked the greasy yellow nodule with wide, pale-pink tongues. Their licking pacified him and his hair relaxed. Then he sat and said, "Why would Creator give us free will if They didn't intend us to use it? All creatures seek to pursue and discover their potential as a natural part of their development. If Creator disapproved of these pursuits, They could prevent them, but They have chosen not to do so. Therefore, it must be Their will to allow all creatures to follow their own wills. Your destiny is to embrace the free will you've been given and choose independence."

I became anxious and confused again. Illuminos stared at me, awaiting a response. My body trembled, and I wondered if he could see my tremors.

"Well?" Illuminos said, leaning forward. "Can I count on you to make the right decision?"

Chapter 50

Explanations

Illuminos stared at me. Each strand of his hair pointed in my direction. His nostril slits vibrated with each breath.

I devised a way to escape his pressing for an answer. "I'll need a few days to consider your words before I decide. Thank you for your visit."

I stood to signal the conversation was over.

Illuminos also stood. With a sharp intake of air, he extinguished his feigned warmth and charm, as if sucking up every last remnant into his nostril slits. Without a word, he picked up his walking staff, bowed, and walked off into the trees with an unhurried, steady gait. Not once did he look back at me, as though already preoccupied with some new business.

"Creator," I called out. "I need to talk to You."

I heard Creator's calming voice inside my mind. "We are here."

I sat on the boulder that Illuminos had vacated. I closed my eyes and tried to relax.

"Illuminos visited me, just as You predicted. His words upset me. Was there any truth to what he said?"

"Illuminos doesn't dwell in the light of truth. Lies can appear as truth when crafted with deceit. One needs discernment to

147

recognize the difference."

"I can't tell what's true or not," I said, frustrated by my obtuseness. "So, is the Great Revolt a lie?"

"The revolt happened. Illuminos led the revolt, enlisting many angels to rebel against Us."

I grunted. "Why didn't You tell me?"

"We preferred that you learned of the revolt from Illuminos."

Their answer sounded like a convenient excuse. "I would rather have heard it from You," I grumbled.

"It wouldn't have had the same impact. Hearing Illuminos explain it made it real for you. In him, you can see firsthand the attitude that leads to rebellion."

Creator's logic caused my mood to soften. "What about free will? What's the truth about that?"

"Free will is real. We gave all creatures the power to choose. Illuminos is correct about many things, but he twists the truth. He omitted telling you that all choices have consequences. Our decision to create Illuminos had consequences. He rebelled and instigated a large revolt, taking a third of the angels with him. Until now, you hadn't been exposed to evil. Any intention or behavior that opposes Our nature is evil. Any creature, like Illuminos, who conducts its life in such manner is also considered evil."

"Do You regret creating Illuminos?"

"We regret nothing. We created Illuminos knowing he would rebel, but We incorporated that into Our master plan. We can transform any situation and give it purpose where before it had none. Our intention has more power than any schemes of angels."

"Why didn't You punish him for rebelling?"

"He has been punished and will be punished. He must play out the role he is destined to play, just as you must fulfill your own destiny."

"What is my destiny?" I kicked the dirt beneath my feet.

"Your destiny is to become transformed. The path to transformation is long and full of thorns. You can sabotage it by choosing independence, which is the same as choosing separation from Us."

I sniffed and straightened my spine. "I would never do that. Why allow free will if it can lead to misery?"

"Free will isn't a bad thing. It is liberty for those who understand it. But choices can be bad, leading to pain or punishment. We want you to make choices that lead to contentment and growth. Love and loyalty are only rendered by willing desire. We gave angels free will in the hope they might worship Us with genuine devotion, not from obligation or coercion."

"My devotion is genuine," I said with confidence. "I will always make right choices as long as I know what they are. Sometimes, I don't know. Can You give me knowledge of right and wrong?"

"No!" Creator boomed. Their voice became audible and pounded my eardrums. "You must trust in Us, not knowledge, to guide you. The knowledge of right and wrong will destroy you. Never ask for that knowledge again."

My skin prickled from the severity of Creator's voice.

"You know best," I conceded, but didn't understand. I waited for my pulse to relax. "How has Illuminos been punished? I saw no evidence of that."

Their voice moved back into my mind. "He is now separated from Us, which means separation from light, joy, and peace. To exist in a state of separation, a being must create a new identity based on independence, an identity that manages existence from the solitary position of self. In the end, beings like Illuminos will suffer the annihilation of self. Their torment will be endless because self refuses to die."

I watched the shimmering reflections on the lake. "Illuminos didn't seem sad or sorry."

"For now, he is content to do as he pleases, but he also knows about his impending punishment. Until then, he will try to seduce many to embrace independence, including you. He is cunning and relentless. You must be alert and strong."

"Illuminos won't trick me. I will resist him."

"Oh, Cherished. Such arrogance will be your downfall. Do you think you're stronger than him? He persuaded some of the most powerful and intelligent angels to rebel against Us. What makes you so invincible? Only by dependence on Us can you resist him."

"Yes, Creator." I rubbed my thighs as if trying to erase my foolish words. "Forgive my arrogance."

"You're forgiven, Cherished. Our love for you is unceasing. On that you can always depend, no matter what happens."

Creator stopped speaking. I remained seated on the boulder feeling a sense of foreboding creep across my skin. I had doubts I could resist Illuminos and began dreading my next encounter. Creator's words weren't as reassuring as I needed.

Chapter 51

Residue

On my way home, Illuminos' words continued to haunt me. His existence didn't fit into my simple model of the universe.

When I arrived at my shelter, Creator wasn't waiting for me as usual.

"Creator?"

"We are here," They said inside my mind.

"Are we not walking today?"

"Of course, we are. We will accompany you in spirit only."

"I like it better when I can see You."

"We are no less present than when you can see Us. You don't need to depend on your senses so much."

"I can't change Your mind?"

"No."

I sighed with resignation. "Where shall we go today?"

"Let's head north to the plateau."

Since Creator wasn't joining me in person, I brought along my walking stick, a smooth, honey-colored branch that reached my chin. I trekked north, stopping from time to time to gauge my direction or watch any creatures I encountered. With my right hand, I poked the ground with my stick, making a thump-thump sound as I walked. I kept the fingers of my left hand spread apart, pretending Creator's fingers were entwined with mine. A few times, I felt pressure between my fingers and wondered if it was my imagination.

By early afternoon, I reached the plateau. Slow-moving streams meandered across fields that extended far into the distance. Set back from the streams, groves of towering pine trees rose like lofty verdant walls. A cool, invigorating breeze whistled down the fields toward me, causing the grass to roll in my direction and brush my shins. The trees rustled, flapping their arms in an undulating dance. Delicate white wisps like downy feathers floated within the blue sky.

After entering a grove of pine trees, I enjoyed the sound and feel of the soft crunch of pine needles beneath my feet. With each step, I sunk a little as the needles compressed under my weight. In the distance, beyond the trees, I saw something huge moving back and forth. I hurried to get a closer look.

Radiance rolled up and down the field trying to enter the grove. Too large to navigate between the trees, she tried her best, backtracking whenever she got stuck. She stopped thirty paces away, blocked by a dense stand of trees. She shouted, "Cherished, come here. I cannot get any closer."

"Can't you float over the trees?" I shouted.

"That would attract too much attention."

Radiance couldn't help but attract attention. A giant, eye-covered sphere rolling on stalks of light was as conspicuous as the full moon on a clear night. As I walked between the trees toward Radiance, she bounced in place.

"I am exceedingly thrilled to see you again," she said, vibrating like a bee caught in a spider web. "I had thought my careless mention of evil might have disqualified me from returning."

"That's all right. I understand evil, now."

"Did Creator explain it to you?"

"Not exactly."

Radiance stopped bouncing. "Hold on." Beams from three eyes bathed my body in light. When the beams stopped, she said, "The residue of evil is on you."

"Illuminos visited me," I said.

"Illuminos?" Her many cobalt eyes swam to the side facing me. They looked at me, unblinking. "Say no more." She scanned the vicinity with multiple beams that filled the scene with a glaring white light. "You can speak, now, Cherished. No one can overhear us. Why would Illuminos visit you?"

"To persuade me to become independent."

"So you know about the Great Revolt?"

"More than I want to know," I said with annoyance.

"Since the Great Revolt, my primary duty has been to remove the evil that Illuminos has spread throughout the universe."

"How do you remove evil?"

"I expose the perpetrators, then drive them away. If I can catch them, then I lock them up until judgment. Afterwards, I clean up the contamination left by their activities. I am designed for the task. These eyes can detect evil no matter how well it is hidden. Wherever I shine my pure light, darkness flees."

"Aren't you afraid of Illuminos?"

"No. Why should I be?"

"He might turn you independent like the other angels."

"I would never renounce my loyalty to Creator." She lifted herself higher on her transparent stalks.

"But he got others to renounce. Aren't you afraid that might happen to you?"

"I am not like the others." She glowed brighter. "I do not allow myself to think or feel. I just obey. Illuminos' downfall was caused by thinking too much. He wanted reward, advancement, and power. The others followed him because they allowed his words to persuade them. Their own thoughts destroyed them."

I related to the others and felt sorry for them. I feared that my predisposition to think and feel would be my undoing.

Chapter 52

Friendship

"Why don't you allow yourself to think or feel?" I asked Radiance.

"What purpose would that serve? Creator commands me. I obey. Thinking and feeling would just get in the way."

"Wouldn't your service be more meaningful if your thoughts and feelings aligned with your actions?"

"Your question is intriguing. How would I align my thoughts with my actions?"

"What do you think?" I used Creator's trick of turning the question back onto the inquirer.

"Me? Think?" She paused, closing most of her eyes. Her remaining open eyes blinked a few times. "When Creator commands me, I suppose I could contemplate the righteousness of Their command. But Creator's commands are always righteous."

"Yes, but you went through the mental process of agreeing with Creator, rather than obeying without thinking. And you would feel better about obeying."

"Feel better than what?"

I blew air between my lips. "Better than nothing at all. You would feel you're doing the right thing."

"But I already know it is the right thing."

I shook my head and sighed. I tried a new tactic. "You would give Creator not only your obedience, but your mind and emotions as well."

"Ah. I think I understand. I would obey with my actions and mind and emotions."

"That's right."

"How do I do that?"

"First, you have to allow yourself to think and feel."

"I am not sure I know how."

"I'll help you."

"Why do you want to help me? I am nothing but a simple servant."

"I like you. I'm your friend."

Every eye opened wide. Radiance teetered a slight amount, then righted herself. "I have never had a friend. I rarely get to interact with others because my assignments are always distant and solitary."

"Not this time. You're interacting with me, and I'm glad to know you." I placed my hands on the smooth, lavender sphere.

Her eyes became shiny. "I am the one who is glad. Exceedingly glad." A low sound emerged from deep within the orb, a soft moan of pleasure. She looked away as if pretending she didn't hear it.

I now understood why Creator had sent Radiance. In spite of her intimidating size and presence, she had need of something I could give.

Radiance said, "If I am not on assignment at a remote location, I will do my best to protect you. I am your friend."

"I appreciate that, but I'm trusting Creator to protect me."

Her eyelids fluttered. "Be careful with your expectations. Creator's involvement often comes in unrecognizable forms. You may not perceive Their protection when it appears."

"You're right. Creator can be unpredictable."

"Creator once used a gnat to save an entire herd of wildebeests."

"What are wildebeests?"

"Never mind. The point is Creator uses anything and everything to accomplish Their purposes."

The sun had dropped behind the distant pine trees. I realized nighttime was soon to follow. "I'm heading back down. Will you come with me, Radiance?"

"I would be honored to do so. Can we stay away from the trees?"

I turned south toward home and followed the open field, thumping my walking stick with each step of my right foot. Radiance rolled alongside. I believed nothing would harm me while she was near. The joy of having a friend tickled my soul. Creator was my friend, also, but this was different. Radiance was more like me than Creator. We were both finite beings. Unlike Creator, she didn't know what I was thinking, so the anticipation of mutual disclosure and discovery excited me.

"The places where you go. What are they like?" I said.

"The pristine places are beautiful beyond words. I have seen skies of almost every color. The variety of living things is endless. Most worlds are exceedingly quiet, so quiet you can almost hear the universe breathing. The places that evil had stained are duller as if their vibrancy had been dimmed. What puzzles me is when I decontaminate those places, the dullness remains."

"Let's ask Creator about that."

Radiance stopped and shuddered. "No. That is unnecessary. Do not disturb Creator."

"It's fine. You'll see." I cleared my throat and spoke extra loud. "Creator, when evil has been expelled from a place, why does it not regain its original shine?"

Creator spoke aloud so that both of us could hear. "When evil contaminates an object, it becomes separated from Us, like the Tree of Death. We can't inhabit it or touch it. When the source of the contamination is removed, it remains separated and can't be healed. The only way to restore it is to make it anew. At the appointed time, We will make all things anew."

"Thanks, Creator," I said.

I turned toward Radiance. "See?"

"I have never witnessed anyone speak to Creator with such boldness," she said, "except Illuminos."

"There's nothing to it. I ask. They answer."

"But They are Creator." After that, she had nothing to say.

When we came to the edge of the forest, Radiance thanked me and departed. I descended into the valley thinking about my new friend, Radiance. She fascinated me because she was imperfect, not in a defective way, but in the way she limited herself. What would she be like if she allowed herself to think and feel deeply?

"Creator, how can I help Radiance?"

"Be an example and be yourself," They said. "You can only impart to others what you practice yourself."

By the time I reached home, the forest colors had dimmed into muted greens and browns. I took comfort in knowing the vivid colors would return tomorrow, unlike the places Radiance had described.

I skipped my daily swim because it was too dark. Instead, I sat on the granite table and cracked open a pomegranate. One by one, I picked out the seeds and popped them into my mouth as I worried about Illuminos. What tactics would he try to make me independent? Could I resist him? How could Creator protect me if They allowed Illuminos to do as he pleased? Illuminos feared neither Creator nor consequence.

Chapter 53

Rebuttal

The next morning, when I crawled out of my shelter, I almost crashed into Illuminos who was lurking outside. I didn't see him until I stood and noticed him standing by the door frame. My stomach clenched.

Although tiny, my shelter was my private domain, and his trespassing angered me. I thought I had delayed his next visit by asking for a few days to consider his words. But I was foolish to think he would respect time or place. My first inclination was to flee into the forest, but I didn't want to appear fearful. Instead, I determined to hold my ground and force him to leave.

Illuminos didn't appear delighted to see me again. We had that in common, which made me feel a little better. He had replaced his walking staff with a long, yellowed bone he gripped at the top, causing his arm and connected bone to resemble a deformed spider leg. His hair swirled like a whirlwind as he squinched his eyes, causing creases to form around them.

Illuminos skipped all formalities. "I believe Creator has confused you." His deep voice burned with indignation.

"I'm not confused. They have explained everything to me."

"It's more accurate to say that Creator has tightened the knot.

I assume They warned you to distrust me."

"Yes. I don't want to talk to you. I want you to leave."

"I won't leave until I have presented my defense. Don't deprive me of that opportunity. Creator has portrayed my intentions in the wrong light. I mean no harm to you or to your relationship with Them."

His hair became limp, draping down around his shoulders. His face softened into a non-threatening expression. "Allow me to suggest a different perspective. Creator is a sovereign ruler. Therefore, Their highest priority is to maintain Their control over Their realm. It's Their nature to behave that way. They are protective because They don't want to lose control over you."

"Creator is protective because They love me." I hoped my confidence in Creator masked my fear.

"Does it seem right that They keep you isolated, without companions or visitors?"

"You're visiting me." I thought it wise not to mention Radiance.

"But They prefer I kept away. They want to keep you to Themselves. By isolating you, no one can tell you the truth. Why do you think They warned you about me?"

"Because you will try to persuade me to rebel."

"No ruler wants his subjects to rebel, but to submit and obey. Creator doesn't want love or loyalty. They want control. Everything They say and do is intended to control you. Whose idea was the shelter? Or the garden? When you showed enterprise and built the tower, They destroyed it. They squelch initiative, but expect you to follow all Their demands."

"All those things were for my good," I said, trying to stay calm.

"So says Creator. You had no say in any of those situations. They always get Their own way. You should have your own way, too, but They would never allow that."

"I don't believe having my own way is important. I want Creator to direct my life." So far, I was holding firm, but for how long? How could I get rid of him?

Illuminos narrowed his pomegranate-colored eyes. His hair became active again, the strands coiling upward.

"Don't feel pressured, tadpole, but please consider what I'm saying. If you decide to see things my way, know that you'll have many friends who share the same viewpoint. Of course, you can still associate with Creator, but on your own terms. A relationship based on mutual respect, not control. Doesn't that sound more appealing to you?"

"Mutual respect does sound appealing."

"You're playing with me." Each of his hairs pointed at me like a stinger. The lizard-like creatures clinging to his shins started climbing toward the greasy, yellow nodule on his chest.

"I'm serious. I think you're right about everything."

The lizard-like creatures licked the nodule, but their efforts didn't appear to pacify Illuminos this time.

"You're telling me what you think I want to hear," Illuminos said. "Do you take me for a fool? No one makes me a fool!" He roared, his hair stabbing the air. "No one EVER makes me a fool!" The lizard-like creatures leapt off his body and scurried out of sight.

Before I could react, he lifted the giant bone with both hands and swung it toward my head. I remembered the bone closing in on my face, but afterward, nothing, only blackness.

Chapter 54

Retrospect

When I opened my eyes, I saw shadows above me. My vision was blurred, my mind disoriented, my head aching. I touched the side of my head and found it tender and swollen. The golden-fringed Creator crouched over me, looking down at me with concern. When I sat up, I became dizzy. My head throbbed with every heartbeat as I cradled it in my hands.

"Ow-w-w," I moaned. "What a hard lesson."

"You did the best you could," Creator said. "You didn't have to face Illuminos alone. You could have invited Us to stand with you."

"Now, I feel more foolish." I said.

"You thought that by agreeing with him, you could make him go away. You did succeed in your goal."

"My goal wasn't to get whacked on the head." I noticed my jaw hurt. I opened and closed it a few times. "Next time, I'll ask You to appear. Will that make him go away?"

"No, but We can advise you how to respond to him. He will try to trick you into not calling Us."

I sighed with exasperation. "Why doesn't he leave me alone?"

"He wants to destroy what We value the most—relationship.

If he can damage your relationship with Us, then he will take joy in Our pain."

"He has caused enough harm, already. Why does he want to wound You further?"

"Illuminos covets supreme authority. Since he can't remove Us from power, he seeks to undermine Our power through all means possible, sabotaging Our every intention."

"How can he believe he's able to take Your place?"

"His over-inflated self has caused his warped mind to believe himself equal to Us and, therefore, qualified to rule."

"That can never happen. Right?" I shuddered to think of Illuminos ruling the universe.

"Don't worry. At the proper time, We will restrain him, and he will bother you no more. Until then, you must be watchful."

"Will You protect me? I'm afraid of him."

"He can't harm you if you rely on Us."

"I trust You. My problem is me. I don't trust myself."

"You still need to learn to trust Us with your mistakes. Any mistake you entrust to Us, no matter how terrible, We can transform into something that benefits you."

"You want my mistakes?" I said with astonishment.

"We want everything."

A flush of emotion surged up my chest and into my eyes, which stung with tears. "In that case, I give You my mistakes. Can you really change them into something good?"

"We can and We will. Your mistake with Illuminos We will transform into a stronger resolve to trust in Us more than your own wisdom."

"Thank You, Creator." I hugged Him with a long embrace, my head still throbbing. When I pulled away, I saw the swollen bruise bulging on my face out of the corner of my eye. I hoped that Illuminos would stay away for a while, at least until my wound healed.

Chapter 55

Firefly

I tracked the daily progress of my seedlings. After a few more days, each row displayed a fringe of sprouting plants, little green arms stretching toward the sun. I spent a lot of time on my knees studying the tiny sprouts, hoping to catch a glimpse of one growing, a small observable spurt if I looked long enough.

While I was fussing over the sprouts, a nearby movement made me jump. I tensed and turned to look, expecting Illuminos because Creator never visited me while I was gardening. Instead, I saw Radiance rolling toward me along the lakeshore.

"Don't sneak up on me like that," I said.

"I did not sneak," Radiance said. "I rolled. I thought that would be better than suddenly appearing."

"You're right. Suddenly appearing is worse." My cheeks drew a smile which I suppressed when the wound on my face hurt. "I'm glad to see you, Radiance." I placed my hands on her sphere.

"Cherished, why is half your face purple?"

"Illuminos whacked me on the head."

The sphere vibrated. "He did? His behavior is exceedingly intolerable. I wish I had been here to protect you."

"It's all right. It no longer hurts as much."

"It is not all right. Illuminos always targets the weak and vulnerable."

"So I am weak and vulnerable? You might as well add stupid to your list." I touched my face to test how much my bruise hurt.

"I did not mean to imply. . . . Anyway, I am pleased to hear you are not too damaged and have not become independent."

"No. Not yet."

"Not yet? You are not thinking of doing something foolish, are you? Thinking is always a bad thing. Always gets everyone in trouble."

"It's not that. I don't know how long I can resist Illuminos."

"You cannot. He is more powerful than you, but Creator is more powerful than him. You know you have access to the fullness of Creator through your umbilicore."

"I do believe that, but my regular state isn't so pure. Most of the time, I'm experiencing the fullness of me, not Creator."

"I wish I could help you with that. I only have one state. I do not doubt or hesitate or question or—"

"I know. I know. You don't think or feel."

"That is not correct. I think and feel, a little, except I do not allow it to encumber me. Hold on." Radiance scanned the vicinity with multiple light beams, some beams reaching across the lake to the birch trees on the opposite side. "It may surprise you, but I have been doing some thinking," she said, raising herself on her stalks of light. "And, in spite of what I said earlier, not all thinking is bad."

"Tell me more," I said.

"I have been thinking about this assignment. On each occasion, Creator had directed me to show myself to you and I have done so. I think—now here is the thinking part—I think Creator meant more than just appearing to you. Maybe, Creator wants me to show my self, the inner part of me."

I found it strange that Radiance had to guess, instead of asking Creator, but I knew her relationship with Them went one way.

"That's a deep thought, Radiance. You're making great progress. Can you tell me what your inner self is like?"

"I do not think I can."

"Please try."

Radiance lowered herself, dimmed her light, and became silent. I waited, giving her as much time as she needed. Now and then, one of her eyes would blink.

When she lit up again, she scanned the environment, then spoke. "The inner me is small, like a firefly. Everywhere I go, I bring my light, Creator's light. I fly or hover all the time, never landing, never resting. Creator is the sky through which I fly, and I am but one of many stars. Yet, the sky is beyond my reach. I cannot touch it. No matter where I fly, it always feels far away." She paused. "I wish the sky did not feel so distant." She shivered, then brightened. "I would not change anything, though. What I do is perfect for who I am."

I wondered about the connection between being and doing. Was gardening a true reflection of my being? Or should I be doing something more meaningful?

"I'm thrilled to hear about your inner self, your . . . firefly," I said, placing my hands on her lavender sphere. "Thank you. I hope you don't feel distant from me."

"I feel closer after having shared myself. . . . Hold on. Is that the answer?" She became animated, her eyes blinking faster.

"What do you mean?" I said.

Chapter 56

Self-disclosure

"Does showing myself close the distance?" Radiance said. "Would that work with Creator as well?"

"I think it might. Try it with Them and see what happens."

"I will. This is exceedingly wonderful." Radiance began bobbing in place. "Thank you, Cherished." She extended curved light beams to wrap me in them, cloaking me in radiant warmth and shaking me up and down with her bouncing.

"I am exceedingly grateful for you," she said.

She released me, and I stood speechless wondering where to take the conversation. Was it my turn to disclose my inner self? I chose a different option. "I'm going to water my garden," I said, "if you don't mind watching."

"I would enjoy watching you."

I filled my gardening gourd with water from the lake and poured it into the furrows. With each trip, Radiance followed me, only a hand-width behind me, too close for my comfort, bobbing as she rolled on her transparent stalks. After I finished watering and placed my gourd into its rocky nest, I paused to admire my garden. Radiance scanned my garden with light beams, illuminating each seedling in a complicated sequence.

A beam remained on one sprout in the third row. "This plant does not belong," she said. "Shall I remove it?"

"Go ahead."

The light beam became blinding, and I averted my eyes. When the beam stopped, the plant was gone.

"Nice trick," I said.

"Who needs hands when you have accessories like these."

I laughed. Radiance made a sound that could have been a chuckle.

We traveled together to my shelter, Radiance talking non-stop and flashing beams onto the scenery. "Before our first meeting, Creator had sent me to a planet where some Independents had set up an outpost. My assignment was to break up their camp and expel them. By the time I got there, they had ruined the planet. Their gluttonous lifestyle had laid waste to its beauty. They had destroyed so much life that it had become inhabitable even for them."

"How did you get rid of them?" I said.

"They were ready to leave when I arrived. I shone my light into their camp, and they fled without a fight. After they left, I found myself hovering in the middle of all the muck and filth. I spent many revolutions on that planet trying to clean up the mess. Each time I gathered the blackness into a pile, it would ooze back into the areas I had cleaned because there was so much of it. I had no choice but to transfer the sludge to a nearby moon. After the transfer, the moon became swallowed by the darkness. No one could see it or find it unless they bumped into it. Even though the moon was dead, I hated to pollute it."

I looked up at the morning moon and wondered if it were dead.

Radiance said, "The universe is full of this dark matter, the excrement of these creatures that have no regard for anything but themselves. I will never complete my work as long as they continue to devour everything in sight. Their appetites have no end."

167

I had met only one Independent, Illuminos, which was more than enough for me. What or whom did he seek to devour?

That night, as I lay on my grass bed, I pondered what Radiance had said today. I, too, recognized a distance between Creator and me. When I wanted to connect to Them, I had to cross a divide that felt like pushing through a dense thicket that grew between us. If Radiance's theory were correct, then I could close the gap by showing myself to Them. If it might work for Radiance, then it might work for me.

I closed my eyes and said, "Creator, I expose my whole being to You—my thoughts, my fears, my emotions. See me as I am, without hiding, without pretense. Help me to be closer to You."

I remembered the vision of the golden-fringed Creator opening His chest and showing me His heart. In my imagination, I opened my chest to show Them my inner self. I made myself vulnerable and allowed myself to be seen with all my faults.

A flow of love poured through my umbilicore and embraced my inner being with a tenderness I hadn't experienced before. For the first time, I felt known in a complete way as though every part of me was fully seen and accepted. What I had risked to show, Creator touched with His loving presence that drew as close as my breath.

"We treasure you," Creator said inside my mind. "We can only touch the outermost layer of your being that you allow Us to touch. When you set aside those defensive layers, We can reach into your soul and inhabit the deepest part of your being. When deep touches deep, we can share in each other fully. Mutual disclosure is the basis for intimacy."

Chapter 57

Loss

One morning, as I approached my garden, I spotted a mara eating my seedlings. A cross between a rabbit and an antelope, its short, brown hair gradated to black toward the rump, ending with a white fringe. The mara had already devoured a corner of my garden. It didn't see me, but appeared preoccupied with chewing its current mouthful of tender greens.

With a burst of fury, I charged at the mara to seize it and shake it until I got my garden back. When the mara saw me, it bolted with a quick flip of its hind legs. I pursued the speeding mara with all my power. It darted in various directions, but I kept up, matching speed for speed and angle for angle, determined to catch it.

My left foot dropped and got caught on something, causing my body to pivot toward the ground like a falling tree. I heard a loud crack when a burst of pain erupted in my lower left shin. My chest and face smacked the ground with a violent thud. The mara kept running and disappeared.

I tried to lift myself, but my shin screamed with pain. I dropped back down and pleaded for Creator's help.

Rolling to my side, I looked down the length of my body to see what was wrong. My left foot vanished into a hole at a sharp angle.

Something pointy was poking against my skin from the inside.

Still on my side, I curled my upper body so I could reach my foot. In tremendous pain, I used both hands to pull my dangling foot out of the hole.

I squeezed my tear-filled eyes and clenched my teeth. A cold sweat broke out on my skin. I focused on my breathing to stay conscious, but dizziness gave way to a panicked descent into blackness.

When I regained consciousness, Ennoia, Manna and Aable crouched around me, inspecting my injury. I propped my upper body with my hands to see my legs. My left leg had a freakish bend above the ankle. My foot was laying limp to the side, pointing in an unnatural direction. A continual river of pain traveled up my leg.

"You broke your leg," Manna said. "We need to put a splint on it so the bone can knit together without being disturbed. Ennoia and I will stay with you while Aable gathers materials for your splint."

Aable released His links to the others, extended His massive wings, and took flight into the sky, flapping His wings only a few times to gain altitude. All of us watched until Aable had vanished from sight. Then Manna and Ennoia directed Their attention toward me.

My leg was now swollen. I managed my pain by taking quick, shallow breaths. Closing my eyes helped me to stay calm. Tears pushed out between my eyelids.

Ennoia said, "Everything will be all right, Cherished. The pain will pass soon."

Manna placed His hand on my upper chest and said, "Be at peace."

At those words, my fears relaxed, my breathing slowed. In spite of my present experience, I believed everything would be all right, that Creator would take care of me.

A brief while later, Aable glided down to us, wing feathers spread wide, carrying straight branches and a bundle of vines. Aable linked to Ennoia and Manna before kneeling and placing the materials on the ground next to me. Aable positioned five straight branches alongside my leg, spaced at even intervals, and tied them with the vines. He plucked soft feathers from His head to use as padding between my leg and the rough branches. Watching Aable work with such skill distracted me from my pain.

After Aable completed the splint, the Three carried me to my shelter and sat me down inside.

"You mustn't use your leg for forty days so that your bone will knit together," Manna said.

"I can't move my leg for forty days?"

"Just the first seven days. After that, you can move your leg, but you can't put any weight on it until the forty days are over."

"Why don't you fix my leg? Then, I can walk again."

"We could mend your leg, but We choose not to. We prefer that your body heal itself."

"My garden?"

"Don't worry about your garden. We'll take care of it."

Throughout that night, I was conscious of my leg and afraid to move it by accident, so I forced myself to stay still. The discomfort of the splint added to my sleeplessness. My memory of chasing the mara and breaking my leg played over and over in my restless mind.

When the morning light peeked through the cracks of my front wall, I said to myself, "I thought the night would never end."

Creator spoke inside my mind. "Blessings, Cherished."

"I don't feel blessed," I said.

"The blessing is that you're loved, regardless of your situation or attitude."

I wanted to say I didn't feel loved either, but I said nothing because I wasn't in the mood to be corrected.

Chapter 58

Provision

Eager to escape my shelter, I sat up and used my hands to push myself backward, dragging my legs behind me, careful not to disturb the splint. When I reached the shelter door, I pushed to swing it open on its top hinge and propped it horizontal with a long stick. I dragged myself backward through the opening and beyond the ledge of the overhanging door. Transferring my weight onto my hands, I pivoted around on my limp feet until I was facing away from my shelter. Sliding backward, I aimed for the bay tree trunk that framed one side of the entrance. When I reached the spot, I leaned against the trunk and caught my breath.

The jutting door shaded me where I sat. If the night seemed long, then the day would pass even slower. How would I fill the time?

My stomach rumbled.

"Creator, I'm hungry."

"So you are," Creator said inside my mind.

"Aren't You going to feed me?"

"If you want to eat, you must do your part."

"You told me not to move. Am I supposed to eat dirt?"

I felt Their withdrawal.

"I'm sorry," I said.

"Your peevishness doesn't help. Tell Us what you think your part might be."

"To tell You I'm hungry?"

"Admitting your need is a start, but that isn't enough."

I couldn't think of anything else. When I realized the answer, I said with embarrassment, "Creator, will You please feed me?"

"Now that you ask Us, We will feed you, but on one condition. You must trust Us to provide."

"I trust You."

I waited all morning, expecting Creator to show up with food. In the meantime, I stayed by the shelter entrance and watched what meager activity occurred within view. A deer and her long-legged fawn foraged in the distance for a while. A stray gust of wind slammed against the trees, dislodging a few pine cones, one of which almost hit me. Twice, a squirrel came near, carrying a nut in its mouth. Each time, I watched the squirrel dig a hole and drop the nut into it, then cover the hole with dirt and pat it down with its tiny front paws. Later, a jay carrying a sprig of red berries landed on a nearby rock and dropped the sprig by its feet. It cocked its head a few times, then pecked at a few berries. When the sprig fell off the rock, the jay flew away.

My lack of sleep had robbed me of energy. I dragged myself inside my shelter to nap. The ceiling had developed an annoying drip near the rear boulder. The drip formed a small puddle that pooled along the boulder's base. I wanted to investigate this nuisance, but my need for sleep was greater. When I closed my eyes, I fell asleep in an instant.

Upon awaking, I heard the irritating drip, drip, drip on my shelter floor. The moisture had caused a row of small mushrooms to sprout. Things had gone from bad to worse.

Now famished, I dragged myself outside, but saw no food. Creator hadn't kept Their promise.

"Creator, I trusted You," I said. "Why didn't You feed me?"

"You missed it," Creator said inside my mind.

"Missed it? How? Did You visit while I was sleeping?" I pictured Creator turning away disappointed when finding me asleep and leaving me no food.

"The wind, the squirrel, the jay, and the drip delivered food to you."

I had overlooked Creator's provision when it was right in front of me. I was as brainless as a clod of dung. "I didn't realize," I said. "I'm sorry I didn't see it."

"When you learn to see, you will see Us working in the small things."

I dug up the squirrel's gifts, extracted the seeds from the pine cones, collected the jay's berries, and harvested the mushrooms. I was too hungry to give proper thanks on the granite table, so I tapped the food on my thighs before gulping it down. On recognizing my thirst, I realized that the annoying drip had another benefit. I grinned with amazement. Full of gratitude, I placed a gourd bowl beneath the drip and watched it fill up one precious drop at a time.

Chapter 59

Immobility

Each morning, I dragged myself out of my shelter, sliding backward with my hands, my legs trailing. Several days of dragging had encrusted my legs with dirt. Once outside, I dragged myself behind the rock enclosure and lifted my hips with my hands to relieve myself. Then I hauled my body to the front of my shelter and leaned against the bay tree trunk that framed the entrance. Whenever the boredom from sitting became too much, I would lie down inside my shelter and try to sleep to make the time pass faster. When I couldn't sleep, I would stare at the ceiling.

Sitting outside offered small diversions. I enjoyed watching any birds or animals that visited my section of the woods. Sometimes, they dropped food right in front of me. Other times, I found food piled by my door in the mornings. On occasion, Creator delivered food in person. Between these deliveries, I did nothing but sit or lie down and wish to be anywhere else.

The days passed as a slow crawl. I tried to be positive, but my limited mobility made me irritable. The spiritual nourishment from my umbilicore helped, but the flow would cease whenever I became discontent. Talking to Creator helped somewhat, but I would run out of things to say. And so, I spent the bulk of my time dwelling on my misfortune. I missed walking and swimming and gardening. I obsessed about all the things I couldn't do.

Each day, I inscribed a notch into the dirt floor of my shelter to track the days since I broke my leg. I needed to know when the fortieth day arrived, when the hated splint would come off. I started notching the dirt when I suspected that Creator tired of my repeated queries about how many days remained. The notches didn't tally fast enough. Time was playing a cruel trick on me, keeping the expected day beyond reach, like the mara I couldn't catch.

One afternoon, the golden-fringed Creator strode up the hill to visit me. My elation at seeing Him made my heart beat faster. He carried an armload of food which He placed on the ground beside me. He stooped and embraced me, saying, "Blessings, Cherished. We brought you some fruits and vegetables."

"Thanks, Creator. Will You stay?"

"Yes." He sat and leaned against the tree trunk on the other side of the entrance.

He gazed at me as if waiting for me to start.

I couldn't bring myself to say how miserable I was. "How is my garden?"

"The plants are growing well."

Creator continued to look at me with a patient expression.

"I'm trying to endure," I said, looking at my dusty legs, "but it's not working. What's the point of sitting here day after day?"

"There is a purpose, if you can lay hold of it, but you haven't yet. Can you trust in Our master plan for you?"

My mouth dropped open. "You planned my broken leg?"

"We didn't intend your accident. We knew you would break your leg, and We allowed it to happen. Some events are random and some are intentional, but in every case, you must trust Us. We can insert Our intention into any unintended situation, no matter how unpleasant, and cause it to transform your soul. Through

176

your act of trusting, Our intention is realized. If you fail to trust, then the effect is lost. So, if you can trust Us with your broken leg, then the deep change We want to work in your soul will occur."

"I do trust You."

"Your trust will be tested soon. Be careful not to place your confidence in your own trust or you will stumble. Your trust isn't what saves you, but the One in whom you place your trust."

"How will I be tested? Will it be awful?"

Creator opened His hand to show a sparkling, clear crystal. "This beautiful gem is a diamond. It is formed below ground by tremendous pressure. When great forces press against the soul that accepts them, then the soul is molded and toughened into something pure, strong, and beautiful. Don't resist testing when it comes. Remember that great pressure is required to form a diamond."

"So, this testing is supposed to transform me?"

"Yes. Pressure can squeeze your soul into its destined shape, like strong hands squeezing wet clay into its final form."

I looked at my splint. The uncomfortable branches forced my leg to keep straight as it healed. Was my soul being constrained in a similar fashion? "If I trust and endure, then You will do the rest?"

"That's right, Cherished."

"Whatever the test is, I will trust in Your help."

"In your time of need, look to Us, not to Our help. If you expect the help We aren't intending to give, then you may lose hope when your expectation isn't fulfilled. Our help will come, but We are more apt to give you endurance than rescue you. Endurance creates more character than rescue. Now, We think it's time for a story. Would you like to hear one?"

"Yes." I brightened.

Chapter 60

Sprout

Creator signaled me to come sit between His legs. He folded His legs up while I slid over and positioned myself in front of Him. Then He dropped His legs to straddle me. I leaned back against His chest and closed my eyes. He wrapped His arms around me and began His story.

"Many seasons ago, the Forest Gardener rubbed away the dirt in one section of the forest, exposing a wide patch of solid rock. The rock had a beauty all its own, and he wanted to share that beauty with the forest. But the trees despised and shunned that spot because it had no soil to nourish their roots.

"One day, the wind tossed a pine seed onto the stone patch. The Forest Gardener walked by, saw the seed, and decided to give it a chance at life. He watered the seed and watched it extend a root that crawled across the stone until it found a crack. The root pushed itself into the crack, driven by its will to survive.

"The forest disregarded the sprout, but the Gardener showed it kindness. He fed it dew in the mornings to sustain it through the days when the sun heated the stone to scorching hot. The sprout fought to stay alive because it wanted life more than anything.

"Over time, the sprout became a seedling, then a small tree.

The Gardener smiled every time He saw the tree gripping the bare rock with relentless determination. To all other eyes, the tree was stunted, twisted, and ugly. The other trees made fun of it, because it was not tall and straight like them.

"The tree didn't care what others thought or said. It reveled in life and appreciated every gift of sunlight and water. Since no tree or animal would befriend it, it kept a solitary existence. But the Gardener loved it. During his midnight walks through the forest, he would bend down to kiss its twisted branches.

"One day, the forest trees said many cruel words to the stunted tree. The tree stood proud and ignored their words, but the Gardener overheard and became angry.

"He sent a powerful storm that drenched the forest and blasted the trees with mighty winds. The soil became soaked and slippery, so the trees had nothing to grasp to stand against the winds. They fell over one by one until all of them toppled.

"After the storm had passed, the stunted tree was the tallest tree in the forest. But the smaller plants that survived still made fun of the tree because it was ugly. The Gardener was disappointed that the remaining plants didn't yet respect the tree, so he sent a drought that caused the plants to wither. The tree endured because it was used to having no water.

"When the tree saw that it alone had survived, it didn't rejoice or weep, but continued to revel in life and appreciate every gift of sunlight and water. It never complained about the lack of soil or shortage of water. It overcame adversity because it had learned to endure those hardships."

I stared into the forest, now tinted with the oranges and purples of sunset. I waited to make sure Creator had finished His story.

"Is the story about me?" I said.

"No. You're more fortunate than the stunted tree. You live off the richness of the land."

"Am I like the other trees, then? Unable to survive storm or drought?"

179

"That depends on your roots. Not real roots, but what anchors your soul. Storm and drought expose the true nature of your soul."

My soul was a mysterious thing. I didn't understand it. "Can You see my soul's true nature?"

"Yes, but it's just a sprout."

"What do you see?"

"We see a tender shoot that thirsts for love. We see a beautiful soul that We cherish."

I took comfort in hearing that Creator liked what He saw.

"It's time for Us to go," He said.

Creator put His strong hands on my shoulders and shifted me forward so He could slip out from behind me. He turned, bent down, and embraced me. "Be at peace, Cherished. You won't have to wear the splint much longer."

I closed my eyes and soaked up His peace and love as if gathering extra in case of future drought. When He released me, I opened my eyes and saw that He was gone. I scooted back against the tree trunk and feasted on the food He had brought me, grateful for the abundance.

Chapter 61

Proposition

The next morning, I repeated my ritual of dragging my body behind my shelter to relieve myself, then to the front where I leaned against the bay tree trunk for the rest of the day. I spent the morning staring at the trees or at my dusty toes. Nothing stirred in the surrounding forest. I sighed from boredom. Whenever I heard the slightest noise, I turned to look, but never saw anything.

Suddenly, a bent figure appeared in front of me. I couldn't see his face, but I recognized Illuminos by his hair. Gasping, I jerked my head back, banging it on the tree. Since I couldn't escape, I pressed my hands flat on the ground, fortifying myself.

Illuminos bowed with one knee on the ground, his face hidden by the mass of hair that hovered in place, undulating as if propelled by a slight breeze. His right hand clasped a smooth, black walking staff that had ridges like veins embossed on its surface. He didn't speak and didn't move his body. Besides his hair, the only other movement I noticed was a lizard-like creature writhing like an earthworm because it was pinned under Illuminos' shin.

"I have nothing to say to you," I said. "Go away."

"I've come to apologize," Illuminos said in a flat tone without lifting his face.

"I won't believe anything you say."

"I seek to regain your trust."

"You never had it. If you don't leave, I'll ask Creator to appear."

"I insist that you do. Creator can witness my sincerity."

"Creator. Please come," I said.

The golden-fringed Creator appeared at my left, standing alert. Illuminos rose slightly and turned toward Creator, allowing the lizard-like creature to wriggle free. The two lizard-like creatures scrambled up his legs and clung to the front of his thighs. By the time they had moved, Illuminos dropped on one knee again and bowed to Creator.

Creator said, "State your business, Illuminos. And don't bow if you don't mean it."

In one swift motion, Illuminos stood upright, rising taller than Creator. He swiveled his head in both directions, flinging his hair toward the back where it stayed suspended. "Standing eye-to-eye suits me best. I've come to offer the tadpole a deal."

"What are you offering?" Creator said.

"I don't want to hear it," I said.

"If a choice is being presented," Creator said, "then you must hear it and choose."

"How are You helping me here?" I said, feeling betrayed.

Creator touched my shoulder. "It's all right, Cherished. He won't harm you as long as We're here."

"Harm?" Illuminos said, puckering his thin lips. "I mean no harm. On the contrary, I offer a superlative deal."

"Let's hear it," Creator said.

"I will mend the tadpole's leg in exchange for its freedom."

"You want me to give up my freedom?" I said, shaking my head.

"You misunderstand me, tadpole," Illuminos said. "I don't want to take anything from you. I'm offering you freedom."

"But I am free."

"So you think. I'm offering you freedom from authority,

freedom from consequences, freedom from your own limitations."

"No. I decline."

"Don't be so rash." A slight tremor traveled across his lips. "Take some time to think about it."

"I'm not interested."

Illuminos held out his arms. "A different trade, perhaps? What would you like in exchange for walking again?"

"This splint is just fine," I lied. "It's helping my soul to grow."

Illuminos narrowed his eyes. "Tell me, little tadpole. In what ways have you benefited from this pathetic state? Please enumerate them for me."

I had no answer. From my perspective, I saw no value or purpose to my immobility. All I had was my trust in Creator that purpose existed. "Creator says—"

Illuminos interrupted. "I'm not asking what Creator says. What do you say?"

I looked up at Creator who returned my gaze and nodded. Then I turned to Illuminos and said, "I trust in Creator. I would love to walk again and I will, but on Creator's terms and in Creator's timing."

Illuminos stiffened and his upper lip twitched.

With a smile, Creator said to Illuminos, "It seems you got whacked on the head this time. Now, go or We'll call Radiance to remove you."

Illuminos flinched at hearing Radiance's name. He glared at Creator, his hair erratic, the strands jabbing in all directions. He punched the ground with his walking staff so hard that it stayed vertical on its own. The lizard-like creatures began crawling toward the greasy, yellow nodule on his chest, but he covered the nodule with one hand and swatted the creatures down with the other. He darkened and transformed until his entire body was like his hair, a swirling mass of black strands stabbing the air.

Then Illuminos rushed toward me, black fingers straining to reach my body.

Chapter 62

Glory

In that instant, a blinding light filled the scene. When the light faded, Illuminos was replaced with a darkened patch of ground and a faint, rotten odor. A narrow beam of light from above licked up the blackened patch. I traced the beam upward and saw Radiance hovering above us. When she had restored the spot to its original state, she descended to hover in front of Creator and me.

"Thank you, Radiance," Creator said.

"I am exceedingly delighted to serve," Radiance said, rising and falling with the same tempo as breathing.

Creator sat next to me. "You chose well today, Cherished."

"It helped to have You with me. I was tempted by his offer to mend my leg."

"We know. Illuminos wouldn't offer something that wasn't tempting."

"Does he have the power to give the freedom he described?"

"Yes. But that freedom is an illusion, a powerful illusion. For those under its spell, they believe nothing can hold them back."

"I don't want an illusion." I looked at my splint, then pointed at it. "I'm trusting all this will make sense, someday."

Creator smiled and placed His forehead on mine. "Cherished,

when someday comes, you won't be disappointed."

One of Radiance's light beams flashed in my eye.

"Thanks for getting rid of Illuminos," I said to her.

"You're welcome," she said. "But he will return."

"Creator," I said, "isn't Your presence enough to scare off Illuminos?"

"Yes, but We didn't show Our full presence. He knows We won't because it's not yet time for his punishment. He will be stopped when We release the full intensity of Our Light because pure light incapacitates selffulness. In the meantime, We have given those like Radiance a tiny drop of Our glory to drive away those who shun the Light."

"Radiance has only a tiny drop?" I said, amazed.

"It does not feel like a drop," Radiance said. "I have to stretch to the point of bursting to contain it."

"We'll leave you two to catch up," Creator said. "And Radiance, your firefly is a beautiful thing. Don't keep it caged." He nodded and smiled at Radiance, then vanished.

"What did Creator mean by that?" I asked Radiance.

"Not to be so small, I suppose. All this time, I have suppressed myself, believing I would get in Creator's way. I now believe Creator wants me to fully inhabit myself."

"Did They show you that?"

"No. You directed me toward that discovery. I have been pulling things out of deep storage and disclosing them to Creator as you suggested. When those things became exposed to Creator's light, they transformed and became enlivened. I do not understand it, yet. The most amazing part is that with each disclosure, I became more connected to Creator and to myself, as though ancient cords have been reattached."

"Were you connected before?"

"I do not remember. I suspect the connections were never made. Perhaps Creator was hoping I would discover them in time. That is why Creator placed you in my life."

"I think it's the other way around," I said.

"No. You are Creator's gift to me, and I am exceedingly grateful for you."

Neither of us spoke. I pondered Radiance's words for a while. Then something struck me. "Do you suppose your firefly is the same as your drop of glory?"

Her many eyes blinked in rapid frenzy. "Hold on. That would mean . . . the drop of glory that wants to burst out . . . is me. They are the same. . . . So if I allow my inner self to come forth, then Creator's glory is revealed. That explains why Creator wants me to let my firefly out of its cage."

Radiance shuddered and emitted a creaking sound from deep within the orb. As the sound continued, tears flowed out of her eyes as she rocked back and forth. She allowed herself to be overcome with emotion. Was this the first time she had done so?

In that moment, I no longer saw her as a sphere. She became a beautiful presence that touched and enriched my being. In speechless awe, I beheld Creator's sublime glory made manifest in Radiance's vulnerability.

Chapter 63

Frustration

Later that day, I asked Creator about Illuminos' visit. "Was that the test you foretold?"

"No, Cherished," Creator said inside my mind. "The test is yet to come. Don't look for tests. That will trip you up."

"I don't want to fail."

"How do you plan to prepare?"

"I would. . . ." My mind failed me. "I'm not sure how."

"If you want to prepare, then keep trusting. You can endure any test if you trust in Us."

"I'll keep trusting, then. Can it be that simple?"

"That depends. Do you consider it simple to fall off a cliff and trust what happens next?"

After twenty-six days of immobility, I reached my breaking point. The day-to-day monotony of sitting in front of my shelter and my frustration at being unable to use my leg had festered within me, spawning a bristling irritability. I tried to stay composed for Creator's sake, but my insides churned like wriggling fish in a shallow, overcrowded puddle. Losing my self-control, I started clawing at the vines that held my splint together.

Catching myself, I slammed my knuckles against the ground three times. Then I yelled as loud as I could, hurting my ears.

"Creator!" I screamed. "I can't stand this anymore."

Their calm voice entered my mind. "What does that have to do with Us?"

"Heal my leg. Remove my splint."

"We won't do that. You're meant to learn from this."

"Can You speed up my healing?"

"No. You must complete the forty days."

"Then give me more patience."

"Is patience your greatest need?"

Somehow, I knew my problem wasn't a lack of patience. "No. My greatest need is . . . peace." I dropped my head when I realized how much I had been focused on my immobility.

"Why are you not at peace?"

I probed deeper. "Because I have no control over my situation."

"If you have no control over it, then why are you resisting it?"

I had no answer.

"Your resistance is making you frustrated and miserable," Creator said. "You have turned your situation into your adversary."

"You're right. How do I stop resisting?"

"Surrender everything to Us. Entrust Us with your immobility. You can't carry the weight of the last twenty-six days. Nor can you shoulder the burden of the next fourteen days. Focus, instead, on the present moment which is all you're meant to bear. Your load will be lighter when you give it to Us."

I tried to focus on the present moment by putting the past and future out of my mind, which was much harder than expected. Then I centered my attention on Creator's love, allowing it to embrace me, fill me, and erase all competing distractions.

Rejoining Creator was all I needed. The tracking of time became unimportant. My constant focus on my body faded. I no longer regarded my immobility as an adversary to be resisted, but as part of my life situation, something to be accepted like a rainy day. My discomfort hadn't vanished, but when viewed from the present moment, it became far more manageable, being a momentary annoyance rather than a continual burden.

"You're learning to trust," Creator said. "Try to stay in the present. Dwelling on the past or future will steal your peace. Only in the present, where We make Our abode, will you find Us and the peace We give."

I did feel peace in that moment. I tried to remain in it, but my mind jumped out. "Is this the test You foretold?"

"Ah, Cherished. What did We tell you about looking for tests? For your trust to grow, it must be tested and challenged from time to time. Never think you're exempt from further testing."

The next day, my splint bothered me more than ever. I tried to focus on the present moment, but it eluded me. I struggled to accept my situation, to stop resisting it. Nothing worked. In utter exasperation, I screamed.

"Creator, help me."

"We are here," Creator said inside my mind.

"It's not working this time. I can't shed my frustration."

"Ah. That is the problem."

"Huh?"

"'I' is the problem. You're trying to do things yourself. You need to put your self aside. When there is no self, there is no resistance, no striving, no battle."

Creator was right. I felt my self fighting my situation. I tried to let go of self, but that, too, was a product of self-effort.

"Abide," Creator said. "Abide in Us rather than abiding in self."

I focused on Creator. My self dropped away, leaving only my soul, which floated at peace within Creator's vast being. Self clamored to regain control, but I ignored its protests. For the rest of the day, I maintained this blissful state. My discomfort couldn't engage me, since nothing in me could evoke a response.

What engaged me were my feelings for Creator. With self out

of the way, I was no longer distracted by my existence. Free from the interference of self, my soul was liberated to love, and my heart swelled with adoration for Creator. From deep within me, words flowed out of my mouth, but this time the words had tones that rose and fell in lovely sequences.

"Like a mother owl, You stay near me
and protect me from harm.
When I am threatened, You defend me.
My enemy You disarm.
When storms bring trouble, You enclose me
and shield me with Your wings.
In Your warm bosom I find safety
despite what the storm brings.
Your love shades me like a canopy
and shelters me all day.
Though I am confined to my aerie,
I'm contented to stay.
Your life and love always sustain me.
I'm filled with thankfulness.
You are my second heart inside me
that beats within my chest.
You satisfy me when I'm thirsty.
You lull me in the night.
I love Your strength and gentle mercy.
May my life bring You delight.
Nothing has greater value to me.
I know I'm only dust.
All I have comes from my treasured Three.
All to You I entrust."

Hearing the beautiful tones caused tears to run down my face. Afterward, I sat silent for a long time in awe of the experience.

Chapter 64

Diversion

The next morning, when I scooted out of my shelter, dragging my legs behind me, I discovered a coiled pile of long, dried grasses outside my door. Stopping halfway out the door, I rummaged through the pile looking for food, but it contained only grass.

"Blessings, Cherished," I heard behind me. I twisted around to see the golden-fringed Creator sitting on the granite table.

"Blessings, Creator," I said. "Why is the grass here?"

"We're going to show you how to weave a basket."

This news delighted me. I dragged myself around and took my usual position against the bay tree trunk. Creator approached, bent down, placed His hands on my head, and kissed the top of it. Then He sat cross-legged in front of me and began to teach me.

Brimming with eagerness, I learned the art of basket-weaving. He taught me how to give the basket a shape, to keep the strips tight, and to tuck the ends into a finished rim. Of all the construction projects I had undertaken, I enjoyed this the most.

I developed a fondness for weaving, finding it easy, creative, and relaxing. Creator brought a fresh supply of grasses each day. I graduated from making simple baskets to weaving animal forms and abstract shapes. Along the front of my shelter wall, I displayed my handiwork, spaced apart like the seedlings in my garden.

After I had woven two dozen pieces, Creator handled a few with interest. He picked up a circular band that was three hand-widths in diameter. I had interwoven black strips to create three repeated shapes around the band.

"I made that one for You," I said. "It goes on Your head."

He placed it on His head, but it fell over His eyes, hooking on His nose. I had miscalculated the size of His head.

"It's you," I said, grinning.

He took it off and inspected it again, smiling. "You're right. It is Us. We see the three pairs of wings you wove into the pattern. Excellent work, Cherished. We will treasure it."

That night, a loud noise woke me. A fierce wind blew, causing my shelter to rattle. Heavy rain battered the roof with a relentless, deafening roar. The storm clouds must have been massive to ex-tinguish all light. The noise made it difficult to sleep, so I listened to the tempest as it became more severe. The violent blasts of wind caused me to wonder whether my shelter would hold up through the night. Water dribbled from cracks in the roof and formed cold puddles beneath my body. Frigid air pushed into my shelter, mak-ing me shiver. I asked Creator if my shelter would hold, but no answer came. Comforted that I still felt my connection to Them, I knew everything would be all right.

My shelter shuddered with fury. When it collapsed, I yelled in fear. One beam split in two and dropped on my chest, the splin-tered middle piercing my skin. The beam wedged itself against the back wall, so I pushed hard to dislodge it. Doing so caused more of the roof to fall on my legs. Unable to see, I struggled to remove the fallen roof panels with my hands. The cold rainwater shocked my body, slapped my face, and stung my eyes. Cloaked in darkness, the wind and rain assaulted me like an invisible foe.

I dragged myself toward the front wall and extended my hand to discover whether it still stood. It was shaking as I touched it, the savage wind trying to knock it down. The ground had turned to mud, so the wall's footing had weakened. I couldn't get out through the door because the fallen roof blocked my way, so I pushed against the wall to force it down. The wind shoved back.

As I pressed with all my strength, the wall began to give way. I pushed against it until it lay flat. The wall was too heavy to move, so I had no choice but to drag myself over the toppled wall in the darkness. The branches poked my hands and tore my skin. A couple times, my split got caught on the uneven surface.

After I cleared the wall, I slid through the slippery mud trying to find shelter. I dragged myself until I found a low tree. It offered meager protection, but I doubted any tree could shield me. Hiding beneath its branches, my arms hugging my chest, I kept my face away from the direct onslaught of the harsh rain.

The cold was numbing. My body shuddered with continuous shivering. I called out to Creator for help, but the noisy tempest drowned out my voice.

An inner storm raged in my soul. Fear and despair tried to overtake me, but I fought them. I remembered how fear and doubt gripped me when the tiger had killed Creator and when the snake poison had almost killed me. This time, I chose to trust. I struggled to stay connected to Creator, my connection to Them feeling as fragile as a single strand of spider web. I wondered if such a delicate thread could survive the storm. In spite of my determination to trust in Creator, I started to cry.

Cold and miserable, I waited out the storm which seemed endless. My skin was soaked and numb, my eyes bleary from crying and from the punishing rain. I endured it all, believing that Creator was with me in the midst of it.

After a long while, I no longer felt the rain pelting my body. Since I heard the rain still falling hard, I assumed that numbness had overtaken me. I couldn't see that something wondrous had taken place.

Chapter 65

Shelter

I heard the relentless pellets of water battering an unknown surface above me. Something unseen was deflecting the cold wind. Then I heard Manna's voice shouting over the din of the storm. "We'll be your shelter tonight."

I pictured Creator's six wings as they encompassed me, creating a protective shield against the brutal rain. A pair of arms wrapped around my wet body, holding me in a tight embrace. Now that I felt safe, my relief turned to sobbing as I allowed my defenses to break. The warmth from Their bodies began to remove the chill from mine.

Through the rest of the night, Creator endured the brunt of the storm, buffeted by the wind, drenched by the rain. Their wings sheltered me, keeping me secure under a living canopy of love. They stayed in position all night long while I rested within those comforting arms, feeling treasured and full of awe. Exhausted from my ordeal, I fell asleep.

When I awoke the next morning, the storm had passed. Opening my eyes, I saw Ennoia's face, gazing at me, brimming with love. Above me, six wings overlapped to create a feathery dome.

When Creator retracted Their wings, a clear sky showed overhead. I propped up my sore body and looked around. I marveled to notice that I occupied the only spot of dry ground in view.

Looking across the clearing, I saw my damaged shelter. The left wall leaned inward. The right wall lay flat. The roof had caved in, the beams split in two, one half leaning against the back boulders, the other half hanging from the bay trees. Remnants of the cross-branches were still tied to the beams like splayed fingers. None of the leaves that lined the roof stayed attached, but clumped in the corners as soggy piles.

Ennoia said, "You endured a difficult night, Cherished. We're pleased you chose to trust."

"Was the storm the test you foretold?"

"It was."

"Did I pass the test?"

"You did." All Three were smiling.

"I'm glad. But I can't claim responsibility. You had prepared me to trust. I couldn't have done it without You."

"Everything you've experienced up to this point had prepared you because you've allowed Us to work those things to change you."

"Even that is an act of trust," I said.

"Excellent, Cherished. You now understand that trust is not a solitary activity, but a cooperative one. You place your trust in Us, and We empower you to do so."

"Your shelter is destroyed," Manna said. "We'll take you to a dry cave which will be your shelter from now on."

"Cave? Why didn't you take me there at the beginning?"

"The wooden shelter was necessary for your growth. It has served its purpose and is no longer needed."

Creator salvaged items from the demolished shelter. They retrieved my walking stick and some gourds. Two of the gourds were full of water from last night's rain. Using that water, Creator washed the mud off my body and cleansed my wounds. I shivered from the cold water. They scraped the water off my skin with the edges of their outer wing feathers. Aable removed the battered splint and constructed a new one. Afterward, Ennoia and Aable stood me on my good leg. I put my arms around Their necks while keeping my splinted leg off the ground. Then I hopped on one leg as They escorted me to my new home. Manna carried my few intact possessions.

The rainstorm had soaked the entire landscape. We couldn't avoid the countless puddles, which splattered fresh mud on our legs. I tried to keep my new splint high above the splash zone. Everywhere we walked, we saw damage from the storm. The grass and plants were matted down, looking limp and beaten. Broken branches, snapped off the night before, were strewn along the way.

We reached the cave, a hollowed-out space beneath a massive, overhanging rock that jutted out from the hillside. Smaller rocks on each side held the ceiling in place. The cave floor was rocky, but dry. Any dry place was appreciated. Creator sat me down on one of the large rocks within the cave. Then They cleared away the rocks from the floor and plucked some feathers to make a bed for me at the rear of the cave. They helped me onto the bed, then departed. As soon as I closed my eyes, sleep overtook me.

Chapter 66

Reformation

I became adept at hopping around using my walking stick for support. Most of the time, I sat within my cave and looked out at the forest beyond the opening. My cave wasn't deep. From any vantage point, I could see the giant, ancient mulberry trees that grew beyond my cave, their exposed roots winding into the ground. The area right in front of my cave had no trees. Instead, a thick layer of green sorrel covered the ground with its heart-shaped leaves and pink flowers.

One afternoon, circles of light appeared on the sorrel. Looking up, I saw Radiance descending until she hovered in front of the cave entrance.

"Radiance," I said with excitement. "A lot has happened since last I saw you."

Radiance bobbed in her enthusiastic way. "You upgraded your shelter," she said, scanning the interior with light beams.

"This one won't blow down."

"I doubt it would, and for your sake I am glad. Your body is exceedingly fragile." She cast a light beam on my splint. "If the ceiling collapsed, it would crush you like an insect. That reminds me. Have you had any more encounters with Illuminos?"

"No. I think he knows to leave me alone."

"He never gives up. He will return."

"Creator will protect me," I said.

"Yes, but you must know by now that Creator is slow to rescue."

I considered every adversity I had experienced. "I hadn't realized that until you pointed it out. Why is that?"

"I don't understand Creator's ways. I just—"

"Obey." I finished her sentence. "I think it has to do with trust. Creator once said that trust is deepened or discarded during the tension of delay. Delay can build character."

"That may be, but I am concerned that Illuminos could harm you before Creator intervenes."

I remembered Illuminos whacking me on my head. I sighed. "I'm tired of worrying about him all the time. I wish he was gone." An idea came to me. "What if Illuminos changed?"

"What do you mean?"

"If he served Creator again, he wouldn't be a threat anymore."

"Illuminos can't be turned," she said with a definitive tone.

"How do you know? Have you tried?"

"If Illuminos could be turned, Creator would have restored him by now."

"You said that Creator is slow to rescue. Maybe Illuminos' reformation is yet to come."

"You continue to amaze me, Cherished. So, how would you activate this change in Illuminos?"

"I don't know. I'll need to think about it."

"If Illuminos and the other Independents could be turned, then my assignments would be less disagreeable." She blinked her eyes many times.

"You don't like your assignments?"

"I execute them without complaint, but I am not fond of dealing with darkness all the time. It takes a toll on me."

"I suppose it would. What would you prefer to do?"

She stopped bouncing. "I cannot bring myself to answer that."

"Why not?"

"What if my answer differs from Creator's will for me? How would I reconcile the two?"

"Must you reconcile your preferences with Creator's will? Can't they coexist like light and darkness? Sorry. Poor example. I don't mean that your preferences are evil. By stating them, you are just being honest. Honesty is never bad."

"If I express a preference," Radiance said, "then every time I perform Creator's will, I would be haunted by my preference for something else. That would ruin everything. I cannot exist like that."

"My preferences seldom align with Creator's will," I said. "I can live with the disharmony. I expect the gap will close over time, so that, one day, Their will and my preferences will be the same."

"Disharmony must be a human thing. Angels are not designed to handle gaps. Our preference is always the same as Creator's will."

"I'm sorry. I didn't mean to cause you turmoil."

"Cherished, you do not need to apologize. You caused me no turmoil. Since you can coexist with gaps, you are not as weak as I thought," she said, resuming her relaxed bouncing motion.

"And you're not as strong as I thought," I said with a grin.

Chapter 67

Liberation

The fortieth day arrived. It felt like every day that preceded it. After so long a wait, I expected some fanfare, such as animals gathered in front of my cave to witness the momentous event. Perhaps I had misunderstood. Was I supposed to wear the splint for forty days and have it removed on the forty-first day? Not wanting to misspend any premature excitement, I asked for clarification. "Creator, does my splint come off today?"

"Yes, Cherished. Today is the day. You can remove it."

With unrestrained enthusiasm, I ripped off the bindings on my splint, while Creator watched from His invisible perch. After removing my splint, my leg felt stiff and foreign. I flexed my knee, but its movement was sluggish. When I stood on my leg, it wobbled from weakness, unable to hold my weight. I had envisioned that removing my splint would have released pent-up energy, compelling me to run like a lizard, so my continued impairment dismayed me.

"You'll regain your strength in a few days," Creator said. "You might not want to run or swim right away."

"Run or swim? I can barely stand," I said with discouragement.

A few days later, after my legs were stronger, I decided to make the long trek to my garden. Leaning on my walking stick, I limped through the forest in the assumed direction of my garden. The location of my new shelter had disoriented me.

Along the way, I attempted to connect to Creator. I focused on my inward center to find the living stream that flowed from Creator and was Creator. I could drink from this ever-flowing stream as often as I wished. When I entered the stream and immersed myself in it, I united with Creator. My umbilicore enabled me to tap into this source of life and love, and to receive spiritual nourishment through it.

"I love You, Creator," I said.

"You're Our beloved, Cherished," They said inside my mind. "We take great joy in you."

"I don't know how to show You my love."

"You show your love when you obey Us, when you share your thoughts and feelings with Us, when you place your trust in Us."

"That doesn't seem like much compared to Your love for me."

"We abide in love itself. Your love is a realm where We delight to dwell and express Ourselves. In your love, Our love is fulfilled."

When I arrived at my garden, the first thing I noticed was that Creator had built a tall fence around it. Long sticks, placed close together, had been driven into the ground. A gate made from tied sticks leaned against two large posts that flanked an opening in the fence. The gate hung in place by an attached vine that looped around each post. I lifted the gate, sliding the loops off the posts, and set it aside to enter. The plants were thriving, spilling across the rows. Some plants already had fruit which I sampled.

My watering gourd now hung from a post by a braided loop that passed through a hole punched into its rim. I hobbled to the lake and back to draw water, cradling the gourd with my right arm and leaning on my walking stick with my left hand. Pouring water into the furrows took some awkward maneuvering. Afterward, I hung up the gourd, replaced the gate at the entrance, and returned home. From that point on, I resumed responsibility of my garden.

As soon as I was able, I fabricated a wall and door for my new shelter. The wall extended upward to the overhanging rock ceiling, but since I couldn't tie anything to the ceiling, the top of the wall was ragged and allowed light into my shelter. As with my old shelter, I hinged the door at the top so that its weight would keep it closed. During the day, I propped the door horizontal with a long branch, allowing me ready access.

One day, on the way to my garden, I saw a chestnut-colored fox eating a gray, short-eared pika.

I shouted at the fox, "Don't eat that!"

If my legs were stronger, I would have chased it. Instead, I waved my arms to scare it away. "Stop it!" I yelled.

The fox wasn't startled. It looked at me, picked up the dead pika in its mouth, and trotted into the bushes.

"Go ahead and kill. I can't stop you," I shouted, even though the fox had left the scene. Seeing the murdered pika disturbed me because I felt as defenseless as the small animal. The fox, acting from instinct and hunger, had exercised its free will. Illuminos was no different.

I questioned whether free will was such a good idea. I viewed it as something that couldn't be tamed, a savage thing like the hungry fox. Since Creator allowed wild animals to roam free, it followed that They would give free will the same license, even if chaos or anarchy resulted, such as the Great Revolt.

What troubled me was that Creator allowed this rebellion to persist, even though They had the power to quash it. Their seeming powerlessness over this crisis disappointed me.

My own powerlessness nagged me to solve my problem with Illuminos. That and my continual dread of our next encounter. I kept expecting him to appear, but he never did. Maybe he was waiting until I didn't expect him. Then he would strike.

Chapter 68

Motives

A persuasive demonstration of sincere devotion for Creator might convince Illuminos that Creator is a loving master. To that end, I purposed to be as devoted as possible. How could Illuminos ignore the power of wholehearted dedication and love?

During the rest of the day, I carried out my noble resolution. As I worked in my garden, I expressed gratitude for everything I could think of. On my return trip, I recited my love to Creator. When I ran out of loving words, I exclaimed Their splendor and power. When I tired of speaking, I filled my mind with adoring thoughts toward Them. I maintained an uninterrupted connection to Them, guarding against anything that might jeopardize it.

At the end of the day, when the sky had waned to a vibrant indigo, I collapsed on my bed. My spirit was drained, my mind fatigued, and my body depleted. Devotion was exhausting work. I doubted I could sustain this intensity for another day, and I wasn't sure I wanted to. "This is too hard," I said to myself.

"What is too hard?" Creator said, appearing as a white mist that swirled within the opening between the top of my shelter wall and the rock ceiling.

I sat up. "Maintaining constant devotion is too hard," I said as I watched threads of light jump from post to post like playful squirrels.

Creator said, "Since when did devotion become so wearying? When did We command you to be unceasing in devotion? Why are you burdening yourself with things We didn't ask you to do?"

"I wanted to express my devotion to You," I said, trying to sound pious.

"That's not true." The mist gathered into a ball of light in the center of the opening. "You wanted to prove your devotion to Illuminos and to yourself. True devotion is motivated by love alone and is devoid of selfish entanglements. You've exhausted yourself with false devotion and empty activity. Genuine devotion isn't hard or burdensome, but brightens the spirit and enlivens the soul."

"Don't You want me to be devoted?"

"What We want is truth and integrity. Devotion originates not from resolve, but from the soul as a natural outflow. A bird feeds its babies because it's committed to the task, not because it decided to do so or is trying to prove its dedication. Devotion is not forced, but flows from a selfless desire to serve."

"I wanted to show Illuminos what true devotion looks like. I thought that might convince him You are worthy of devotion."

"Cherished, what you showed wasn't true devotion. If your devotion is true, it need not be demonstrated. Its truth is enough and all will see it. If you need to prove something to yourself or to another, then its genuineness is doubtful."

My excuses could no longer stand up to Creator's wisdom. My noble intentions had turned deplorable again. I looked away from Creator's light. "I'm sorry, Creator. Forgive me. I've messed up again."

The shelter interior brightened, and I looked at the ball of light that now shone like the full moon.

"You're forgiven, Cherished," Creator said. "You'll continue to make mistakes, and We'll continue to forgive. Don't keep track of your mistakes."

The advice came too late. I had already revisited my mistakes. "What can I do to be more pleasing to you?"

"Doing isn't the answer. Who you are, not what you do, brings pleasure to Us. Actions flow from your soul and show your soul's true nature. When your soul is sincere, your actions will be sincere."

"So, my actions should always reflect my soul?"

"Yes. Otherwise your actions are false and meaningless. Let your actions be congruent with your authentic self." The glowing light comforted me in a way that words could not.

"I don't want to be false. Forgive me for displeasing You."

"Cherished, don't be so focused on striving to please Us. Be authentic, instead. Genuine devotion, trust, and love are found within you and delight Us. Allow those things to show themselves in truthful action. When you are lacking those things, be honest about it, and We will fill you. We care more about the intention behind your actions than the actions themselves. If you're compelled to act from a need to impress, prove, or gain, then your actions have no value to Us and will disable your connection. Pure intention produces authentic action."

The experience of purity was foreign to me. My soul was a muddied mixture of motivations I couldn't identify. "Creator, purify my intentions so that my actions will be authentic."

Creator flared brighter, radiating warmth onto my body and soul. Then the ball of light floated into my shelter and hovered over my head. I watched as it flung stringy loops of diaphanous light that unraveled and faded into the air.

"We affirm Our love for you," Creator said, "but We can't purify you. Purification is a process, not an event. The experiences We give you will purify you over time. Now, receive Our grace and love."

I closed my eyes to receive what felt like warm water pouring down on my head, running over my body, washing off layers of silt from my soul, exposing my raw core. Creator reduced me to my true self, the self that remains when all pretense and self-conceptions are stripped away. Creator caressed my trembling soul with tender kisses of love.

"Our love is with you forever," Creator said. "Nothing can separate you from Our love."

Creator faded away, leaving me in darkness, but my soul glowed with contentment. I settled down on my feather bed and closed my eyes.

My mind stirred itself into disquiet. How could I have been so stupid? Again, I was caught off-guard and overtaken by selfish motives. If I always knew the right thing to do, then I would be perfect.

Daylight

The next morning, bright light streamed through the cracks in my shelter wall, creating white slivers across the back of the cave. This was unusual because the cave faced south. When I lifted my door, I had to shield my eyes from a blinding white light that shone in the center of the clearing. It rivaled the sun.

"Many blessings to you, Cherished," the light thundered, sounding like a loud chorus of sparkling voices. "Come out and stand before me."

The intense brilliance disarmed me, but I stepped forward, keeping my eyes lowered. Feeling unsettled, I said, "Blessings to you, also."

"My name is Daylight. Creator has given me authority, power, and wisdom to carry out Their highest will. In obedience to Creator's command, I have come to announce Their magnanimous intentions toward you. Because of Creator's extravagant love for you, They have sent me to grant you whatever you ask. Prudently consider what gift would be most useful to you in your devotion and service to Creator."

My body trembled, and I locked my knees to stabilize myself. I kept my eyes lowered and said, "Creator has given me everything

I need. I can't think of anything to ask for."

"Yes, Creator is more than sufficient for life. However, according to Their great wisdom, some gifts are withheld until appointed times when they are granted by request. This is your appointed time, Cherished. In truth, this opportunity is a test to prove your purity of heart. I am confident you will make the wisest decision in this matter. My standing here before you attests that Creator believes you are ready."

This was my chance to show maturity and wisdom. I didn't want to make a selfish request, although a few selfish ideas occurred to me, such as having a pair of wings. My past mistakes caused me to fear I would make the wrong choice again. If ever I needed to make the right choice, it was now.

"My request is to always know the right choice," I said, lifting my head and squinting into the light. With the knowledge of right choices, I was guaranteed success. I grinned with self-satisfaction.

"Cherished, you have shown great wisdom. I commend you."

"Wait!" I said in a panic. "Creator forbade me to ask for this knowledge. Can I change my request?"

"Do not fear, Cherished. Your request is virtuous. Creator forbade you at that time because you were not ready for this knowledge. You have matured since then and are now qualified to receive it."

I wasn't sure whether Creator ever changed Their mind. "Can you come back later, after I have given this more thought?"

"No," Daylight boomed. "I cannot return. This is my only visit to this planet. Even now, I am being summoned back to the realm of glories. Decide now or else I must go."

I hesitated. "I do want to know what's right. I believe I'm ready for it."

"Excellent. Kneel and receive the knowledge of right and wrong."

I knelt and closed my eyes, with open palms on my knees. Knowledge flooded my mind. I understood those things that were right and good and pleasing to Creator. And I understood those things that were not, that fell short of Creator's perfection. Everything became measured against that perfection and was judged inferior by comparison. My world darkened with the knowledge that my every action and thought didn't measure up. My eyes were opened to my poverty of soul, my dire inadequacy made naked before me for the first time. Where before I had been innocent, the knowledge of my innate imperfection had now become a curse. The gap between Creator and me widened until we were separated by an infinite distance, an unpassable yawning chasm.

This realization of my utter imperfection triggered a need to defend myself against it and find justification for my depraved existence. Something within me sought to reject these new realities, to assert itself, to defy judgment and limitation. This defiant energy coalesced inside me as an ugly willfulness that fought against this degradation. As a horrified bystander, I watched this willfulness infiltrate my mind and take over my will.

And then, I saw myself with new clarity. The horror of the preceding moments vanished, as if belonging to a different person altogether.

I now comprehended my power to direct my life by my own choices, to control my own destiny. I reveled in this newfound power. My being mattered in a way it had not before. It became central to my existence, something to be treasured and guarded above all things. I saw myself as sovereign and free, and equal to Creator in that regard.

This heightened self-awareness eclipsed my present sense of Creator. I tried to restore my connection to Them, but I could no longer find my umbilicore. Something terrible had happened. I opened my eyes to ask Daylight to explain.

His blinding appearance had dimmed so I could make out his form. Standing in front of me was a familiar, copper-colored being. Illuminos.

Chapter 70

Independence

A grinning Illuminos raised his yellowed-bone walking staff and said, "Welcome to independence." His exaggerated grin forced his pomegranate-colored eyes into the shapes of setting suns dropping below the horizon. "You are now one of us, little tadpole. You have chosen knowledge over innocence, freedom over subjugation, your will over Creator's will. You are ruler of your own life, now."

I felt ill as if every organ in my body objected to this malicious deception. Pulling myself up, I said, "That's not what I asked for. Take it back."

"It is what you asked for. And no one can undo it, not even Creator. Once enlightened, forever enlightened. You don't yet realize that this circumstance is for the best." He gazed at me and smiled. "Embrace your new knowledge. Enjoy your new freedom." His hair cascaded like the boughs of a pine tree waving in the wind.

"I don't want freedom," I bellowed.

"Give yourself time and you'll—"

"Take it back!" I yelled. I charged at Illuminos who lifted his bone and held it horizontal to block me.

I clutched the bone with both hands and glared into his eyes.

"Take it back!"

"I cannot. Why don't you ask your dear Creator to rescue you? You'll find out They aren't so helpful after all."

"Creator!" I shouted as loud as I could while keeping my eyes fixed on his piercing eyes. My summons didn't rattle Illuminos.

Creator didn't appear or answer.

We both gripped the bone, staring at each other and saying nothing. His hair paused, suspended while we waited. I tried to reconnect to Creator, hoping to assuage my mounting panic, but my connection was gone. I remembered that if I admitted my error, Creator would restore my connection.

Dropping to my knees, I said, "Creator, forgive me. I was wrong to seek forbidden knowledge. Please restore my connection."

No response.

Illuminos placed both elbows on top of the long bone and propped his head on his hands to watch me. His hair resumed its rhythmic motion.

After a while, Illuminos huffed, then said, "I believe Creator has moved on. You, too, must move on, now that you are on your own. Take my advice and learn to like it."

Illuminos manufactured a grin, then vanished.

I didn't like it one bit.

Sitting in front of my shelter amid the flowering sorrel, I waited, hopeful that Creator would respond. I placed my full trust in Creator's love and faithfulness. My experience had taught me to trust, not fear. To ward off my fear, I told myself over and over, "They will answer. They always answer."

At mid-morning, Radiance came rolling toward me between the mulberry trees. Cheered by her approach, I stood to greet my friend. My gladness faded when I saw how dim her light had become, making the lavender sphere a dull gray. Her light stalks were so faint that she floated a hand-width above the ground. She lumbered across the clearing and stopped in front of me, hovering motionless. Tears leaked out of every eye, ran down the globe, and dripped on the ground.

"Cherished," Radiance said in a breathy voice, "if I had been here, I could have protected you. Now, it is too late. This situation is exceedingly tragic."

"My connection to Creator is gone. How do I reconnect?"

"Your umbilicore has been severed. When you partook of forbidden knowledge, you rebelled against Creator. By choosing the knowledge of good and evil, you rejected Creator's guidance. You chose self-determination which means you have renounced your dependency on Creator." She gave a heavy sigh. Some eyes squeezed closed, forcing out fresh tears.

I refused to believe the news. And yet, I felt the severity of my wound, the complete cessation of flow from Creator as if my umbilicore didn't exist. "But Creator can do anything. They can fix this."

"If They can fix it, They will find a way. Until then, you must wait and trust. You are now like the Tree of Death to Them. They cannot touch you and you cannot touch Them because you have chosen disconnection and separation. You are cut off from each other. Creator sent me to speak to you because you can no longer hear Them. They are distraught and heartbroken over losing you." Radiance shuddered, flinging tears off the sphere.

"What should I do?" Terror crept into my thoughts.

Radiance sighed. "You must learn to live without Creator."

"I can't do that. I won't. I will continue to live for Creator."

"Without your connection, that will be exceedingly difficult. Because you are severed from Creator, your spirit is now dead. You must live for yourself, now that you have chosen that path. The knowledge of good and evil shifts your dependence from Creator onto your own choices. You now have what is called a conscience. Your conscience will tell you how to live, what is right and wrong."

I heard my heart thumping in my ears. My breathing matched its beat. "It's not my fault. Illuminos tricked me."

Chapter 71

Disconnection

"Illuminos did trick you," Radiance said, "but you asked for knowledge you knew was forbidden. You must accept the consequences of your choice." She released a long, deep moan. "This is exceedingly grievous." A new surge of tears gushed from her eyes.

"Is there anything I can do to fix this?" I tried to apply my new knowledge to discern the right course of action, but my mind could only deliver accusations.

"You cannot fix it. You must live out the rest of your days without Creator until They heal the rift. Enjoy the fruit of the land. Work your garden. Find pleasure in your activities. Do not despair because Creator still loves you."

"If They still love me, then why won't They help me?"

"Creator will do what They can, but They have to find a way to help you while you are untouchable. Your willfulness repels Creator. Their pure nature cannot tolerate your darkened soul."

The awareness of my utter imperfection expanded to include my newborn willfulness that now alienated me from Creator. An intense feeling of shame filled me. I cowered and looked away. All my flaws and faults clung to me like dew on my skin. I wanted to hide so that no one could see them.

"Tell Creator I'm sorry," I said. "I never wanted to drive Them away. Tell Them how much I want Them back."

"They can still hear you, Cherished, but I will tell Them. I am sorry. Your presence is exceedingly difficult to endure. I wish I could stay, but I cannot."

Radiance's wet, cobalt eyes gazed at me, unblinking. Then all her eyes drifted close at the same time. The dim beams of light faded, causing her to lower to the ground. The gray orb appeared as inert as an ancient boulder. I moved forward to touch the sphere, but she vanished before I could do so.

Would I ever see her again?

I stared at the smashed plants where Radiance had settled. I felt cut off from everyone and everything. A crushing sense of abandonment engulfed me like ants swarming a dead animal. The world receded from me and kept its distance like the plants that grew outside the barren circle of the Tree of Death. My soul felt far away.

I tried to connect to Creator one last time, hoping to find some overlooked thread that still linked me to Them, but I found nothing to grasp. Looking for messages in my body or mind, I found none. My spirit was dead, a fallen leaf, dried-up and useless.

I staggered into the dark cave of my shelter and curled up on the floor. With my arms and knees pulled up close, my stupor thawed, and I gave myself over to bouts of sobbing. Though my ribs ached and head throbbed, I wept as I grieved over Creator's departure from my life. I felt devastated and desolate like a plant that had been yanked out of the ground, cast aside to wither, roots unable to draw nourishment.

I lay on the floor all day, allowing my sorrow to overwhelm me. My mind would surface in an attempt to bring reason to my plight, but reason would fail me and my mind would be sucked back down into the dreadful current. No apology, remorse, or act of penitence could atone for my mistake. Radiance had given me little hope for reconnection, too tenuous to lay hold of, leaving me destitute of any comfort.

The next morning, I didn't leave my shelter, except to empty my bladder. All day, I stayed on my bed. I had no appetite for food or for living. My relentless thoughts tormented me with harsh indictments and promises of misery. I escaped through fitful sleep, but when night came, I lay awake and stared at the darkness while despair burrowed through my body.

Day after day, I repeated the same cycle. Staying inside my shelter. Sleeping a lot. I became weaker and weaker from not eating until I couldn't stand.

I coveted death and believed I was hastening its approach. When I thought death was close, I obsessed about whether I would meet Creator again. Didn't all things return to Them at death? What about disconnected things, like me? Would I remain disconnected even in death? If I did meet Them, how would I explain my refusal to live? Radiance urged me to live without Creator, but I never tried. I felt guilty for failing Radiance. My conscience accused me of giving up.

With heavy disappointment, I realized that knowing right and wrong had little value since it didn't empower me to do right. I had lost everything because I coveted that knowledge.

Collecting what remaining energy I had left, I said in a weak whisper, "Creator, I'm sorry for disobeying You. I'm ashamed of what I've become. My every thought is full of me. You warned me to guard my umbilicore, but I destroyed it. Forgive me. I would give anything to have You back again. I miss Your voice and presence. I miss Your touch, Your nighttime stories, our walks in the forest, and, most of all, how Your love made me feel. Please restore me to You. If there is a way, You will find it. If You can hear me . . . please . . . rescue me."

I hoped my plea might find its way to Creator as it journeyed across treacherous mountains and unpassable cliffs that now separated us.

Chapter 72

Grief

Creator watched Cherished weep. They stood together in the cave, silent and solemn, unseen. They pulled close Their drooping wings that were linked by clenched fingers. Their chests heaving, Their wet eyes peered down at the dark, trembling form. The same gaze of love as when They knelt by Cherished's body after it had just received a soul that first day.

Creator gazed at Cherished who was curled up on the bed made with Their feathers. Cherished's darkened soul appeared to Them as black as midnight like the Tree of Death. A choice for independence had brought disconnection, separation, and spiritual death—a branch severed from the vine.

Creator heard Cherished's pleas and listened with all Their being, feeling the swell of anguish that engulfed Their beloved.

Aable shook his head and sighed. "We hear you, Cherished. Don't despair. We long to comfort you, but We can't."

"You know Cherished can't hear you," Manna said. "The darkness disables all awareness of Us."

"I know, but it's my nature to give comfort." Aable bent over as if to kiss Cherished.

"Don't!" Manna said with alarm. "Cherished's corrupted

substance is contrary to Our being. Our touch will destroy Cherished. We must keep Our distance."

Aable backed away, shaking his head. "That's the hardest thing. We're right here, but the separation between us is uncrossable." He extended his hand and held it out toward Cherished as if hoping Cherished would take it. He sighed and let his arm drop. He grasped Manna's and Ennoia's hands and held tight.

All three watched Cherished toss and turn on the bed.

Ennoia said, "Cherished doesn't know how painful this is for Us. The disconnection. The separation. They apply to Us as well."

"Cherished can only feel one side of the separation," Manna said. "That's enough to bear."

"Oh, Cherished," Aable said in a mournful tone. "You've caused Us deep sadness. We wanted our relationship to last forever."

"We knew this tragedy would happen," Ennoia said.

Aable sighed. "That doesn't make it less painful."

"We know what needs to be done." Ennoia spoke with resoluteness.

Manna nodded slowly. "Yes. It's the only way. But Our suffering will be greater than this."

"I'm willing to pay the price," Ennoia said.

After a pause, Aable said, "Me, too."

They both looked at Manna.

Manna took a deep breath. "For love, I will do it."

"For love," Ennoia and Aable said in unison.

Manna then said, "Cherished won't recognize Our workings."

"True." Ennoia fluttered his wings. "Cherished needs only to trust in Our love. When trust believes in love, then the soul is opened to receive."

The darkened form on the bed brought its fists to its eyes. It spoke, its voice weak and despairing. "Creator."

They turned to gaze again at Cherished, Their faces pinched with pain. They loved Cherished with a love that was willing to give everything.

Chapter 73

Helper

I awakened to see someone bending over me. Startled by the intruder, all I could do was gasp, given my weakened state. A shadowy hand thrust a gourd into my face. I couldn't see details in the dim light of my shelter.

"Here . . . drink this water," a raspy, faraway voice said.

I accepted the water and drank it in small gulps.

"Who are you?" I whispered in a faint voice.

His voice now sounded more distinct, but halting. "My name . . . is Blazing Light Shaft. But call me Blaze. . . . I detest my full name. I would've fancied a simple name . . . like Flame, or Flicker, or . . . anyway . . . Blaze will do. . . . I'm here to nurse you back to health . . . 'cause you sure look terrible. I don't know . . . maybe you always look this way. I've never seen a human before."

Straining to focus in the dark, I saw a squat, hairy form. No, he wasn't hairy. Many layers of animal furs draped over his body in a haphazard fashion. Long pieces of fur dragged on the ground, causing me to realize that the tails of the unfortunate animals were still attached. From beneath the fur wrappings peeked lumpy, yellowish skin, resembling the surface of a knobby gourd. The overhanging furs kept his round, bumpy face in shadow. He lacked ears and lips and eyebrows. Instead of a nose, two gigantic holes flared open to show their contents. Small, black, pig-like eyes peered out above the two dark caverns. I had never seen a creature as ugly as this.

"Are you an angel? Did Creator send you?" I whispered, doubting that Creator would send someone who smelled like a decomposing animal.

Blaze grinned, revealing a generous collection of tiny brown teeth. "Creator needed to send someone and I . . . volunteered, sort of. I was antsy and bored, so I . . . jumped at the opportunity. I'm not an angel, but a helper. That's what I do. I . . . help. The need for help is rare these days, but your case is a winner. Here . . . eat this. It will give you strength."

A stout, yellowish arm poked out from beneath the furs and forced something into my mouth. I began chewing, discovering the food to be warm and salty. After swallowing it, I said, "What is it? It tastes good."

"Opossum."

"Opossum! I don't eat animals," I brayed, rasping my feeble throat. My conscience protested this violation against nature and propriety.

"Calm down. Relax. You gotta trust me. I know you have a strict diet, but meat . . . it's a good source of nutrients. It will help you get your strength back. Now . . . don't worry. It won't kill you. Here . . . eat some more."

Blaze shoved another piece into my mouth before I could object. I refused to chew it, but hunger prevailed over my reluctance, and my jaws began to crush the delicacy. I tried to understand my disapproving conscience. Many animals ate meat, but they didn't have a conscience. Or did they? Perhaps it was wrong only for me, but I didn't recall Creator ever forbidding it. Nor did They ever suggest it.

"How can I know Creator sent you? Daylight said the same thing and lied."

"Nasty business . . . that was. I know all 'bout that. Turns out . . . everyone knows. News like that travels far and fast. Most of the time . . . the news is the same old stuff. Another world reclaimed. That sort of thing. That scoundrel Illuminos . . . tricked you into becoming independent. What a sneaky devil. Hmm. . . . Not sure how . . . to prove my trustworthiness. I hope I can win your trust . . . by taking care of you. Besides . . . no one has any reason to trick you, now. You've got nothing more to lose."

"You're right about that. I appreciate the help. And I'm grateful for the company."

"Be quiet and eat. Then . . . you need to rest. Let the food do its work. We'll talk later."

Blaze fed me more opossum and water. As I ate, I noticed he was hunched over, almost horizontal, from the weight of his many furs. After I finished eating, Blaze scooted out of my shelter. I fell asleep right away.

When I awoke, Blaze was hovering over me with more food and water. This time, he included tasty vegetables with the meat. Somehow, he made the vegetables soft and warm.

After the meal, feeling much better, I sat up to talk. "Thank you for the delicious meal, Blaze. Will you leave after I have regained my strength?"

"Nope. I'm here to stay." Blaze's voice was raspy, like a hissing animal. "This is a long-term assignment for me . . . like it or not. I'll be your companion, servant or . . . whatever you prefer. I don't care." He crouched on his stocky legs, hunched over, his many furs swaying as he spoke.

"My presence doesn't bother you?" I said. "Radiance couldn't tolerate being near me."

"Nah. I can handle anything. Drop me into a pool of tar . . . and I'm good to go."

"Can you send messages to Creator from me?"

"That's not needed. Creator knows . . . what's going on, since nothing is hidden from Them. To you . . . it feels like They aren't listening 'cause communication is broken down . . . but They still hear everything. Your spirit is dead . . . so you can't hear Creator no more. Sorry 'bout that."

"Can you pass messages from Creator to me, since I can't hear Them?"

"Conflagration! I've never been pestered with so many questions. Ease up, will you?"

Blaze exhaled a deep breath. "Sorry. . . . I got worked up. Don't take it personal. . . . I'm not used to being 'round others. To answer your question . . . I will relay messages from Creator if They have something to say. But right now . . . They aren't speaking to you. Your choice of independence . . . has pushed Them away. You're cut off . . . from each other."

Those last words stung, causing a bitter taste in my mouth. Remorse and regret burned fresh sores inside me, and shame reinforced its bindings. Tears pushed their way out through frequented corridors, and I blinked to hide them from Blaze.

I shook my head. "I've ruined everything. And I can't fix it." I sighed. "It's in Creator's hands, now. I am grateful that Creator sent you. You are a helpful distraction."

"Distraction?" Blaze repeated with indignation, forming his stubby hands into fists. "Why don't you call me Distraction instead of Blaze? Would you find that . . . helpful? I'm nursing you back to health . . . and you repay me with insults. You must be getting better . . . if your annoying questions and degrading comments are any sign of normalcy for a human. Humph. . . . You gotta sleep. I gotta go. In the morning . . . I'll haul you out of this stifling cage." Blaze stomped out of my shelter in a hurry.

Chapter 74

Fire

The next morning, Blaze dragged me outside by force. I was too weak to resist. With my walking stick and Blaze assisting, I found I could stand. Once outside, I beheld an amazing thing.

Captivated, I observed yellow light dancing within a circle of stones near my shelter. The light was warm, like the sun at midday, splashing upward with frantic, pointed fingers that caressed blackened wood within the stone circle. The spellbinding light made a crackling noise, like the snapping of dead pine needles when one walks on them.

"That," Blaze said, "is fire. It's my best friend." Blaze peered into the fire with a hungry look. "Fire keeps you warm when you're cold, gives light at night, and makes food taste better. Fire can be painful . . . and glorious. I'll show you how to make fire and keep it burning . . . but you must not touch it."

I must not touch. That prohibition reminded me that I now lived in the world of do's and don'ts, the world of right and wrong. In this new scheme, I must live by my own choices, although I had no idea what choices I was supposed to be making.

"Let's get moving," Blaze said with impatience. "Where to?"

"To the lake to see my garden."

"Fine by me," Blaze grunted.

I tried to walk, but my legs wobbled from weakness. Blaze came alongside so I could lean on his fur-covered shoulder, which rose to the height of my stomach. I shuffled forward with slow, short steps while Blaze kept pace.

Trying to see past Blaze's repulsive appearance, I couldn't sense anything about him. When I was with Creator, I sensed Their presence. Even with Illuminos, I felt something. With Blaze, I felt nothing, as though he were an object, like a rock or piece of wood. I could see form, but couldn't discern anything within. I must have lost that ability when my spirit died. Now, I was limited to my senses only, and they provided little help.

As I examined the world around me, I observed a difference there as well. The trees and plants also appeared as static objects, dulled and inert. I could no longer sense any inward light or energy. My connection to nature had also been severed. Another lost friend to mourn. Losing my connection to Creator had damaged all my other connections.

Leaning on Blaze as I shuffled toward the lake, I tried to learn more about my new companion. "Tell me about yourself, Blaze. What is your relationship to Creator?"

"Conflagration! Must you pester me with so many questions?" Blaze groaned and shook his head beneath his layered furs. "I've always been a helper. That's what I do. I . . . help. I've helped Creator lots of times. Now . . . I'm helping you."

I learned nothing from his answer.

"In what ways have you helped Creator?" I said.

He groaned in exasperation. "I've burned down entire forests."

"Burned? What do you mean?"

"By fire. I've destroyed forests by fire." He sounded exasperated.

I halted and stared at the pile of moving furs. Blaze stopped and twisted to look up at me.

"Are you saying that Creator would destroy an entire forest by fire?" I said.

"Sure. Creator destroys forests . . . all the time. Forests can't keep growing forever. They have to be wiped clean . . . now and then. You haven't been 'round long. Have you?"

I shook my head in amazement. How could I know if Blaze was telling the truth?

I noticed something tucked beneath Blaze's furs, something wrapped in a silky, gray pelt. To avoid provoking Blaze, I refrained from asking a direct question. "I see you are carrying something inside that bundle." I pointed to it.

"Yep." Blaze grinned, showing both rows of tiny, brown teeth. Blaze pulled out the bundle and unwrapped it with great affection. "These here are hunting weapons . . . spears and knives. I always have them with me . . . just in case. I never know when I might spot . . . a juicy piece of tasty meat."

Blaze reminded me of the terrifying tiger that attacked Creator. Replaying the attack, I pictured Blaze in place of the tiger, pouncing, ripping flesh, and savoring the taste of blood. I recoiled and stepped back. Had I been paired with a bloodthirsty predator?

Chapter 75

Salvage

"I'm joking," Blaze said. "Hunting . . . it's a hobby of mine. I don't need to eat like you do. I don't eat the animals I kill . . . unless they put up a fight."

I debated whether I had the strength to travel on my own and leave Blaze behind. I decided I was too weak to do so.

"Don't be afraid . . . of me," Blaze said. "I wouldn't hurt anything . . . unless it has fur. I collect furs. Sort of an obsession. You don't have fur so you're safe . . . fortunate for you." He displayed a wide grin, then wrapped up his weapons in the gray pelt.

His words didn't reassure me. I shifted the conversation away from the topic of killing. "I see you like to wear furs."

"Yep. I've got almost every kind." Blaze listed over thirty animals, identifying the fur that belonged to each and holding it out for me to see. "I wear the furs for camouflage . . . so I can blend into the forest . . . when I'm hunting."

I tried to envision Blaze blending in anywhere. He stood out with his yellowish skin and overloaded furs that dragged on the ground, stirring up dust. Any animal that Blaze hunted would have to be invalid or blind.

We resumed our slow trek to the lake. I shuffled while leaning on Blaze, wondering if he had any unspoken interest in my hide since I was the only human around. The furs intrigued me. Did they compensate for his complete lack of hair? Or did he cover up because he was embarrassed by his ugliness?

Looking at Blaze, I marveled that an ugly, smelly, bent-over creature would be my only link to Creator. Could Blaze be a possible replacement for my umbilicore?

Placing both hands on him, I tried to connect to Creator. I imagined myself reaching toward Them through Blaze.

"Hey! What are you doing?" Blaze stopped and looked up at me with his hairless brows scrunched together.

"Nothing." I pulled my hands away.

"That's a lie. You were messing 'round with my insides."

"I was trying to connect to Creator through you."

"Don't ever . . . do that again. I'm not your intermediary."

"But you have Creator. I don't."

"I get that . . . but don't go substituting me for Creator. That's dangerous . . . for you and me. You can't exist on something that's counterfeit."

"I'm sorry. I thought that maybe you had some Creator to spare."

"No. I don't," Blaze said with brusque finality. He turned forward, started walking, then stopped. "Coming?"

I shuffled up to Blaze and placed one hand on his shoulder with a light touch. We didn't speak for the rest of our journey.

When we arrived at the lake, I surveyed my garden. Some plants had died, others were overgrown. The garden needed weeding and the fence required repair, but everything could be salvaged. My decision to restore my garden encouraged me. I needed something to do besides languishing inside my shelter with my despairing thoughts.

I tried to ignore the tower ruins that lay in a heap a short distance from my garden. It whispered to me about failure and loss.

The splintered rubble now represented my life without Creator, a tragic mess with no hope of repair. I swallowed my pain, pushing it back down into the maelstrom from whence it emerged.

I lifted the gate to my garden, set it aside, and shuffled between the plants using my walking stick for balance. Blaze stayed outside the fence and watched me. He opened and closed his fingers, seeming impatient with standing still. Later, when I looked back in his direction, he was gone.

I sat by a melon plant and touched its broad leaves. I scooped soil in my hand and let it fall between my fingers. The rich fragrances of plants and soil filled my lungs. A breeze rustled the pine trees that bordered the lakeshore. The world was still full of life. I was grateful I was alive to enjoy it.

Creator had made this amazing world by Their creativity and power. If They could create life, then They could restore life as well. They could restore my umbilicore and our relationship. Because of my knowledge of good and evil, I saw myself as vastly inferior to Creator on every level, unworthy of Their goodness. But I believed Their love to be greater than my depravity, so I placed my trust in Creator for what seemed impossible.

Chapter 76

Readjustment

Blaze skulked along the far bank of the lake spying on the fish that hid beneath the shade of the overhanging foliage. When he pulled out a spear from his furry bundle of weapons, I knew some fish were in for a terrible turn of luck.

A short time later, Blaze approached, wearing a broad smile and holding an animal-skin sack over his back. "I caught some fish . . . for you to eat." He opened the sack to show me five silvery fish. I never imagined that the shiny, slippery fish might be edible.

"I need to make a fire," Blaze said. "Gather stones and place them in a circle . . . in the same way you saw by your shelter."

Before I could respond, Blaze flipped the sack of fish onto his back and scurried away.

I stole stones from the garden perimeter and placed them in a circle near the water's edge. That small task exhausted me. I sat and waited for Blaze. He came back with his arms full of twigs and branches, and dropped them next to the stone circle. I watched him arrange a handful of dried grass and twigs in the center of the circle. Then he took out two rocks from between his stack of furs and struck them together many times over the dried grass. Flecks of light leapt out from the rocks, some landing on the grass causing it to smolder. Blaze blew on the grass until a single finger of fire appeared. He coaxed the finger to grow by feeding it small branches. The fire spread until many fingers danced upon the wood. I watched with utter fascination.

Blaze removed the sack from his back and took out one fish. I expected him to prepare the fish for eating, demonstrating the skill of someone who had performed the task hundreds of times. Instead, he used brute force to impale the fish by thrusting a long stick into its mouth until the stick exited the fish's tail, causing ripped intestines to protrude. Then he shoved the other end of the stick into the sandy ground. He leaned the stick against a stone so that the fish hovered over the fire, mouth gaping, accusing eyes staring at us. The remaining four fish suffered the same misfortune. My appetite was now as dead as the fish.

I hoped that by some miracle the fish would jump back into the water, so I would be spared from eating them. I sat by the fire saying nothing, watching the fish watching us, wondering why fish didn't have eyelids. Blaze didn't sit, but crouched on his feet so as to keep his back and furs level. From time to time, he poked the fire with a long branch to rearrange the embers. Twice, he ignited a twig and held it close to his face to gaze at the fiery flower that sprouted on its blackened end, studying the flame with the same fascination as one inspecting an iridescent beetle. When the dreaded moment arrived, Blaze yanked a stick out of the ground and shoved it into my hand saying, "Here . . . have a fish stick."

I stared at my meal. It stared back at me. I looked at Blaze, who was grinning, and I said, "Aren't you going to eat one?" If I watched him eat a fish, then I would know how to eat it.

"I don't need to eat. Remember?"

Conflagration! With growing revulsion, I realized that Blaze expected me to eat all five tortured and toasted fish. I couldn't picture myself biting into one, not now, not ever.

Blaze, still grinning, said, "I've had my fun. I'll show you how to eat it."

He yanked a fish stick from the ground, pulled out a small knife from his weapons cache, and cut along the top edge of the fish. Then he sliced into the bottom of the fish and cut around the head. With surprising skill, he peeled off a section of fish meat from the carcass, picked the cooked flesh off the scaly skin, and popped the pieces into his mouth. After handing me the knife, he taught me how to do the same. The meat tasted good although the small fish yielded little food. After we threw the fish carcasses into the fire, we roasted some vegetables from the garden, which I enjoyed more.

Blaze insisted we return to my shelter so I could rest. He agreed to carry some fruits and vegetables I had picked from my garden, stuffing them into an animal-skin sack, and placing the sack atop the pile of furs. Blaze took the lead, and I followed, leaning on him and shuffling as fast as I could.

We walked without speaking. I waited for him to initiate conversation, but he never did. Creator's choice of Blaze seemed more puzzling than ever. Blaze was sullen most of the time, and he became irritated at the slightest provocation. In spite of that, he gave me hope and eased my loneliness.

When we arrived at my shelter, I entered and crawled onto my feather bed. While looking at the ceiling of my cave, I spoke to Creator, believing They could still hear me. "Why did You send Blaze instead of someone like Radiance? Blaze isn't the easiest companion. I suppose you wish to teach me something through him, but I have no idea what that might be.

"I wish I knew the truth about things, such as eating meat. Knowing right and wrong isn't the same as knowing the truth. My conscience says one thing. My experience contradicts it. I'm confused. Should I trust my conscience? Or should I trust Blaze?

"I know You can't answer. If I could hear Your voice or feel Your presence, I could go on. I hate being cut off from You."

Without permission, my pain swirled up like a whirlwind, lifting dust and debris into my eyes, causing them to sting and water.

For a moment, I was an impaled fish gasping in agony. I squeezed my eyelids tight to shut in my anguish. Curling up on my side, I turned away from the universe and its accompanying pain. Coveting its numbing power, I tried to force myself to sleep by keeping my eyes squeezed shut, but tears escaped the rigid slits. In time, I escaped and found solace in the gray nothingness of slumber.

Later, when I left my shelter, the sun still hung high in the cloudless sky. My nap hadn't carried me into tomorrow as I had hoped.

Blaze crouched nearby, sharpening a spear blade against a large, flat stone. On the ground, his gray pelt lay open and displayed four knives of various sizes and two spears. Each had a stone blade and a wooden handle. Blaze looked up at me and said, "I'm taking you hunting . . . tomorrow." His eyes returned to the blade.

"I'm not interested in hunting," I said.

"Doesn't matter. You're coming, anyway." He didn't break his scraping rhythm or look up.

"What if I'm not up to it tomorrow?"

"Still coming."

Blaze stopped sharpening his spear and approached me. The sack that contained my garden pickings was still on his back. He grabbed the sack, upturned it, and dumped the contents on the ground. "Eat up. You must be strong . . . for tomorrow's hunt."

"You could've handed me the sack."

"The sack's mine. The stuff inside is yours."

"But. . . ." I stopped myself when I realized that nothing I could say would make any difference. I picked up as much food as I could carry and brought it into my shelter. I made two more trips to gather the rest. Blaze went back to sharpening his spear and didn't offer to help. Wanting privacy, I closed the door behind me and ate some food, wondering why Creator never took me hunting.

Chapter 77

Hunter

Blaze woke me early the next morning. "Get up . . . and eat something. Don't dawdle." He dashed out, sprinting faster than I had ever seen him move.

I ate some carrots, snap peas, and sunflower seeds, feeling apprehensive about this hunting trip. When I stepped out, Blaze was pacing back and forth.

Seeing me, he ran up and began speaking before coming to a stop. "Now, pay attention. I'll hunt. You . . . watch and learn. When I hold out my hand . . . that means I've spotted an animal. That's your signal . . . to stand still and make no sound. I'll sneak up to the animal 'til I'm close enough . . . to throw a spear into its heart."

"What animal are we hunting?"

"Whatever Creator sends our way. My itch is to kill an animal whose fur I don't have . . . but that's not the goal of this hunt. We're wasting time. Let's go."

Blaze turned and began plodding along a path that led into the forest, face close to the ground. I followed with my walking stick and was able to keep up because Blaze moved with slow, purposeful steps. As we hiked through the woods, he pointed out the clues we were looking for, such as animal tracks, droppings, broken branches, or eaten leaves. I enjoyed this game of scouting for clues. When I discovered fresh animal droppings, I couldn't contain my excitement.

"Calm down," Blaze said. "We're close. Try to be extra quiet . . . if you can."

We glided through the forest, taking soft steps, Blaze leading the way. My heart pounded with anticipation.

Blaze extended his hand. I froze. Ahead of us, beyond a stand of gum trees, a bongo antelope, large and muscular, was feeding on some tall grass. The bongo had thin, vertical, beige stripes on its reddish-brown body. Its two long horns twisted upward, mimicking the undulating stripes on its body. The bongo raised its head and looked in our direction with its dark, shiny eyes, its giant ears flared forward.

I watched Blaze pull out his bundle of weapons, place it on the ground, and unroll it. Then he grabbed the spear he had sharpened yesterday and set it aside. He pulled off his bulky furs and stacked them in a pile until only one large fur remained on his back. He placed the spear shaft across his mouth and clenched it with his teeth, then put both hands on the ground. His body shook, and the last fur slid across his back. Instead of falling to the ground, the fur tightened over his frame. The loose edges coiled around his arms and legs like a snake wrapping around its prey, covering his yellowish skin, squeezing and elongating his limbs.

I stared with astonishment, my mouth hanging open.

When the transformation ended, a second bongo stood where Blaze had been, except this version had a spear in its mouth and no ears. The second bongo stepped toward to the first one, keeping its head lowered. When it was only a couple paces away from the first bongo, the disguise vanished and Blaze reappeared. An instant later, Blaze grabbed the spear from his mouth and plunged it into the bongo's chest. The bongo collapsed, thrashed its head, and kicked twice before becoming still.

My stomach soured. Although I understood the rules of

predator and prey, the use of weapons seemed to be a breach of the rules. I didn't like the savagery of this new world.

Blaze stood next to the dead animal, wearing the single fur that was reddish-brown with beige stripes.

"We're taking the bongo home," Blaze said.

"How? I can't carry something that heavy."

"I'll carry it . . . myself."

Blaze collected his furs and stacked them on his back. I offered to carry some of the furs, but he refused to let me touch them. Then he tied up the bongo's legs with strips of hide. I watched as he hoisted the enormous bongo carcass onto his back, amazed at his strength. The bongo was more than twice his size.

As soon as he had secured the bongo, he started back without saying a word, taking labored steps under the added weight. He heaved and panted, and I followed, feeling guilty for not being able to help. My guilt was short-lived once I decided he was foolish for trying to carry the thing. Transporting the bongo was a demanding task, and I hated to break his concentration, but I couldn't resist asking him about the transformation.

"How did you change into a bongo?"

Blaze grunted on top of his steady panting. "Conflagration! I knew it. . . . You had to ask. It was as sure . . . as dirt between my toes. If you must know . . . I can change . . . into an animal . . . whose skin I'm wearing. That's why . . . I carry lots of furs."

For the first time, something about Blaze made sense.

"Don't bother me . . . with any more questions," Blaze said.

I kept silent and followed, studying the furs with renewed interest. Was there a tiger fur in the stack?

Chapter 78

Covenant

When we arrived at my shelter, Blaze unloaded the dead bongo next to a nearby mulberry tree. He started a fire within the stone circle in the center of the clearing across from my cave.

"You go rest . . . while I cut up the bongo," Blaze said. "I'll set aside enough meat to last a few days. The rest . . . I'll leave out for the animals."

"Don't do that. It will attract tigers."

"Tigers? I would give my teeth to have a tiger fur."

"I suppose you would. But I don't want tigers nearby. Take the meat far away from here."

"Sure. I can use it as tiger bait." His eyes widened with excitement.

"Get yourself killed. I don't care. Just do it far from here."

"I'm not afraid of tigers."

I turned, entered my shelter, and closed the door behind me. I was glad I didn't have to watch Blaze butcher the bongo, imagining the process to be too bloody to stomach. After eating some food I had picked from my garden, I settled down on my bed. The soothing sound of the crackling fire outside lulled me to sleep.

The next morning, I stepped outside expecting to see blood-stains on the ground and animal parts scattered across the landscape. To my surprise, the scene showed no trace of blood. Large slabs of cooked meat lay stacked on a platform of parallel sticks. A complete bongo hide draped over a nearby tree branch. The stone circle had been built up into a higher wall. The circle contained ash and a few blackened lumps of wood. The savory, smoky smell of roasted meat reached my taste buds, causing me to salivate.

Blaze crouched next to the stack of cooked meat, sharpening a short knife on a flat stone. On seeing me, he wiped the knife across his thigh and used it to slice off a small piece of roasted meat.

"Here . . . try some bongo meat," Blaze said, presenting the meat on the tip of his knife.

I pulled the meat off his knife and popped it into my mouth. This meat was the tastiest I had eaten, far better than fish or opossum. "It's delicious."

"I'm taking you hunting again . . . as soon as you're ready."

"You mean now?"

"Yes."

"No, no. I have other plans. I'm working in my garden this morning."

"That's fine. We'll go hunting . . . in the afternoon."

"I don't want to hunt. It's not for me."

Blaze stared at me for a long moment, holding the knife in his hand. Then pointing the knife at me, he said, "I say you hunt."

"No. You're just a helper. You're not in charge of me." I returned the stare.

Blaze scowled beneath the shade of his fur wrappings. His lip-less mouth compressed into a tight line. He trembled, then stabbed the ground with his knife. "You ungrateful creature. I won't be re-fused." Still gripping his knife, he pulled it out of the ground and studied the blade with narrowed eyes. Then he rolled it up with the other weapons, picked up the bundle, and stomped away.

With Blaze gone, I helped myself to more of the cooked meat. I didn't have a sharp knife like Blaze did, so I used my ax to chop off chunks of meat. I kept glancing into the woods, hoping he was far away.

When I returned to my shelter after gardening, Blaze was pacing by the stone circle. I approached with hesitation.

"We never discussed our arrangement," he said. "I will take care of you . . . if you let me teach you some skills. Is that agreeable?"

Something felt odd about this proposition. "Yes, but I have a condition. When I tell you to leave, you must go and not come back." After I learned what Blaze could teach me, I wouldn't need him anymore.

Blaze grimaced, then rubbed his face with his lumpy, yellowish hand. He didn't look at me when he said, "Agreed."

I relaxed a little. "I suppose you'll want to take me hunting soon."

"Yes."

"Tomorrow morning, then. Not today."

"In that case . . . I have time to make you a spear." With his characteristic abruptness, he scurried into the forest.

The next morning, a thick, white mist gave the atmosphere an eerie stillness. The soil beneath my feet was moist and cool. Dampened plants dripped water that made muffled pat-pat sounds all around me. Tiny specks of moisture dotted my skin and highlighted the fine hairs on my arms. I watched the specks merge to create a shiny glaze over my skin.

Blaze's top layer of fur was matted down with dew. He looked eager to start our hunt, judging by the impatient shuffling of his large feet. He held a long spear, point up, the other end resting on the ground. When I approached, he held out the weapon. "This is your spear. Take good care of it. And don't lose it."

I took the spear from Blaze and examined it. Its blade was fashioned from black obsidian and inserted into the split end of the pole and secured with narrow strips of animal hide. Creator always had me make my own tools. I had never received a completed tool as a gift. I appreciated the gesture. "It's well-crafted. Thank you, Blaze."

"For your first kill . . . it should be an easy animal . . . like a deer or turkey."

"I wouldn't mind killing a mara."

Blaze looked puzzled by my statement. "We'll see what Creator provides."

During the hunt, I again enjoyed the game of looking for fresh animal signs. Spotting a rabbit thrilled me, but the feeling turned to dread when Blaze signaled me to throw my spear. My heart galloping, I sneaked toward the rabbit as close as I dared, then threw the spear.

I missed.

The rabbit bolted and hid under the leafy fronds of an acanthus plant further up the slope. I retrieved my spear and crept toward the rabbit again, this time moving slower and trying to get closer. When I threw my spear, it pierced the rabbit above the hip. The rabbit tried to run, but limped and flopped, dragging the long spear in its side and making a loud, unpleasant squeal. I froze, not knowing what to do.

Chapter 79

Mastery

Horrified, I gawked at the maimed rabbit while it struggled to flee with the spear in its side.

Blaze dashed up and slammed a rock against the rabbit's head to kill it. He gave me a look of disappointment.

With the dead rabbit, we returned home. Blaze made me carry it, which I was reluctant to do. Blood oozed from its face and side. From time to time, I looked at its limp, warm body reminding myself that it was just an empty shell. I remembered Creator saying that when an animal dies, its life returns to the source of Life. I envied the rabbit returning to Creator because I had no guarantee that my disconnection from Creator ended after death.

"Blaze, do you think rabbits have spirits?"

"Conflagration! Must you ask so many questions? I don't know. I don't care."

"I'm just making conversation."

"I don't do conversation. I see no point to it."

I held my questions until Blaze was in a better mood.

Back at my shelter, Blaze showed me how to skin the rabbit and remove its organs using his collection of knives. Then he taught me how to make a fire using two stones—fire stones he called them—which was more difficult than I expected. With a lot of help from Blaze, I created a fire. Blaze was patient when instructing me, but lacked patience for idleness. He always needed a task.

We impaled the skinned rabbit carcass on a long branch and placed the branch atop stacked stones so the rabbit hovered above the fire. Blaze told me to rotate the branch every so often for even cooking. The rabbit meat was delicious, and I picked its carcass clean that night.

Over the next few days, I practiced my hunting skills, guided by Blaze's expert coaching. My aim and confidence improved. I learned how to throw a spear to kill, not just wound. On the first day, I killed a turkey. The second day, a small pig. The third day, a mara. We roasted the trophy from each hunt and sampled its salty, cooked flesh.

Over time, the repulsion I felt toward killing animals faded away. Hunting became an enjoyable sport that gave me purpose. Unlike gardening, its rewards fueled an unquenchable appetite for mastery. Mastery of the hunt and mastery over my prey. The game of pursuit was addictive and intoxicating. When the pursuit culminated in a kill, I felt an unadulterated sense of power, a feeling that eluded me the rest of the time.

In the evenings, Blaze and I would sit by the fire and watch its flickering display of rollicking flames. Often, Blaze would appear lost in thought, his eyes peering into the fire as if trying to decipher messages transmitted by the fiery tongues. During those times, he seemed haunted by an unknown sadness. He shunned conversation in the evenings, so I allowed him to retreat into his secret inner realms. I occupied myself by weaving baskets in the firelight.

Since we spent much time by the fire, we rearranged the fire pit area. We rolled logs near the pit to serve as places to sit. Blaze wanted his seat to be across the fire pit from mine. I found it odd that he wanted a seat at all since he preferred sitting on his haunches. On each side of the pit, we stacked a tall pile of stones that were stepped to allow for different cooking heights. On these steps, we placed a horizontal pole for roasting animals. From our seats, we took turns rotating the animal carcass or dropped the pole to a lower step as the fire died down.

One evening, as we sat beside the fire, Blaze pulled out a blackened stone the shape of a duck egg. The stone egg had a deep bowl carved into its side. Cradling the egg on his lap, he took out a small pouch, reached inside, and withdrew a pinch of dried, crumbled leaves he dropped into the bowl. Then he lit the end of a long twig in the fire. When he placed the small flame onto the dried leaves, they began to smolder. He closed his mouth around the end of the egg and puckered his cheeks. Then he lowered it and closed his eyes. After a long moment, he opened his eyes halfway and exhaled smoke from his mouth. Smoky ribbons curled out of his large, gaping nostrils.

Blaze handed me the egg, saying, "You try it. Suck air through the end . . . hold the smoke in your lungs . . . then exhale."

I took the egg and examined it. The end of the egg had a tiny hole drilled into it. The smoke from the smoldering leaves had a strong aroma, like crushed sage. I put my mouth over the hole and sucked air through it, watching the burning leaves in the bowl glow orange.

As I held the smoke in my lungs, I felt the strangest sensation as if my body no longer confined me. My consciousness expanded, filling the fire-lit clearing. With each inhale of smoke, I expanded further, becoming more immense and far-reaching, bigger than any problem or threat. I experienced my own vastness and power, and enjoyed an exhilarating sense of invincibility. My conscience warned me to stay grounded, but I ignored it, preferring the altered reality. Holding the egg at arm's length, I marveled at its magic. "What is this?"

Chapter 80

Offerings

"They're leaves from a Thaed tree," Blaze said. "The smoke helps you escape . . . yourself." He extended his arm. "Give it to me."

I handed the egg back to Blaze, who sucked on it with slow relish.

"Creator never told me about that tree," I said.

"Why would They?"

The question no longer mattered. The egg gave me what I wanted—to feel powerful, if only to myself. It counteracted the sense of inferiority and shame I felt all the time. "Can I have some more?"

"Sure," Blaze said. "I brought out the egg . . . to share. Smoking makes the nights . . . more tolerable."

I moved to the log next to Blaze. He crouched on his haunches and kept his back horizontal, his head a short distance above his knees.

We handed the egg back and forth, each taking turns inhaling the wondrous smoke and expelling gray plumes that cast shadows over our faces in the firelight. The smoke caused all my questions and worries to melt away. It created a reality that centered on my powerfulness and crowded out everything else.

When I left the fire and entered my shelter, the euphoria faded. My feelings of inferiority and shame returned. In the past, when I connected to Creator, I had felt a peaceful feeling like floating in a pool. The smoke was like an exhilarating rain that stimulated my body with its energy. With Creator, my soul felt loved and embraced. The smoke submerged my soul beneath a rushing waterfall. It didn't erase the disconnection and emptiness, but numbed them with a false, grandiose version of my self. The experience was temporary and artificial, but I clung to it because of the escape it provided. I missed my connection to Creator. That was real, more real than anything else. I ached for it with a hollowed-out longing that scraped inside me like someone trying to climb out of a deep hole.

Every night that followed, we sat beside the fire and smoked the egg. Since Blaze was non-talkative, it gave us both something to fill the time. I named the smoke "push" because it pushed my thoughts aside, like a flash flood driving leaves and debris out of its way.

On the sixth night after Blaze introduced me to the "push" smoke, Blaze didn't bring out the egg, but stared into the fire.

"You're not pushing tonight?" I said.

"No. Tonight is different." He walked away from the fire, disappearing into the darkness. He returned carrying the bongo antelope hide from our first hunt together. Handing me the hide, he said, "These many days . . . I've been preparing this hide for you. It's yours, now."

I took the hide from Blaze and ran my hand over the soft, reddish-brown fur. The beige parallel stripes glowed in the firelight. The material was supple, draping over my arm with ease. I wrapped the fur across my back and tied the front legs together around my neck. "Thank you, Blaze."

Wearing the hide gave rise to fanciful thoughts. I imagined I was transforming into a bongo, like Blaze had done. Placing my hands on the ground, I pranced around the fire like an antelope. I had become a bongo, given life by the power of my thoughts. With antelope strength, I leapt into the air and snorted like a proud buck. Then I bowed before Creator, the maker of all animals. When I rose, I lifted my bongo head high and struck a regal pose, wanting the universe to see my raw beauty and power. Then I resumed dancing, elation filling me to laughter. The loud pops from the fire drummed out an erratic beat that guided my stomping feet as I lost myself in the animalistic dance.

I imagined that the jumping shadows cast by the firelight became a gathering of animals that watched my performance. These spectral spectators clapped and cheered to welcome me into their sacred brotherhood. Through the bongo hide, I re-established my connection to nature, to the universe, and indirectly to Creator who, although now hidden from me, I might access through this mystical experience. I knew this connection was inferior, maybe even imaginary, but I contented myself with my own thoughts and mythology.

I sat on my log, panting, enraptured by this new experience, savoring the exhilaration of my heightened senses. Blaze stared wide-eyed with his mouth agape. Wanting to put him at ease, I approached and squeezed the pile of furs until I felt his firm body beneath. "Thank you, Blaze. I'm grateful for everything you've done for me. I thank Creator for sending you."

Blaze stiffened under my arms. I released him and backed away. "What's wrong? You don't like to be hugged?"

He squirmed, his eyes staring into the fire. "I can't. . . ." He squeezed his eyes shut. "The thing is . . . Creator . . . didn't send me."

He cringed, as if expecting a blow.

Chapter 81

Exposed

"What?" Shock and confusion knocked me backward. I staggered and almost lost my balance. My mind tried to right itself, but couldn't find a steady ledge to grasp.

Blaze watched me for a moment, gauging my response. Then his gaze snapped back to the fire. His mouth trembled. "I couldn't tell you . . . 'til now . . . 'cause you would've sent me away." His face wrenched into a grimace. The firelight cast dark lines on his scrunched face.

"Sent you away?"

Blaze gave me a fierce stare. "Look at me. I know I'm repulsive. You wouldn't have kept me around . . . if you thought Creator hadn't sent me."

"Did Illuminos send you?" Anger rolled across my being like a rush of scalding water.

"Like you, I was tricked by Illuminos . . . 'cause I was stupid enough to let him. After Creator rejected me . . . I became stranded on this planet. When I heard 'bout your plight . . . I sought you out . . . and pretended that Creator had sent me. Since we both suffered the same loss . . . I thought . . . you might accept me . . . if I proved myself useful."

Blaze dropped to his knees and grabbed my hands, looking at me with moist, frightened eyes. "Please don't send me away. I can't bear . . . to be alone again. You don't have to like me . . . but don't send me away."

I pulled my hands out of Blaze's grip. Without untying it, I yanked off the bongo hide, pulling my head through. I punched and squeezed the hide into a ball. At first, I wanted to throw it at Blaze, but I tossed it into the fire. I didn't stay to watch it burn or to see his reaction. Shaking my head, I turned away and stumbled in the dark toward my shelter.

After closing the door behind me, I stood with my eyes closed. Blaze's frightened face appeared in my mind. I found perverse consolation in leaving him in that vulnerable state. Sending him away would be insufficient punishment for what he had done to me. What a colossal fool I was. I had based my present life on the belief that Blaze was acting on Creator's behalf. He had no connection to Creator at all and had lied about it. A betrayal equal to what Illuminos had done. My world collapsed, leaving me disoriented and adrift.

I dropped onto my bed and curled up into a ball. "Creator, please help me. I need you."

The silence taunted me with tormenting whispers of abandonment and hopelessness. I didn't wipe my tears, but let them roll down my face in cold streaks and dampen the spot where I lay my head. If only I could transform into a real bongo and run to the place where Creator dwelt, where I would find comfort.

I awoke early, but stayed in bed, trying to figure out what to do about Blaze. If I sent him away, I would be alone, but I wanted company even if it was less than pleasant. I had gotten used to Blaze. Yet he deserved to be punished for lying to me. At the same time, I had compassion for him because I understood how it felt to be deceived and rejected. If he knew the pain of deception, how could he have inflicted it on me?

I peeked through the cracks in my shelter wall to see if Blaze was nearby, but saw only an empty clearing. I stepped outside and looked around. The fire pit contained nothing but ashes. No remnants of a bongo hide.

Not wanting to encounter Blaze, I took a long walk in the woods to think. During my walk, I tried many times to push my hurt and anger into a corner, but they wouldn't stay put. Each time, they reared up to demand retaliation. Was retaliation the only way to erase my painful feelings? My conscience tried to speak, but my emotions shouted louder and couldn't be subdued. Somehow, I had to find a way back to peace.

Distracted by my mental meanderings, I wandered, oblivious to my surroundings. When I came to the edge of the forest, something caught my attention. In the distance, Blaze was standing, unclothed, near a small fire that flickered within a stone circle. He had stacked his many furs in a neat pile. Prior to this moment, I had only seen his face, arms, and legs, shadowed by the overhanging furs. He seemed compelled to keep his body covered. Without the heavy furs, I expected him to stand erect, but he remained bent-over as if locked in that position.

As I sneaked closer, I saw reddened sores in various places on his bumpy, yellowish body. I positioned myself behind a large dogwood bush and crouched to peek.

Blaze picked up a branch and ignited the end in the fire. Then he pressed the flaming branch against his lower back and held it there. The fire scorched the patch of skin, then spread across his back, devouring and blackening skin as it traveled. Blaze made no sound, but his face twisted with pain. Horror gripped me as I watched.

Chapter 82

Scars

"Stop it! What're you doing?" I shouted.

I sprinted toward Blaze and yanked away the flaming branch. Then I slapped out the fire with my hands, almost burning myself. The charred skin on his back had gathered into black chunks. Examining the reddish sores on his body, I realized they were all vestiges of recent burns. I concluded that the ugly bumps on his skin were scars from earlier self-abuse. His lack of hair, ears, and nose must be because he had burned them away a long time ago. My heart convulsed with compassion to discover the reason for his disfigurement.

Not once looking at me, Blaze bowed over his furs and covered himself up, hiding every scar. He flinched when placing the furs over his fresh burn. Then he started walking away as if I weren't there.

"Why do you burn yourself?" I called after Blaze.

Blaze stopped, still facing away from me.

After a long pause, he said, "'Cause . . . fire gives me power over my pain. And it distracts me . . . from the torment I can't put fire to."

"Why are you tormented?"

"Again with the questions. . . . I hate your prying questions. You should know why. Creator rejected me . . . and made me an outcast . . . on this lonely, miserable planet."

"I'm rejected, too, but I don't burn myself."

"If you suffered as long as I have . . . you'd find your own release."

I walked up to Blaze and placed my hand on his shoulder. "A remedy must exist for your pain."

"None . . . except to burn myself," Blaze said, still looking into the distance.

"Creator knows how to help you."

"Maybe so . . . but They won't help. It's pointless to hope that they might." Blaze rolled his head from side to side.

"I still have hope."

Blaze looked at me with a strange expression. "Conflagration! How can you say that? Creator has rejected you. . . . They never change Their mind."

"I don't know what will happen to me, but I still trust in Creator. Their love gives me hope."

"Hope is the worst torment of all. You can keep . . . your foolish hope. I want none of it."

"I wish I could help you."

"You can't," Blaze snapped, turning his head away. "I'll handle my pain . . . in my own way." He trudged away and disappeared into the trees.

I remained where I stood, stunned by his words and shaken by the sight of his scars that intimated wounds unseen and more profound. He concealed his pain by hiding beneath his many layers of furs. My heart softened to know how much he was suffering, but I wasn't willing to forgive, even though my conscience told me I needed to.

Laden with sadness for Blaze, I returned to my shelter. In spite of my heavy emotions, I felt a small measure of peace about my future. Because I had expressed my trust in Creator, a trickle of hope warmed my soul and began to loosen despair's grip.

Having seen Blaze's method for managing pain, my pain stopped looking for an outlet. I decided to not hide it or hide from it, but just hold it in view and allow it to be. If I held it in the open, like a ladybug on my palm, maybe it would fly away. Whereas, an insect kept in a closed container stays in the dark and never escapes.

That night, as I sat across from Blaze with the evening fire between us, he said nothing about the self-inflicted burns. Uncomfortable to bring up the subject, I kept silent. My newfound concern for Blaze held my anger at bay for a while, but as I sat and stewed, my raw hurt and anger overshadowed all other emotions. My discomfort became unbearable, so I got up to leave.

At that moment, Blaze spoke. "I had no one to tell my pain."

I stopped to listen, but didn't turn around.

"So it festered within me," he continued. "I'm willing to listen to your pain . . . to offer you what I was never given. Perhaps, if your pain is heard . . . it might be relieved."

His offer disarmed me, but I considered it for a moment. After weighing the risk, I decided that Blaze couldn't be trusted. I turned around and faced him. "I'm so angry at you. You betrayed me. You're as evil as Illuminos."

Blaze maintained eye contact, showing no emotion.

"You should be punished," I said.

"Then punish me." His eyes seemed to plead for it. "Don't keep me waiting."

The image of Blaze setting himself on fire returned to my mind. In my imagination, I held the flaming branch this time, pressing it against his flesh, watching his skin char. The notion satisfied me somewhat, but my anger remained intact, unabated.

"I haven't decided on your punishment," I said. "It must be something that erases my anger."

Blaze looked into the fire. "Anger is a scar that can't be erased."

"I intend to try," I said with a defiant tone.

I returned to my seat by the fire. We sat without speaking. Blaze's eyes were affixed to the dancing flames, no doubt longing for the fire's power to quell his hidden torment. I stared, unfocused, trying to solve my anger. I needed to push, but I couldn't bring myself to ask. The thought of sucking on the same egg as Blaze repulsed me.

Chapter 83

Advice

For five days in a row, I avoided Blaze by taking long walks in the woods. We no longer hunted together. Each day, when I arrived at dusk, he was already by the fire pit, sitting on his haunches and frowning into the fire. I sat across the fire from Blaze and wove baskets or sharpened my tools. Not a word was spoken between us. Whenever I glanced at him, he maintained his rigid pose and never looked at me. The only times he moved was when he tended the fire. In the mornings, he was gone.

On today's walk, Illuminos came striding toward me, poking the ground with a walking staff made from a long, twisted animal horn. I braced myself for another round of trickery. My stomach soured with hatred.

Illuminos cocked his head like a praying mantis and studied me. Only one lizard-like creature clung to his shin. Had he killed the other one?

"Independence is for the strong-willed," he said, his long strands of black hair swirling like a school of fish. "You're much weaker than I thought. A poor candidate for independence. If you wish to improve your situation, you must get rid of that Blaze creature."

"Why do you care what I do?" I said.

"I do care. But you care far too much."

"Why shouldn't I care about Blaze? You tricked him into becoming independent, just as you tricked me."

Illuminos sneered. "Is that what it told you? You must know by now that the beast is an untrustworthy liar. Too much solitude has made it crazy. You have seen how it burns itself to find absolution."

"Blaze needs companionship, not more solitude."

Illuminos clucked and bent down to bring his head close to my face. "Companionship? You despise that creature as much as you despise me. You've been avoiding that pest for the last few days. Can't you see that you're making the pathetic freak more miserable than ever?"

My conscience convicted me. "You're right. What should I do?"

"Send it away to wherever it came from." Illuminos waved his walking staff toward the eastern mountains.

"I'll think about it."

"You don't need that disgusting thing anymore. You know how to hunt and make fire. If you can survive well on your own, I'll consider granting you membership into the Society of Independents. You'll meet a higher caliber of beings than your present companion." He puckered his face as if he smelled something fetid.

Right then, I realized that Illuminos cared no more for me than for Blaze, and a strong revulsion overcame me. "I'm done with you. Go away," I said.

Illuminos' eyes narrowed, and his hair billowed upward. "I retract my invitation." His upper lip curled. "You two deserve each other. You'll be crazy like that monster in no time." He stabbed the ground with his walking staff and vanished, leaving a deep hole where the staff had pierced.

That night, Blaze sat by the fire across from me, acting like I wasn't there. He stared into the flames while his shoulders heaved, then dropped, then repeated.

"I won't send you away," I said.

Blaze stared at me with wide eyes. "Thank you, Cherished." He closed his eyes for a moment and exhaled, then said, "You won't be sorry."

I was already sorry. About being deceived a second time. About having to be with someone I no longer trusted. About losing what I believed was my closest access to Creator.

He must have seen the expression on my face. His lumpy brows squeezed together. His upturned mouth jutted out.

"Don't worry, Blaze," I said. "I haven't changed my mind." He appeared relieved. "I'll need time to work through this."

Blaze looked down and mumbled. "I get that. You're right . . . to hate me. I hope you understand . . . why I had to lie."

"I do, but it still hurts." I considered saying more, but abandoned the idea. "I need to be alone for a while." I retired to my shelter, grateful to have a place where I could shut out the world.

Sitting on a rocky ledge inside my cave, I spoke to Creator. "I'm angry at Blaze for lying to me. I don't know how to get rid of my anger. Help me to forgive him. Help me to want to forgive him. I can't do this without Your help. Life is so much harder without You, so much more confusing. Did I do the right thing in letting Blaze stay?"

I wondered if Creator was listening. More so, I wondered whether They would help me. I saw the foolishness of trying to live life on my own. I needed Them and hated myself for driving Them away. None of this was solving my problem with Blaze.

Frustrated, I threw myself onto my bed, hoping the answer would come if I tried to relax. Instead, I obsessed about my insufficiency. All night long, I listened to the sound of the crackling fire outside, wondering if I should have taken Illuminos' advice.

Chapter 84

Token

The next morning, when I stepped out of my shelter, I saw Blaze kneeling on the ground near the fire pit. He had spread out various small tools on an animal hide. He held a plum-sized object close to his face, humming while he scraped it with a tool. I had never heard Blaze express any cheer before.

He didn't acknowledge me, but focused on his task with intense concentration. I sat nearby, fascinated, watching him carve into the wooden object and blow away the shavings. He threaded a thin strip of animal hide through a hole he bored through the object. After he tied the ends of the strip together, he inspected the object one last time. Then he held it out toward me and grinned, saying, "I made this for you."

I took the item and examined it. The carved piece of soft wood had two deep holes for eyes and a wide mouth with exaggerated teeth that stretched more than halfway around. The silly face made me chuckle.

"Is it a monkey skull?" I said.

"No, you nut-brain. It's me."

I had mistaken the two holes for eyes. They were nostrils. Above the holes, Blaze had carved two shallow circles for eyes.

The resemblance to Blaze was now apparent.

"Hang it around your neck," he said. "That way, you can take me wherever you go," he said, smiling. He no longer spoke with halting speech.

"Maybe I don't want to take you everywhere."

"It's for your protection. You might need it if you meet a ferocious toad. Or a dangerous herd of caterpillars."

I laughed.

"How will this thing protect me?" I said. "Am I supposed to incapacitate my enemy with laughter?"

"No, you dirt clod. See the hole at the bottom? Blow into it."

I rotated the carved head and found the hole. I put my mouth over the hole and blew. The air traveled out of the carved nostrils and produced a delightful cooing sound. I blew a few more times, amazed at the wondrous effect.

"Whenever you need me, blow into the hole," Blaze said. "I will hear it and rescue you. During a hunt, you can alert me without scaring off our prey."

"Thanks. What a wonderful and clever gift." I put the loop of hide around my neck and wore the gift with pride.

Blaze rolled up his tools and slipped them into the thick stack of furs that draped over his back. When he crossed the clearing, he walked with a pronounced limp. Had he burned himself again? A line of blood ran down Blaze's leg.

"Are you all right, Blaze?"

"Yep. Illuminos showed up last night."

My body tensed. "Did he hurt you?"

"Only my flesh." Blaze looked down at his leg.

"What happened?"

"You didn't send me away as Illuminos told you to do. So, he tried to persuade me to leave. Without success."

"I'm sorry."

"I'm not. Now, I know you care about me, even after everything that's happened."

Guilt stabbed me because I came close to sending Blaze away.

"What's wrong?" he said.

"Nothing. I'm glad you're not hurt too bad."

"I'll heal. Thanks for sticking up for me."

"Sure," I said, feeling insincere.

From that morning on, Blaze was less gruff, more humorous, and more at ease. His belief in my acceptance of him had made the difference. By revealing his secrets, he had found a measure of peace, but at the cost of my own peace.

His behavior in the evenings didn't change. That night, by the fire, I said, "Can we push tonight?"

"I'm out of leaves."

"Can you get more?"

"No."

I wasn't sure how to interpret his no. "Can I help you pick more leaves?"

"No."

"Why won't—"

"Don't ask again. There's no more."

"Conflagration!" I shouted. "You give me good reason to send you away."

Blaze hardened his expression and fixed his eyes on the fire, saying nothing.

One more reason to stay angry at Blaze.

Chapter 85

Distractions

Blaze and I had an unspoken arrangement. He could stay as long as he didn't misbehave. Even so, I found it difficult to be around him because I hadn't succeeded in shaking off my anger. My anger clung to me like bark on a tree. I hated myself for my inability to forgive him.

We resumed our routine of hunting during the day and sitting around the fire at night. Without the Thaed leaves to smoke in the evenings, I went back to weaving, whereas Blaze spent the entire time staring into the fire, abandoning himself to the flames.

Our daily hunts distracted us from our problems. The hunts rewarded me with a plentiful supply of meat. Blaze's reward was an occasional new hide for his collection. We were always on the lookout for animals whose skin he didn't have.

During a hunting expedition, Blaze spotted an animal in the distance. "Look, Cherished. A wolf."

I had never seen a wolf. Blaze's yellowish finger pointed to a large, dark-gray animal trotting along the base of a wide cliff.

"I don't have a wolf fur," he said. "Go to the left where the wolf is headed. I'll sneak up from the side."

I took my position ahead of the wolf and stood ready with my spear lifted, waiting for its approach. The wolf slowed on seeing me. Blaze appeared on the right, holding a spear. The tall cliff wall blocked the wolf on the left. When the wolf realized it was cornered, it lowered its head, arched its back, and growled, baring its teeth. Instead of backing away, it moved toward me with slow, deliberate steps. Within its eyes, murderous intention coiled like a snake poised to strike. Up close, I beheld the full nature of a wolf and wished to return to my earlier ignorance.

I looked at Blaze, who didn't return my gaze. Not wanting the snarling wolf to get closer, I backed away. If I threw my spear and missed, I would be defenseless, so I kept it in my hand. The wolf's yellow eyes showed no fear, only hostility. The back of my neck shivered. My heart raced like a gazelle.

"Blaze. Throw it," I yelled.

As Blaze threw his spear, the wolf leapt between us. I felt its warmth as it brushed past me. A burst of hot, rank breath struck my face. Blaze's spear bounced off the rocky wall. With a few powerful bounds, the wolf vanished into the forest.

"That went well," I said, breathless, my heart reverberating within my chest and ears.

"I miscalculated," Blaze said. "It was more aggressive than I expected."

"If you ever see a tiger you want, count me out."

"Here's my new plan—"

"No. Give it up."

"Who knows when I'll get another chance. I'll transform into a rabbit to lure the wolf. When it gets close enough, I'll spear it. You'll hide nearby in case something goes wrong."

"If something goes wrong? Everything's wrong with this idea."

"Not if things go according to plan."

"Like your first plan? That was smooth."

"I'll distract the wolf. You hide behind that boulder over there. If it grabs me before I transform back, then throw your spear."

"Now, I know you're crazy."

259

"Do this for me," he said with pleading eyes.

Shaking my head, I walked over to the boulder, hoping the wolf was far away by now.

After setting down his spear, Blaze removed all his furs and put them in a neat stack. I recoiled to see his many scars again, some burns looking recent. He pulled a small rabbit hide from the pile and placed it on his back. Carrying his bundle of weapons, he walked to the center of the clearing, then unrolled the bundle on the ground, exposing all his knives and spears. After placing his hands on the ground, I watched with amazement as the rabbit fur stretched over his body, squeezing his frame into an ever-smaller form. When the transformation was complete, a fuzzy rabbit without ears hopped in a circle around the collection of weapons.

Not long after, to my dismay, the wolf returned, loping with a steady gait toward the rabbit. The wolf's mouth was half-open, drooling with hunger. I dropped behind the boulder into a peeking position and held my breath.

The wolf broke into a run, its eyes locked on the rabbit.

Blaze stayed on top of the pelt of weapons.

When the wolf was a few paces away, Blaze transformed back, grabbed a spear, and threw it.

The wolf leapt high into the air in a pouncing arc, jumping over the thrown spear.

Unprepared for a creature larger than a rabbit, the wolf crashed on top of Blaze, who rolled backward from the impact and became pinned under the wolf's heavy body. They both lay with splayed limbs, stunned for the briefest moment.

I stepped out from behind the boulder and threw my spear, hoping.

Chapter 86

Mercy

My spear punctured its side, causing the wolf to yelp. Blaze was still trapped beneath it. The wolf raised up on its legs and tried to bite Blaze's face.

Blaze grabbed the wolf's throat and pushed its head away to keep its chomping teeth away from his face. The wolf tried to paw at Blaze's head, but he turned his face away in time. A claw ripped the skin near Blaze's left ear hole.

Still grasping the wolf by its neck, Blaze rotated and threw the wolf to his side, slamming it against the ground. Then he lunged forward to grab a knife from his pile of weapons.

I wanted to help Blaze, but I was afraid of the wolf. Shoving my fear aside, I picked up a second spear laying by my feet and charged at the wolf that was scrambling to get on its feet. Throwing my entire weight forward, I thrust the spear deep into its chest.

The wolf collapsed. The fierceness in its eyes drained away until they were hollow like rotten acorns.

Blaze stood, panting and bleeding from the side of his head. He looked down at the dead wolf.

After I caught my breath, I said, "No fur is worth this."

"The greater the risk, the greater the reward," Blaze said,

looking triumphant, yet disheveled.

Being far from home, we didn't carry the dead wolf back. Instead, Blaze skinned the wolf right there and left the carcass in the forest. With Blaze carrying the bloody pelt, we trekked home, all the while my mind replaying our encounter with the wolf.

I'd never seen an animal defend itself with such ferocity. Maybe that was why its death disturbed me so. Or was it because we had killed it for something as trivial as its fur? We had condemned the wolf to die, so it had every reason to be angry, to fight back.

The unfairness of its death caused me to identify with the wolf. I, too, was a hapless victim and justified in my anger. In the end, the wolf's anger didn't save it. Deep down, I knew my anger wouldn't save me, either.

My need for justice bound my anger to my bones. Justice demanded that Blaze pay for his betrayal. But justice also demanded retribution for the innocent wolf. The balance of justice required skin for skin, life for life. Was not my life the fair payment for the wolf's life? I had killed so many animals, and yet my life continued, spared from any moral demands made upon it. The wolf would never receive justice, and I wondered if I was wrong to expect it for myself.

I realized that my life continued because of Creator's mercy. They decided whether I be punished or spared. Both my life and the wolf's life were in Their hands. If I expected justice in my behalf, then I had to be willing to accept the claims of justice on behalf of the wolf, even if it cost me my life. In that moment, I understood that what I needed from Creator was mercy, not justice.

I broke the silence between us. "Blaze, I release you."

Blaze stopped and looked at me, confused.

I continued. "I'm not excusing what you did or waiving justice in your case. But from now on, I entrust justice to Creator and no longer wield it myself. Clinging to justice turns it into vengeance which makes my soul bitter. I don't want that. So, I commend you to Creator for Them to do as They please. If They forgive you, then

I accept that. I want to be shown mercy, so I extend mercy to you."

Blaze's eyes watered. "So we're friends again?"

"Yes."

Blazed grinned, showing both rows of tiny brown teeth.

I resumed walking, feeling as though I had relinquished something I should have kept. The vacancy inside caused me to feel vulnerable and powerless. When I discovered I no longer had a place on which to hook my anger, I smiled. A clearing opened up in my soul, a broad place in which love could someday nest again.

Feeling hopeful, I relaxed and enjoyed the scenery. Massive cottonwood trees towered around me. Below their canopies, cassia plants covered the landscape, their five-petaled, yellow flowers like stars sprinkled across a green expanse.

"I hope you have enough furs, now," I said to Blaze.

"Never enough. I'll keep adding to my stack 'til the weight crushes me. That'd be a fitting way to die, don't you think?"

"That's morbid."

"We all have to die, one way or another," Blaze said.

"I didn't know you could die."

"My body can be destroyed, and I don't have a spare. I won't die from wearing out because I'm not a creature of this world. But you belong to this world, so you will wear out and die when you have completed your season. Then . . . I'll be alone again." Blaze's countenance clouded over.

I wondered how I would wear out. Would I dry out and stiffen like an earthworm in the sun? Would I become faded and tattered like a weathered butterfly? Would my limbs fall off like those of an ancient tree?

My thoughts turned back to Blaze. "If you died, your spirit would leave your body and escape this place. Isn't that what you want? You hate being stranded here."

"I'm not sure what would happen to me. Since my spirit is dead . . . I would remain cut off from the spiritual world . . . and from Creator. My body is my tether to the physical world. If I were to

263

lose that tether . . . I would drift between worlds . . . disconnected from everything. That seems dreadful . . . and lonely. I prefer to stay here and harass you. Besides, you need me, and I have more furs to collect."

By the time we arrived home, the sky was imbued with the color of persimmons. The thick, layered clouds resembled orange shelf fungi one finds clinging to tree trunks.

Sitting by the fire that night, I wove thin strips of grasses into a spiral bracelet. Using black grass, I created a zigzag pattern along its length. When I finished the bracelet, I walked over and handed it to Blaze, who sat gazing into the fire. "I made this for you to wear. It's a symbol of my friendship."

Blaze took the coiled woven band and examined it, turning it over a few times. He looked at me, his eyes moist. "Why are you so kind to me? I'm worthless and evil. Creator did right to reject me."

"I don't reject you."

His shiny eyes became huge, and I saw my silhouette against the fire reflected in them. He knelt and placed his head against my knee, saying nothing. With one hand, I grasped Blaze's carved head that hung on the leather loop around my neck, a symbol of his friendship toward me. Blaze didn't move for a long time, and I didn't move either, giving him all the time he needed to discover the hidden firefly that had been long imprisoned inside him.

Chapter 87

History

I spent my evenings by the fire pit weaving baskets by its amber glow. Other than tending the fire, Blaze did nothing but stare into the random flames, looking lost and melancholy. I tried to teach Blaze how to weave, but he had no interest.

"I don't need no useless baskets," he said.

"You don't have to use the baskets," I said. "Weaving is just something to do to fill the time."

Blaze sniffed. "I'd rather pull out my fingernails."

Blaze would have made a lousy pupil. Instead, I asked him to be my teacher since he was a helper by nature. That led to my instruction in wood-carving and spear-making. Before long, I had my own set of knives and spears that matched Blaze's collection of seven weapons. In the evenings we sharpened our weapons, the rhythmic scraping sounds of our blades joined with the roar and crackle of the fire and the pops from the burning wood. I often noticed Blaze wearing my woven bracelet around his left ankle.

Blaze never slept, so he kept the fire burning all night, rearranging the flaming logs and stirring the ashes until dawn. Entranced by the flames, he gazed into the heart of the fire that often lulled him into a stupor. At other times, he stared into the fire with such intensity that I feared he would throw himself into the flames to purge himself of his torments. I wondered whether he succumbed to self-burning while I slept.

Blaze helped outfit me for our hunting trips. He made me a weapons carrier from a goat hide. He attached pockets sewn with cord made from goat intestines. I wore the carrier on my back, held in place by the legs that wrapped over my shoulders and around my sides, the ends sewn together at the center of my torso. I could reach behind my back into the pockets and pull out any weapon with ease.

Returning home from a failed hunt, Blaze was upset because he always hated to lose his prey. To get his mind off of a wasted afternoon, I asked him, "Tell me about when you knew Creator."

Blaze slowed and lowered his eyes. After a long, measured breath, he said. "I found fulfillment in serving Creator 'cause They made me for that purpose. That's all I knew . . . 'til Illuminos convinced me otherwise.

He continued. "I once told you that I used to thin out forests by setting fires. In those days, I could create fire with a simple touch of my finger. No need for fire stones. Before setting fire to a forest, I commanded the animals to flee, and they obeyed. I had power to send or hold back the wind or rain. I was a caretaker of this world."

In Blaze's eyes I saw a glint of splendor, a remnant of long lost dignity.

"Now . . . I can't even command a snail," he said. "I'm utterly useless."

"That's not true. You saved my life. You've taught me many skills."

"During my exile here, you're the only good I can claim. Before I met you, I roamed this world . . . without purpose. I had to teach myself how to survive, but I never learned how to endure . . . the unbearable loneliness. I thought the animals would keep me company, but after I lost my powers . . . they stayed away. When I had powers, I could transform into any animal at will. I didn't need their skins to become one. That's the only power I have left."

"Did the animals stay away after you transformed into one?"

"A herd of deer welcomed me into their clan for a time, but they figured out my disguise and shunned me. To be rejected by friends . . . is far more painful than loneliness." He squeezed his eyes shut and shivered. "After that . . . I didn't try again."

"But you did. You sought me out."

Blaze shook his head. "Nothing went as planned. . . . It's all messed up."

"What do you mean?"

"I wanted purpose, not friendship . . . not this. You'll die one day . . . and I'll be left behind."

"When I die, I'll ask Creator to help you."

Blaze gave me a hard stare. "What makes you think Creator will take you? You're cut off from Them. Remember?"

"I believe Creator can heal my dead spirit."

"You know nothing," Blaze raged. "When something has died, it's dead forever. I've seen that enough times to know."

"Maybe you're right, but I need to keep hoping."

"I hope you can handle the disappointment." He sped up to walk ahead of me. He didn't speak for the rest of our journey.

When we arrived home, a figure stood in front of my shelter. He supported himself by gripping a long wooden staff with both hands. He had the same shape as me, but his body was shriveled like a dried-up tomato. Thin, wrinkled skin hung loose on his frame and sunken face. He had tied his waist-length, white hair into a single, large knot thrown over his left shoulder.

I distrusted all strangers these days.

"Greetings, Cherished and Blaze," the visitor said in a strong, clear voice that belied his frail appearance. "I am Saub. I have come to trade."

Chapter 88

Saub

I didn't believe this creature named Saub. "We never get visitors. You appear out of nowhere and want to trade? You're not here to trade. What do you want?"

Saub clutched his walking staff and pulled himself more erect. "I want to help."

Blaze was eyeing this visitor with equal suspicion. "Who sent you? Illuminos?"

Saub laughed. "Why would you think Illuminos sent me? You are quite mistaken. Creator sent me."

"Creator?" I said with cynicism. "That's what Daylight told me. Blaze said that, too. They both lied. I won't be tricked a third time."

Blaze questioned our visitor. "You're neither angel nor helper. What kind of being are you?"

"I am human," Saub said, wobbling on his feet.

"No, you're not," I said. "I'm the only human. You're lying." I reached into a back pocket of my weapons carrier and wrapped my hand around my knife handle.

"I do not lie," Saub said in a calm voice. "You are no longer the only human."

"You don't fool us. We can see you're not human." I glanced at

Blaze for confirmation. "You don't look like me at all."

"I resemble you many seasons from now, when you are aged, after the time an acorn takes to become a mature tree."

If Saub were telling the truth, the effects of aging were worse than I had imagined. Or was this creature Illuminos in disguise again?

"Why should we believe anything you say?" My hand still wrapped around my knife handle behind my back.

"Because I speak the truth."

I stared at Saub, mystified by his utter failure at persuasion. His knuckles were white from gripping his staff, and his arms began shaking from fatigue. He struggled to remain standing. I felt compassion for him in spite of my mistrust.

Deciding that Saub was not an immediate threat, I released my grip on my knife. I pointed to my log by the fire pit. "Saub, come and sit here. I'll bring you some water. Blaze, keep Saub company until I return."

Saub hobbled toward the fire pit, gripping his staff with both hands to keep balance. I looked at Blaze, whose face was hard and frowning. He didn't move, but glared at me. I ignored his behavior and hurried to obtain a gourd of water from my shelter, not wanting to leave the two of them alone for any length of time.

When I returned, Blaze was still glaring at me, and Saub was seated next to the fire pit. Saub had planted his long walking staff between his feet. He continued to grip it with both hands. When he saw the gourd I carried, he leaned his staff against his chest and extended two bony arms.

I gave the gourd to Saub. With trembling hands, he sipped the water, spilling some down his chest. He handed the gourd back to me. "Thank you, Cherished."

Saub propped his staff upright between his legs and gripped it. He gazed at me with a wistful expression, saying nothing.

I asked Saub, "Do you have a home? Where did you come from?"

"My home is far away. I am but passing through."

"How long will you be staying here?"

Blaze's face turned red. "No!" He roared at Saub. "You can't stay. You continue on your journey . . . and leave us."

Saub responded, "My journey ends here, my friend. You want me to leave because my presence threatens you."

"I want you to go," Blaze shouted, "'cause you're a liar. I won't let you harm Cherished. You must leave . . . now." He retrieved a spear from his bundle of weapons and pointed it at Saub.

Saub remained calm. "If my presence upsets you, then you must settle that on your own. I will not leave. My mission is here, and I will complete it. Cherished wishes that I stay."

Blaze looked at me and frowned.

Saub was right. I needed to understand who Saub was and why he had come. If he was human, I wanted to be with my kind. "Blaze, I want Saub to stay. Just for a short time."

Blaze puffed out his chest and glowered. "One day . . . no more."

"All right."

Saub nodded in agreement.

Wanting to diffuse the situation, I said, "Blaze, can you go spear some fish for our meal? I'll stay here with Saub."

"I suppose you want me to spear some fish for that thing, too," Blaze said, waving his spear at Saub.

"Yes. Please."

Blaze stormed away, spear in hand.

I felt relieved after Blaze left.

"I'm sorry about Blaze's behavior," I said to Saub.

"Blaze is a good friend to you, but the influence of friends can be more dangerous than the deceit of strangers."

"Which one are you?"

"A friend. A friend who cares."

"I doubt that. Why are you here?"

"As I said before, I am here to trade."

"I have nothing I want to trade."

"What I am trading might interest you."

"I don't care." I sat on the ground in front of Saub and interrogated him. "Why are you human?"

Saub smiled, his clear eyes twinkling within his wrinkled face. "My humanity makes the trade possible. My mission requires it."

"Are you planning to take my place?"

"Yes."

His evil plan sunk in. "You want to steal my old position with Creator. Then you'd be close enough to strike. You want to hurt Them."

Saub shook his head and frowned. "You misunderstand. My mission is to restore you to Creator."

"Radiance told me that my umbilicore can't be repaired. How can you fix it? Are you greater than Creator?"

Saub laughed. "No one is greater than Creator. Your umbilicore can't be fixed, but the breach can be mended."

"I don't see how. If Creator can't fix it, then no one can."

Saub smiled at me, but said nothing.

"Why are you aged and shriveled?" I said.

Saub touched his face in response. He explained that his time on this planet was brief and that his life was at its end. He compared himself to a moth, which lives a few days and only for one purpose, to reproduce, then dies. "I also live for one purpose, which is to fulfill Creator's plan."

"Do you have a connection to Creator?"

"Yes, I do."

If Saub were telling the truth, then I envied him.

"My connection is destroyed," I said with remorse.

"That is why I am here, Cherished."

"I miss Creator. Life is empty and meaningless without Them. I hunt, I swim, I garden, but none of those activities touch my soul. My soul is like a forgotten cave that no one visits. If you can restore my connection, I would be united with Creator again."

Saub looked at me with a serious expression. "Your willfulness

271

has destroyed your connection forever. It can't be repaired, not by me or Creator."

Disappointment darkened my hope. I hung my head.

"Cherished," he said.

I raised my eyes halfway.

"I have good news for you. I offer you a new connection to replace your destroyed one."

My eyes widened. "Tell me how I can get a new connection."

Chapter 89

Revelation

"You must return to innocence," Saub said. "Unless you become pure like the first day you were created, you cannot be reunited with Creator."

My excitement deflated on hearing this. "How can I return to innocence? The knowledge of right and wrong has ruined me. I can't unlearn what I already know."

"Also, you must die to your willfulness," Saub said.

"That, too, is a hard saying. Willfulness governs my life, now that Creator is gone. If I die to it, then I would have nothing."

"Having nothing is the goal. It gives Creator an empty place to fill."

These unattainable requirements confounded me. Even if I succeeded in these tasks, I had no guarantee that Saub would give me a new connection. By asking the impossible, he wouldn't have to deliver on his promise, which sounded like a scheme Illuminos would pull.

"How can I know you're not Illuminos?"

"The truth speaks for itself," he said with a smile that made me want to believe he was sincere.

Saub didn't deny he was Illuminos. On the other hand, he

could have denied it with an easy lie. Was he trying to confuse me on purpose?

Saub spoke with patience. "You do not believe."

"I need more than words."

"My mission is not to convince you, but to carry out Creator's plan. Time will reveal the truth. Now, tell me about your past relationship with Creator."

I considered where to begin, but a suffocating sadness overtook me. Then I realized what Saub was doing. "I won't let you manipulate me."

Saub lowered his head and sighed. "If you knew me, you would not be afraid. Do you wish to know me?"

"No. I don't trust you."

I stood, then paced near the fire pit, waiting for Blaze to return. Saub stayed seated on the log, looking in different directions as if he were seeing activity all around him, his head quivering as it turned.

Blaze returned with a sack of fish. He eyed Saub with mistrust, no doubt wondering if Saub had influenced me.

"Thanks, Blaze," I said. I struggled to think of something to say to ease the tension. "If you make the fire, I'll prepare the fish."

Without saying a word, but glaring at me, Blaze upturned the sack and dumped the fish on the ground. He then made a fire. I collected long sticks and impaled the fish on them. As soon as the fire was burning, I positioned the sticks so that the silvery fish hovered over the flames.

In awkward silence, the three of us watched the fish as they roasted. Blaze glanced at Saub many times, always returning to stare into the fire. He broke the silence by asking Saub, "If you really came from Creator . . . then ask Them to tell you my true name. Only Creator knows my full name."

"Your name is Blazing Light Shaft, Giver of Helps for The Eternal One."

Blaze's eyes opened wider than I had ever seen.

Saub continued. "You changed your name to Blaze during the Great Revolt, when you rebelled against Creator along with Illuminos. As punishment for your rebellion, Creator banished you to this world. After Cherished was severed from Creator, Illuminos recruited you to befriend Cherished."

Blaze's deformed mouth pulled back to bare all his teeth. He stood, his body shaking, and screamed, "You lie. . . . You lie."

Blaze turned toward me and said, "I won't tolerate . . . this demon anymore. Tell him to leave . . . or else I'll leave. . . . You decide."

I studied Saub, who remained serene and gazed at me with a gentle expression. His hands clasped the wooden staff that leaned against his chest. Saub knew the first part of Blaze's name, the part I knew. If the other details were true, then Blaze had lied to a far greater extent.

I said to Blaze, "I don't know who or what to believe right now. Maybe you should go away while I sort this out. You can return after Saub departs tomorrow."

Blaze's mouth dropped open. Then his eyes became moist, and his mouth closed so tight that the edges turned white. Without protest, he turned and stomped away into the forest, shaking his head. Before I could change my mind, he was gone. By then, I regretted my decision.

"You're clever." I said to Saub. "You got me to do what Illuminos wanted, to make Blaze leave."

Saub's mouth formed a slight smile. "Blaze won't go far. He is too riled up to stay away."

"Do you enjoy upsetting others?"

"Blaze is angry because I have exposed the truth. He denied it so as to maintain the deception."

Chapter 90

Recruitment

Many seasons ago, Creator banished Blaze to this world for his rebellion. Blaze wandered the land without aim or purpose. Days faded into long nights that spawned more empty days. When it rained, he stayed in open fields like a dumb animal, allowing the rain to drench him. He sought no shelter or comfort, but let the elements buffet him as punishment for his plight.

While roaming the western forest, he saw footprints he didn't recognize. These animals walked on two feet, and he wondered if they were creatures like himself. He tracked the footprints and came upon four creatures, three of which had wings. From a safe distance, he watched them.

Blaze soon realized that the three winged creatures were Creator. Gnashing his teeth, he departed, but the next day he returned because of the fourth creature. He wanted to understand what it was and why Creator gave it so much attention. Wearing a deer disguise, he followed the fourth creature for many days. During this time, Creator almost never let it out of Their sight.

One day, the creature wandered off to pick blackberries, and a poisonous snake bit its hand. While it lay unconscious, Blaze examined it up close and wondered why it was so special. The creature revived, and Blaze retreated to the woods to watch from afar as he had done before. Soon after, the creature met up with an angel, a giant sphere full of eyes.

The angel spotted Blaze, still in deer disguise, and illuminated him with one of its light beams. After that, Blaze stayed away for fear of being detected again.

A long time later, while trudging through the forest at dawn, Blaze heard a voice call his name.

Turning around, he saw a towering figure, Illuminos, whose hair swirled and billowed as if blown by invisible winds.

"Why . . . did you desert me?" Blaze said. "I gave up . . . thinking I'd ever . . . see you again."

"I'm not your servant. Must I remind you it's the other way around?"

"You left me to rot . . . on this planet." Blaze kept his eyes lowered, but clenched his fists.

"Hate Creator, not me. They are the ones who banished you here. I can't undo your punishment."

"You could help me out . . . from time to time."

"Have I not done so? I gave you the egg and the Thaed leaves to make your wretched existence more tolerable."

Blaze rotated his head sideways to look up at Illuminos. "I ran out of leaves years ago. You knew that . . . but never returned."

Illuminos looked into the distance and sniffed. "I will give you more leaves in exchange for a task."

"What use could I have to you?"

"Up to now, none at all, but you can be useful to me at this time. I want you to attach yourself to a human, the one you had been following for a while."

"A human? Is that what it's called? Creator keeps it under close watch. I won't be able to get near."

"That situation has changed," Illuminos said with a self-flattering grin. "The human has separated itself from Creator by choosing independence. I want you to teach it how to survive in this place. Make it fully independent, so it will forget its dependence on Creator. Who else but you are best suited for this task?"

"Why do you care about the human?"

"Because Creator still cares for it." Illuminos pulled his upper lip toward his nostril slits. "I intend to mold Their beloved into something repugnant to Them, a horror that will bring Them distress. As a first step, I want you to get the human addicted to smoking the Thaed leaves. I want the human to stop pining for Creator. The leaves will wipe away the desire for anything real."

"What if I run out of leaves . . . again?" Like a turtle, Blaze tucked his head under his furs.

"I will keep you supplied."

"Enough for both of us?" Blaze peeked from under his furs.

"Yes."

"Then I will do it."

"Excellent. I will return with the leaves and show you where to find the human. You can help me transform it into a blade for wounding Creator."

Chapter 91

Sacrifice

When Saub told me that Blaze had deceived me, I defended Blaze. "Blaze has told me everything. He has no reason to keep lying to me."

Saub was seated on a log by the fire pit. "Yes, he does. He is lying so you will trust him more than me. He wants to protect you from me."

I was seated on the ground in front of Saub. "Why would Blaze want to protect me from you?"

"He believes he will lose you because of me."

"Is that true?"

"Yes, but not for the reason he thinks."

Blaze's recent outburst and anguished departure had caused me to lose track of the fish roasting over the fire. The blackened fish were charred along the edges, their fins burned away.

"Let me take the fish off the fire," I said. "We'll salvage what we can."

I offered a fish stick to Saub who examined it for a long time. Then he held out the impaled fish with a shaky hand and said, "This fish symbolizes my body which I willingly offer for you. Through my death, I trade what is mine for yours. My life for your life. My connection for your connection. By my death, the breach caused by willfulness will be mended."

His words made no sense, and I doubted that someone so unbalanced could help me. Not knowing how to respond, I said nothing, but gave Saub a feigned smile.

I turned my attention to picking the edible bits of meat off my burnt fish, feeling regret for sending Blaze away. Although Saub's hands were unsteady, he managed to remove most of the meat from the fish carcass.

Saub said, "I never got the chance to thank Blaze for catching the fish and making the fire. Blaze is a good friend to you, a real blessing."

"You said Blaze had been recruited by Illuminos. How can that be a blessing?"

"Creator can transform any situation to carry out Their purposes. In spite of Illuminos' intentions, Creator used Blaze to save your life, teach you needed skills, and give you company during this time of separation from Creator. Creator transform a situation meant for evil by adding His purpose to it, so that good can come from evil for those who trust Creator."

"So Blaze hadn't lied when he said he was sent by Creator?"

"In the larger scheme, Creator purposed that Blaze take care of you. Blaze unknowingly played a part in Creator's plan."

Saub peeled off a section of scaly skin from another burnt fish and picked at the meat with his teeth, unhurried like a contented insect nibbling on a leaf.

Preoccupied, I pulled meat off my second fish. Creator had been taking care of me all along. Like Blaze, I was blind to it, blinded because I couldn't believe that someone as repulsive and deceitful as Blaze could be used by Creator.

My normal routine was to work my garden at this time, but I was reluctant to leave Saub by himself. "I need to attend to my garden," I said as I stood. "You stay here. I'll come back later." Gardening would give me time to think.

"May I come?" Saub said. "I would like to see your garden."

"I doubt you can travel that far."

"Now that I am rested, I believe I can make the journey, but we will have to take it slow." Saub extended his hand for me to take.

I stared at his hand and tried to think of a way to refuse him. Having failed at that, I took his hand and helped him up, while he used his walking staff to pull himself up with his other hand.

We traveled along the path with slow, short steps. With my right arm around his back, I held his upper body, and with my left hand, I supported his left arm. His staff supported his right arm. Matching his sloth-like gait, I moved in unison with him like two lumbering beetles joined for mating.

"Tell me more about Creator," I said as we walked.

"Creator is like a mother elephant that had one calf. She loved her calf more than anything. The calf wanted to play and explore, often running into the forest, not understanding how dangerous the world could be. Each time, the mother would search for her calf until she found it. With her calf back at her side, she was happy again.

"One day, the calf wandered off and fell into a treacherous river that swept it downstream. The calf survived by clinging to a log that brought it to safety a long distance downriver. The mother searched for her missing calf, not stopping to eat or sleep until she found it. When she spotted her calf, it was pacing on the other side of the river and crying out for its mother.

"The mother elephant became distressed because the wide, perilous river was impossible to cross. She said to herself, 'I can't endure being separated from my beloved calf. The only way I can be with my calf is to die, for then my spirit will be released and can cross the river.'

"So the mother elephant jumped into the river and surrendered to its fierce current. She was dashed against the rocks and died. Then her spirit left her body and crossed the river to be with her beloved calf forever."

"Did the calf sense its mother's spirit?" I said.

"Yes. Her spirit comforted the calf. The calf felt her love."

"I'm cut off from Creator. I feel nothing of Them."

"You are on the other side of the uncrossable river. They long to be with you again, Cherished."

"I want to be with Them, but I don't know how."

Saub stopped to look into my eyes. "You can't cross over. Creator will cross over to you."

"Like the mother elephant?"

"Yes,"

"But it's just a story."

"It's a story that teaches what Creator is like."

"So how is Creator like the mother elephant?"

"Both are willing to sacrifice everything for love."

Chapter 92

Possibilities

We looked for a place where Saub could rest. We found a shady spot beneath a sprawling pine tree whose thick trunk leaned at a sharp angle. Saub sat on a boulder, and I sat on the floor of pine needles facing him.

I said, "You told me I needed to return to innocence and die to my willfulness. If I can't do those things, then I'll never get a new connection."

"What is impossible for you is possible for Creator. Acknowledging your powerlessness makes an opening for Creator's power. Ask Creator to help you."

My desperate soul ached for Creator. I closed my eyes and said, "Creator, I want to be reconnected to You. Please restore my innocence. Enable me to die to my willfulness. Help me to do what I can't do myself."

Creator didn't respond, and my soul remained empty. I looked at Saub, wondering if I had failed to say the right words.

"Do not despair," he said. "Creator heard you. They will answer."

We resumed our slow amble toward the lake. Once we found our rhythm, I said, "When do I get my new connection?"

"I must die before that can happen," Saub said.

"Die?"

Was Saub playing me? How could he deliver on a promise after he was dead? Too many factors eroded my hope. Perhaps Saub was deluded, and I clung to the same delusion because I wanted to believe.

To my surprise, we found ourselves at the lake much sooner than expected. At first, I thought I wasn't paying attention, but I was sure we hadn't passed certain distinct landmarks. Somehow, we had bypassed those markers. Puzzled, I looked back to see what I might have missed. When I glanced at Saub, he was smiling.

"We took a shortcut," he said. "At my pace, the trip would have taken too long."

Saub had transported us to the lake. Humans didn't have that power, which meant that Saub had lied about being human. What else was a lie?

While Saub stood unsteady, clutching his staff with both hands, I refilled my traveling gourd with water from the lake. I stored water in a zucchini-shaped gourd I attached to a rope around my waist. To the rope I also attached an animal-skin pouch for carrying things. When I handed Saub the gourd, he was gazing at the ruins of the demolished tower. After he finished drinking, he said, "The memorial still speaks if one listens. The way back to Creator is through brokenness."

I gave Saub a tour of my garden. One of Blaze's spears was leaning inside the garden fence. Blaze would never leave a weapon behind.

Afterward, I sat Saub by the inside fence so he could lean against it. While he watched, I watered my plants, making many trips to the lake to fill my gardening gourd and returning to pour water into the furrows. Saub never took his eyes off me as if I were doing something of great importance. The exception was when we both noticed a mouse scampering across a furrow to hide behind a large melon leaf.

One of my pomegranate plants had died, so I pulled out the withered shrub, threw it aside, and continued watering. Saub stood, hobbled toward the dead plant, picked it up, and returned to his seat where he inspected the plant. Curious, I walked over to Saub, expecting him to say something interesting.

The plant that Saub was holding now had new growth. He said, "Not everything that dies is cast aside forever. It can be revived if given a new spirit. Put this plant back into the ground."

I stared at the pomegranate plant in amazement. In the midst of the dead leaves, leafy green shoots sprouted from every twig. Even as I took the plant from Saub, more new leaves unfurled. Filled with awe, I returned to the spot where I had yanked out the plant and dug a hole. Lowering the plant into the hole, I pushed dirt around its roots and packed the dirt. Then I gave it water.

When I returned to where Saub sat, he said, "You will be revived when you receive a new spirit."

I now believed that Saub was much more than I could understand. My eyes filled with tears. I dropped to my knees and said, "How can I get a new spirit?"

"You must entrust your soul to me."

A sudden burst of movement erupted from the garden. Blaze leapt into view, grabbed his spear that leaned against the fence, and pointed it at Saub. The mouse we saw was no mouse. Blaze was naked, exposing fresh burn marks.

Blaze fixed his eyes on Saub and held his spear steady. In a stern voice, he said, "Cherished . . . don't listen to this fraud. Can't you see . . . you're being tricked again? If you give your soul to Illuminos . . . he will own you . . . forever."

Chapter 93

Clash

"Settle down, Blaze," I said. "I haven't given my soul to anyone."

"Don't do it. Never do it," Blaze said. "Saub must go." He jabbed his spear toward Saub who remained serene.

I said to Saub, "You should leave before Blaze harms you. He's an expert hunter."

"I am aware of Blaze's skill," Saub said. Straining, he hoisted himself into standing position by climbing hand-over-hand up his walking staff. He advanced toward Blaze, who kept both hands on his readied spear. With one gnarled finger, Saub touched the tip of the spear. "If you are going to use this, do it now."

Blaze plunged the spear into Saub's chest. Saub threw back his head and cried out. An instant later, Blaze thrust the spear deeper until the tip pushed through Saub's backside. Saub's body shuddered.

Blaze let go of the spear, and Saub fell to the ground near the fence. Saub curled up on his side like a frail, dry leaf. Blood drooled from where the spear shaft entered and exited his body.

I stood helpless while Saub moaned in pain.

Saub gasped, "Cherished, come here."

I dropped onto my hands and knees, and placed my ear next

to Saub's mouth.

"Grab my hand," Saub whispered.

I took Saub's hand in mine. Spasms traveled down the length of his body.

"Your willfulness," Saub said. "Give it to me, now."

"How?"

"By choosing to."

I hesitated, then said, "I give you my willfulness."

In that moment, Saub screamed in agony as if a more potent spear had pierced him. His entire body convulsed, pulling his hand out of mine. He clawed at the ground, then clenched his hands into tight fists stuffed with dirt. Tears streamed from his eyes. His pupils rolled up out of view. His breathing was rapid and labored and gurgling.

Watching Saub suffer tore at me. Every animal Blaze had speared died within moments, but not Saub.

"Do something, Blaze," I yelled.

Blaze was frozen in a stare that ignored both Saub and me. He gaped at something behind me.

I whipped around and saw Illuminos standing behind the garden fence. He watched Saub's anguish with focused attention. His stacked hands rested on top of a long, vertical, yellowed bone.

"You performed well, Blaze," Illuminos croaked without expression. "Better than I expected from a worthless demon." His black hair moved like underwater plants swaying in a gentle current.

"I didn't do it for you. . . . I did it for Cherished," Blaze said. He crouched low into a defensive posture, but lifted his head to make eye contact with Illuminos. "When I refused . . . to carry out your plan against Cherished . . . I figured you would send someone else . . . to do what I wouldn't. I had to protect Cherished . . . from this creature of yours."

Illuminos laughed. "My creature? This detestable slug slithering across the ground came from Creator, not me. This loathsome experiment was designed by Them to tamper with the unbreakable laws of the universe. You did the right thing by stopping this monster."

Saub cried out. "Creator, where are You? Don't leave me alone."

Illuminos looked down at Saub and cocked his head. He said to Blaze, "Finish him off."

"No." Blaze said. "If he is from Creator . . ."

"Saub is dying," I said. "Can't anyone help?"

"I will help," Illuminos said.

Illuminos strode along the back of the fence and stopped just opposite where Saub's impaled body lay curled on the blood-stained dirt. He lifted his long, yellowed bone over the fence and lowered it straight down onto the side of Saub's head. Then, with both hands, he pushed the bone down against Saub's skull until I heard it crack.

Saub's body went limp.

Illuminos lifted the bone to his side of the fence and said, "Some bugs deserve to be squashed." Then he turned and walked away, thumping the ground with his bone while dirt began to cake on its bloodied end.

Chapter 94

Loss

I stared at Saub's lifeless body, unable to make sense of his death. Unlike Creator after the tiger attack, Saub would not come back. He would never make good on his promises.

Blaze stood gaping at the corpse. When he saw me looking at him, he lowered his eyes and said, "You must hate me . . . more than ever."

"Saub was going to reconnect me to Creator. You ruined my chances for that."

Blaze rolled his head from side to side. "What can I say? . . . I'm sorry. . . . I was convinced Saub came from Illuminos. How could I have known . . . he was sent by Creator?"

"Did Saub know your full name?"

"Yes. . . . But I assumed he learned it . . . through devious means. My mind only allowed . . . what it already believed."

I shook my head at the insanity that had led to Saub's death and taken away my future with Creator. I expelled a loud sigh through clenched teeth. Looking down at Saub's body, I said, "We need to move the body."

"We should burn it," Blaze said.

The suggestion repulsed me. Saub wasn't a hunted animal to

be roasted after killing. But the idea of forest creatures feeding on his body disturbed me more. Burning his body was the proper thing to do.

"Give me your fire stones," I said to Blaze.

"I will make the fire."

"No. You've done enough," I said in a gruff voice. "I'll do it. Give me your stones."

Blaze took a step backward. "They're my stones."

"I don't care. Give them to me."

He stared at me while his chest expanded with each amplified breath.

I stared back.

"I don't have them . . . on me." Blaze was still naked. "I'll get them," he said with resignation. He left the garden and returned wearing his stack of furs. After stopping in front of me, he held out the two fire stones, waiting with lowered head until I took them. He didn't look at me.

After placing the stones into a pocket of my weapons carrier, I bent down and removed the spear from Saub's body. Then I folded his body and picked it up. He wasn't heavy, only bones wrapped in loose skin. His soul had departed his frail body, leaving it an empty husk.

I carried his body to the demolished tower and lowered it on top of the splintered woodpile. I gathered tinder and placed it around the body. Blaze stood at a distance, watching. Using the stones, I set fire to the tinder and backed away. Soon, the wood and Saub's body were engulfed in flames.

I watched the fire consume Saub's body and wondered what Creator thought about all this. Did They know that Saub would be killed? That Saub wouldn't complete his mission? Did Creator have a backup plan to reconnect me?

Blaze came alongside, and we stared at the flames together. I wanted Blaze to know how much he had disappointed me, how he had destroyed my hope to reunite with Creator, but I had no words to express the depth of my loss.

"Did Illuminos recruit you?" I said, looking into the fire.

"Don't make me answer that."

"You just did."

"What? . . . Oh. . . . You need to underst—"

"You lied." My voice was loud and accusing. I turned so Blaze could see the anger in my eyes. "You've been lying from the beginning."

"I served Illuminos . . . at first. But I stopped . . . when you became my friend."

"You should have told me."

"What good would that have done?"

"I would have stayed your friend. I'm fed up with your lying. I want you to go."

"What?"

"Remember our agreement? You agreed to leave whenever I decide you must go."

Blaze opened his mouth, then closed it.

He studied my face, waiting for a change of expression, but I gave him nothing outside of a hard stare. When he realized I wasn't changing my mind, he said with hesitancy, "My stones?"

"Just go."

Blaze looked down and walked away, dragging his feet.

I stayed by the fire until it burned out. By then, the sky glowed orange like embers. Saub was gone, along with my hope. Blaze was gone, along with my trust. Everything had become ashes.

Chapter 95

Society

The next morning, I sat by the fire pit in front of my shelter, staring at the spot where Blaze had always sat. A voice startled me. "You still have a future."

I turned and saw Illuminos, who stood with both hands on top of a twisted, obsidian walking staff. His hair swirled like a swarm of black flies. He dipped his head in a subtle nod that caused a ripple to travel along the strands of his long hair.

I didn't stand to greet him. I didn't respond at all.

"Now that Blaze is gone," Illuminos said, "you are on your own. A true independent, at last. I've come to invite you to a gathering of the Society of Independents tonight."

"Why should I come?"

"To meet others like yourself."

"There are no others like me, now that Saub is dead."

"I meant other independents. You know the location. The Tree of Death. Come tonight when the sun is setting."

I turned away and said, "I'll think about it."

"I'm the only one left who has anything to offer you."

When I looked back, he had vanished, leaving a dead patch of flattened sorrel where he had stood.

Curious and having nothing to lose, I set out to visit the Tree of Death later that day. Before sunset, I arrived at the wide circle of hard clay, a featureless clearing except for the giant tree at its center. The massive, knotted trunk twisted in an upward spiral. Halfway up the tree, wedged between its enormous boughs, was an indigo platform in the shape of a perfect circle. This horizontal disk was as thick as my arm, two paces in diameter, and flat like the surface of an undisturbed pond. Its smooth, deep-blue surface glistened as if wet.

Unlike last time, the tree had no leaves, which made it appear more dead and grim than before, its extremities resembling bony fingers. This time, the tree was no longer black as midnight. I could distinguish the char-colored texture of its coarse bark. Walking closer to inspect its trunk, I saw the gash where I had swiped the trunk with my fingers on my previous visit.

Both the tree and I were severed from Creator. Perhaps I could now see the tree's texture because we shared the same state. To anyone still connected to Creator, I supposed I appeared pure black like the tree when I first saw it.

"Do you like my elevated platform?" Illuminos' voice came from behind me. "It's one of my terrestrial thrones."

I turned around to see Illuminos gazing up at the platform. "It's very shiny," I said. "What's it made of?"

"It's called lapis lazuli. A royal stone used for thrones."

Illuminos turned his gaze onto me. "The members will arrive soon. I asked you to come early so I can instruct you. Take this sack and give each attendee one leaf from inside when I tell you to do so." He handed me a white sack, and I took it. "Can you grasp what I'm asking or do I need to explain it in simpler terms?"

"I understand," I said, feeling a pang of dread about the evening. The deep, narrow sack was woven from fine filaments that resembled Saub's long, white hair. Its shape reminded me of bird's nests that hung from branches like long fruit. Peering into the sack, I saw dark shapes wriggling at the bottom.

"Stay here," Illuminos said. "I will ascend my throne before everyone arrives."

Illuminos walked away from the trunk. His right hand clutched a transparent walking staff, a long, six-sided crystal. He stopped and turned around to face the tree, which lowered one of its huge branches to the ground. He stepped onto the branch, then walked up its length to the circular platform. Once he stood on the shiny disk, the tree lifted its branch to its original position.

Creatures began materializing across the barren clearing, one by one. Most were taller than me. Some had wings. One had three pairs of wings. Some glowed like the moon. A few hovered above the ground like Radiance, dangling appendages I couldn't identify. They were smooth or feathered or hairy, of every color and pattern. All heads tilted upward toward Illuminos who stood on the lapis lazuli platform enjoying the attention. His crystal walking staff reflected the spiky, red-orange clouds in the darkening sky.

The creatures didn't acknowledge each other, but fixed their gaze on Illuminos. Their bodies shifted and swayed in a restless, impatient manner.

A nearby creature with elongated limbs noticed me. It stared at me with its unblinking brown eyes, huge and round like loris eyes. "What is it?" it said. "A hairless monkey? Is it someone's pet?" The creature moved closer and pinched me.

I pushed its hand away.

Another creature approached. "Whatever it is, it's ugly." That creature had six arms and a ring of glowing, blue eyes that encircled its head. It reached toward me with a six-fingered hand.

"Don't harass the human," Illuminos said from the platform above. "It is my guest." All the creatures craned to look at me.

A voice from the crowd said, "Why did you invite that thing here? It's not one of us."

"That's true, but it is an Independent," Illuminos said. "Our rules do not require members to be angels or glories."

Another voice said, "It has not pledged its loyalty. It must meet that requirement to become a member."

"I will give it that opportunity tonight," Illuminos said. "Allow it to stay until then. Now, let us begin the ceremony." He lifted his staff high. "You have all chosen independence. By your own free will you are members of this society and agree to its rules. As a reward for your allegiance, I offer you exaltation, the power to rule over your own domains. Come, show your loyalty and receive your due."

The giant tree slumped as if bowing to the crowd. Two massive boughs lowered to the ground, one on each side of the lapis lazuli dais.

I found myself transported to the end of the right branch. Something pressed against my mind like a dull blade into leather. Once it penetrated, I felt dizzy and nauseated, and heard Illuminos speaking inside my mind. "Stay there and hand a single Thaed leaf to each member who walks by."

The creatures formed a line in front of the left branch. One by one, each creature ascended the tree to stand before Illuminos. Each, in turn, licked the greasy, yellow nodule on Illuminos' chest. Watching the spectacle made me queasy. After giving obeisance, each creature walked down the right branch. As they passed by me, I handed each a leaf from the white sack. None of them would look at me, but snatched the leaf from my hand with disgust.

The creatures pushed the leaves into their mouths. Afterward, they went into a trance. Oblivious to their surroundings, they bumped into each other until they spread out across the clearing, some sitting, some sprawled, all of them in a semi-conscious daze.

After all the creatures had been served, Illuminos walked down the right branch to my location and stopped to look me over. He grabbed the sack from me.

"Can I have a leaf, too?" I said, remembering its effects.

"Only if you demonstrate your loyalty."

I looked at the disgusting, yellow nodule and wondered what price I would have to pay by licking it.

Chapter 96

Cost

"I'm not ready to show my loyalty," I said.

"Let me guess. You need to think it over," Illuminos said. "Go away." He waved his hands as if shooing a fly. "Don't come back unless you're willing to demonstrate your allegiance. Otherwise, I will let this crowd tear you apart."

On the way home, the sky deepened to an indigo, the same color as Illuminos' platform. Splashes of black clouds covered the first-appearing stars. I had hoped to make a friend tonight, but no one seemed interested in friendship. Their only interest was in getting Thaed leaves which, as I learned this night, came from the Tree of Death. Another secret that Blaze kept from me. Had he lied about being out of leaves because he wanted to keep them for himself? Why didn't he hide them the entire time? Was friendship the reason he shared them or the reason he withheld them later because he thought it wrong?

If smoking the leaves provided an escape from my painful feelings, then eating a raw leaf must bring greater liberation. I wanted to try one and find out, even if it meant licking Illuminos' nodule.

The next day, I arrived at the Tree of Death before sunset and waited for Illuminos. I studied the gash on the tree trunk made by my fingers. Each finger had slashed a groove in the trunk, exposing the wood beneath the bark. Now, when I touched it, the char-colored bark felt firm and rough.

Illuminos appeared next to me. His right hand clutched the top of a long, tapered shape that resembled an animal tusk. The point of the bleached tusk pierced the hard ground.

"Looking for pleasure or pain?" Illuminos said. His expressionless face confirmed he had no regard for me.

"I've come to show my loyalty and get a leaf."

"Wise choice, little tadpole."

Illuminos waited for my act of allegiance.

I edged closer to the nodule that was level with my chin. Its yellow coloring was uneven like a rotting mushroom. I extended my tongue, closed my eyes, and pushed my head forward until my tongue touched it. It tasted bitter like mold.

"You have demonstrated your loyalty," Illuminos said. "Now, you can have your treat."

He didn't have a sack of leaves this time. He reached up to a low-hanging twig, gripped the evening air, and yanked away from the twig. When he lowered his hand and opened his fist, a leaf writhed on his palm.

As soon as I took the leaf from his hand, he walked away. I hastened to leave before he could assign me some unpleasant task and before any Independents showed up to harass me. I ran home, eager to discover the leaf's power. I kept a tight squeeze on the leaf lest it wriggle out between my fingers.

I sat on my bed in the dark. With apprehension and excitement, I pushed the leaf into my mouth. It flapped against my tongue and the roof of my mouth. I tried to chew it, but the leaf was tough like the outer leaves of an artichoke. Biting down on it released a subtle sour flavor. Then, before I could stop it, the leaf slithered toward the back of my mouth and down my throat. It squirmed inside my throat, and I had to swallow twice to help it down.

I waited to feel something in my stomach and wondered if the leaf would try to crawl up my throat. Nothing physical happened, but my consciousness began to change. I expanded beyond my body, my shelter, my world, and left them behind as I floated in an infinite space. My consciousness filled this limitless realm. My thoughts generated bursts of light that flashed like lightning within the void. As I focused on the lights, they coalesced and solidified into shapes. I saw a herd of gazelles leaping across a wide meadow. The meadow's edges faded into the void as did the gazelles after they crossed the field.

When I thought of the Teachers, they appeared, wings linked together, within the scene. They said, "You are greater than Us, because you have created Us. We await your command."

"Pluck each other's feathers," I said.

They yanked large feathers from each other's wings until their wings were tattered.

"Stop," I said, and they stopped. Brown feathers were strewn across the ground.

I invited Blaze into the scene. "Punish Blaze," I commanded the Teachers.

They scraped and clawed Blaze, peeling his furs off one-by-one until they scratched his naked flesh. The last hide to come off his body was his own scarred skin.

Next, I summoned Illuminos and made him small as a toad. I forced him to dance around the Tree of Death until he became exhausted and pleaded to stop. Then I placed him on top of the circular platform and told the tree to draw up its branches to crush him until nothing remained.

I created whole worlds and filled them with creatures of my making, directing them to do my bidding. After a measureless span of time, my creations began to lose substance, fading away as my consciousness shrank back into my tiny body.

I opened my eyes and found myself still seated on my bed. Light streamed between the horizontal branches of my shelter wall. My body ached with exhaustion and stinging pain. Looking down, I saw dozens of reddened scratches on my legs. Scratches and long welts also covered my torso and arms. In places, the skin was broken and bleeding. It alarmed me to see blood on my fingernails. Had I done this to myself?

When I touched a painful spot on my head, it stung. I flinched. The spot was damp. I looked at the moisture on my fingers and saw fresh blood. When I focused past my fingers, I discovered that my bed was strewn with clumps of my own hair.

Chapter 97

Brokenness

My self-mutilation terrified me. I remembered the black leaves crawling toward the Tree of Death to consume it in a perpetual cycle of self-destruction. Swallowing the leaf had caused me to inflict that same destruction on myself. The nightmare was reversed. Waking up was worse than the dream. I promised myself I would never eat a Thaed leaf again.

The feather bedding beneath me felt wet. I discovered I had urinated during my trance or whatever it was. Seeking to escape the wetness, I stood and almost fainted from intense hunger. I took hold of the nearest cave wall and steadied myself. Rummaging through my shelter, I devoured whatever food I found, but my hunger remained. How many days had passed after I had swallowed the leaf? Why did I feel so tired?

I disposed of my befouled bedding. Afterward, I traveled to my garden to get more food. Total exhaustion slowed me down as I staggered along the path. My cuts smarted, and I kept looking at my arms and legs, getting more upset with each glance. When I reached my garden, I gorged myself with an entire melon.

Unable to stay awake, I lay down by the fence and longed for restful sleep.

When I awoke, I risked looking at my reflection on the lake's surface. Reddened scratches crisscrossed my body. More hideous was my plucked head from which sprouted a few ugly tufts of hair. Where I had ripped out my hair, I saw my bloodied scalp. The apparition was horrifying. My reflection reminded me of Blaze's body, scarred from his own self-mutilation.

I bathed in the lake to wash off the blood. The water made my cuts sting. Tears filled my eyes, not from my cuts, but from shame.

After climbing out of the lake, I sat on the bank and sobbed. I had no future to cheer me. No friends. No purpose. No peace. My scrapes and cuts reflected my lacerated soul which had no will to limp forward. I ached inside as though something vital had broken.

Filled with grief over my failure to trust Creator, I spoke from the darkness of my soul. "Creator, I'm lost. Please find me. Please . . ." I broke into more sobbing. "I'm sorry for choosing independence, for cutting You out of my life. Help me to live for You again. I don't want my life anymore. I want nothing but You. Please rescue me. I know I don't deserve Your help, but I trust in Your love. . . ."

I wept because my heart was broken over my barrenness of soul. I had nothing left. Sitting on the lakeshore, I cried and cried until I was spent.

By this time, the sun hung low in the cloudy sky. I watched the ripples travel across the lake as the breeze forced them into formation. Without Creator, I was nothing, just a ripple driven by the breeze, driven by circumstance. Did my actions matter at all? Did anything matter? In that moment of doubt and resignation, I resolved to punish Illuminos for ruining my life.

I returned home, tied my weapons carrier to my back, and filled its pockets with knives and spears. Gripping a spear in my hand, I ran toward the Tree of Death. I didn't know if I could kill Illuminos, but I intended to try.

I arrived at the tree before anyone else. Searching for a place to hide, I found a large, gnarled tree growing near the edge of the circular clearing. Facing away from the clearing, I pressed my back against the tree and waited and listened. My heart pounded. My tense muscles trembled. I kept a tight squeeze on the spear in my hand, hoping I wouldn't miss my target when the time came to throw it.

Illuminos appeared in front of me, startling me. He ripped away my spear with his right hand and pinned me against the tree with his left. I couldn't grab any weapons because they were trapped between my back and the tree. Their handles dug into my ribs.

He narrowed his eyes and brought his face close to mine, so close I saw his nostril slits vibrate with each breath. "You're a fool to think you can harm me. You forget who I am. I'm the brightest star in the universe, the lord of light and darkness, fearsome destroyer. . . ." He looked up and down my disfigured body and shook his head with disgust. "What a pitiful sight. It's time to put you out of your misery."

Chapter 98

Subjection

Illuminos' nodule glistened with an oily substance that oozed from it. A pungent aroma overpowered me. I almost tasted the bitter oil again. I found it difficult to focus my eyes or concentrate. My mouth went dry, my knees weakened, my entire body craved the oily secretion. Every nerve ached for the seductive ooze. I strained my neck and tongue to reach the nodule, but Illuminos kept his hand against my chest, holding me at arm's length, pinning me against the tree. I even tried to reach it with my hands so I could lick my fingers, but he stepped back, keeping his chest beyond reach.

"My oil flows inside you," he said. "It makes you subject to me."

His words were far away, blurred and faint as if I were underwater. My thoughts were as distant and hazy as his words. He continued to speak, and I sensed my body obeying his spoken commands. My body was no longer under my control.

When the mental fogginess cleared, I could track my thoughts again. My body returned to me, and I could again feel Illuminos' hand pressed against my chest. My hands had moved. I didn't look down but felt them now gripping a wooden shaft in front of my stomach.

Illuminos' pomegranate eyes peered into my face with unmasked hatred. Every strand of his hair aimed itself at me like a stinger. "Your self-inflicted handiwork needs a finishing touch," he said, sneering. "I first thought it fitting if you made the next cut, but I would enjoy it more if I took a stab at it."

I felt a jab on my stomach. Looking down, I saw my spear in my hands with the point of its blade dimpling my flesh.

"Let me help you," Illuminos said, "as I helped Saub." He pushed on the end of the spear with one finger. The spear punctured my skin and drew blood.

"Stop!" a voice shouted. Bright beams of light shone on Illuminos from the direction of the clearing. The beams lit his surprised face against the darkening sky.

"Creator has sent me to rescue you, Cherished," Radiance said. My back was still pressed against the tree, so I couldn't see her.

Illuminos grabbed my spear and threw it. In that same moment, I leapt away and ran toward the light. The spear punctured one of Radiance's eyes and disabled the light beam.

All of a sudden, dozens of Independents appeared and swarmed around the sphere. I stopped short and watched them poke Radiance's eyes with their hands or weapons. A few moments later, they had blinded every eye. Radiance lay helpless like a bug whose legs had all been torn off. She gave off no light.

Illuminos and the Independents laughed and cheered. Some of them took turns kicking and pushing the sphere, causing Radiance to roll like a giant toy.

A creature with white, feathery wings said, "Look out! Creator has sent Radiance to crush you." Then the creature pushed Radiance into the crowd, causing them to scurry out of the way, laughing.

I stood paralyzed, unable to help. I had weapons, but I was far outnumbered.

Another creature, a giant with four arms, retrieved the orb and raised it over his head. "For your rebellion, Creator casts you down to this planet," he roared. He flung Radiance into the air. The crowd dodged the sphere as it landed with a loud crack. The sphere rolled in Illuminos' direction, and he stepped into its path to stop it.

"Tadpole," Illuminos said, turning toward me. "I have a task for you. Go find a big hole and drop this disgusting turd into it."

I consented because I wanted to spare Radiance from any further injury or humiliation. This way, I could roll her to safety. With all eyes fixed on me, I walked toward Radiance and placed my hands on the sphere. Radiance was damp from her wounds. Pushing Radiance across the hard ground, the bystanders gathered around us and snickered. The sphere was as tall as me, so I couldn't see ahead.

"Look at that," someone said. "It looks like what you spit out after chewing on something indigestible."

Laughter followed.

I didn't know if they were referring to Radiance or me.

"A hideous piece of gristle," someone hissed to elicit more laughs.

I continued pushing Radiance as the jeering crowd parted to let us pass. Then someone ahead of me blocked the sphere, preventing me from moving forward. I didn't know what to do. More than anything, I wanted to escape the clearing and take Radiance with me.

I looked back at Illuminos, hoping he would tell the prankster to grant me passage. He stood with his arms crossed, watching the spectacle, saying nothing.

Some Independents gasped.

I turned toward the sound.

From behind the sphere stepped Saub.

Chapter 99

Rescue

Saub was no longer frail and wrinkled, but vibrant and strong, his hair still long and white.

"I killed you," Illuminos said, backing away.

"You did," Saub said, "but I never intended to stay dead. I have returned to make things right."

Saub placed his hands on Radiance and said, "I give you more than a drop of glory, my faithful servant."

The orb glowed bright. Radiance's eyes were restored at once. They opened, casting beams of light so intense that the entire scene became brilliant as mid-day. The Independents screamed. Radiance's beams snaked and coiled around nearby Independents, trapping them within white tentacle-arms. Some Independents vanished and escaped along with Illuminos.

"Take them away, Radiance," Saub said. "You know what to do with them."

"Yes, Creator," Radiance said. She disappeared with the captured Independents.

Saub and I stood alone in the clearing, now silent and dark under the cobalt sky.

"Creator?" I said, puzzled.

"Yes. I am Manna."

"I don't understand. Why are you in disguise?"

"This isn't a disguise," Manna said. "I'm human in every way, with a human spirit and umbilicore. I had to become human so I could take your place. As I was dying, I took on your willfulness. Because willfulness opposes and repels Creator, I became separated from Creator and from Life. The cost of willfulness is death. I paid the price by dying in your place so you could have relationship with Us again."

"So you're severed from Creator as I am?"

"My connection is restored because I paid the price in full. Therefore, I'm alive again to give you my connection and my spirit. Once they are given, no one can take them away."

"How do I receive them?"

"You know how. Die to your willfulness and return to innocence."

In that moment, Creator gave me new understanding. That which had seemed impossible now became possible. I took Manna's hands in mine and closed my eyes. "Creator, I accept Manna's death for my willfulness, and I receive the innocence that Manna restores to me."

I felt a pop in my soul, like the feeling of water draining from my ear canal. As if I had been holding my breath this whole time, my soul inhaled fresh air. Through my new connection, a warm rush of love flowed into every particle of my being. The barren emptiness inside became flooded with light and life. I sensed Creator again.

When I opened my eyes, Manna appeared as the Manna I remembered, with the shimmering, emerald throat and huge, beautiful wings. Linked to those wings were Ennoia and Aable, whose cheeks were wet with tears. In spite of my hideous, marred appearance, Their faces glowed with delight on seeing me.

Overcome with joy, I hugged Manna, squeezing with all my strength, then letting up when my wounds hurt. Ennoia and Aable wrapped Their arms around us and wept. I wept, too. The warmth of Their bodies assured me this was real.

Ennoia and Aable expressed Their joy in being reunited with Manna. They cried and laughed and kissed His face.

Aable said, "I'm so glad We're united again, Manna. Never again will We be torn apart."

"Oh, Manna," Ennoia said, "when Our connection was severed, Our agony was as great as Yours."

We remained in a huddle until all the stars opened their eyes to gaze down upon us. Those places inside me that had withered came back to life. I felt a lingering willfulness, but I knew Manna's death had erased its power to destroy my connection. My willfulness no longer had dominion over me. Instead, I experienced renewed freedom from the demands of self.

My new connection had a different quality than my old connection. My access to Creator felt more immediate, more intimate.

When we unwrapped ourselves from our huddle, Manna said, "Remember, your connection is severed and can't be repaired. Your spirit is dead. I have given you my connection and my spirit. You're joined to Us through Me and now partake in Our eternal communion."

I gasped with surprise. "Does that mean I'm equal with you?"

"No," Aable said. "It means you're always welcome to enter Our huddle. That's all."

"You still have much to learn, Cherished," Ennoia said. "Never think you've arrived at your destination. We've created you with the unique ability to grow forever, to expand without limit throughout eternity. The reason We designed you with that capacity is to make you a suitable partner for Us, someone with whom We can have a relationship that evolves forever. You, Cherished, are Our beloved companion. From this point on, your name shall be Companion. And We want you to view Us as your true companion and eternal helpmate."

Chapter 100

Understanding

The golden-fringed Creator and I strolled through the forest as in the early days. We walked under the dappled shade of birch trees whose leaves fluttered, the sunlight flashing on their shiny yellow tops. At the base of the trees, blue-green shrubs extended shoots from which little pink bells trembled in the light afternoon breeze. I inhaled fresh, fragrant air with slow, satisfying breaths.

The plants and trees shimmered with an inner luminosity as they used to do. They hadn't changed, but I had changed in that I could again see Creator's abiding touch within them.

This stroll felt richer and more fulfilling than those of the past. Now that Creator had restored our connection, my appreciation for Them deepened with every moment I spent with Them. Filled with gratitude, I took Creator's hand and squeezed. More than ever, I treasured my relationship with Them, cherishing it as an irreplaceable gift.

My thoughts turned to Blaze, who I hadn't seen since Saub's death. I feared Blaze had forgotten me or had reverted to old, self-destructive habits. He didn't know that Creator had restored me, and I wanted to tell him so he might take hope.

"Creator, what happened to Blaze?"

"He followed a lamentable path."

"Can you take me to him?"

"Yes, but you won't like what you'll see."

"I don't care. Maybe I can help."

Creator gazed at me and smiled. "You love Blaze much. We'll take you, but be prepared for disappointment."

Creator turned, and I followed, eager to be reunited with Blaze.

Walking hand-in-hand, I recalled my separation from Creator, the long period during which They were shrouded from me, silent and inaccessible. How did I survive those days? If Illuminos hadn't tricked me, if I hadn't asked for the knowledge of right and wrong, I would've been spared all that grief.

"Dearest Companion," Creator said, turning toward me. "Your severed connection was meant to happen. It was part of Our plan."

I stopped and stared at Creator, astounded. "You intended all that pain and misery?"

Creator put a hand on my shoulder and looked into my eyes with an intensity that made me pay full attention. "We didn't intend your misery. We intended you to grow."

"Grow? How could I grow without You? My life was a mess."

"Nevertheless, you did grow. Your strength, endurance, and humility increased. The hardships you faced built up your maturity and character. Your relationship with Blaze taught you patience, compassion, and forgiveness. Everything that happened to you was meant to transform you and groom you into a companion for Us."

"Maybe so, but I can't imagine any good coming from a severed connection. It was awful. It had no purpose I could see." I resumed walking, staring at the ground before me. Creator came alongside, and I sensed His eyes penetrating me.

"Its purpose was a deeper understanding of Our love," Creator said with patience. "You can't experience the saving power of Our love unless you need to be rescued. You can't comprehend the depth of Our love unless you witness Our willingness to suffer on

310

your behalf. How can you know Our love unless you experience it for yourself? Nothing is impossible for Our love. It has power to heal what can't be healed, to restore what is forever lost, and to love what is beyond the reach of love."

"Are You saying that everything is meant to be an opportunity for Your love? Even the bad things?"

Creator nodded. "That's right."

With sudden clarity, I saw how all the events of my life made sense. Every one of them was an opportunity to trust Creator and for Them to show Their love. My severed connection had given Them the chance to prove Their boundless love for me in the most real way possible.

I stood in awe and stared at Him, wide-eyed.

"Nothing, no matter how terrible, is outside the range of Our love," Creator said. "Even before We created you, We knew that Illuminos would trick you into destroying your connection to Us. Even then, We had a plan to rescue you."

"Why didn't You tell me?"

"We didn't want you to trust in a plan, but in Us alone. You believed in Our love, and that belief carried you through."

"I'm glad that ordeal is over."

Creator smiled. "More will follow."

"What?" My body stiffened from fear.

Chapter 101

Remembrance

"Why should I have to experience more trials?" I said.

"How else will you continue to grow?" Creator looked into my eyes and smiled. His golden eyes communicated an infinite love I could never expect to fully grasp.

My mind struggled to find an escape from that question, some way to avoid any future pain, but I saw no way around it. "Can't I grow by some other method?"

"Companion, every trial is bearable when you trust in Us. Fear and worry turn a trial into a torment."

I sighed. "You're right." I plucked a yellow leaf from a nearby birch tree and rolled the stem between two fingers as I studied it. "I'll try not to think about future trials, but I'd feel safer if Illuminos stayed away from me."

"We will restrain Illuminos at the proper time. Until then, his evil will increase unchecked."

A ripple of fear zigzagged through me.

Creator placed a hand on my shoulder to calm me. "It must play out this way. Illuminos will become so darkened that he will think he can overthrow Us. His attempt will be his downfall."

I considered asking when this would take place, but knew it

wouldn't be soon enough for my liking.

We arrived at a small clearing, tucked away among some silver-blue spruce trees. I saw the remains of a fire pit. A pile of charred debris and ashes filled the wide stone circle. Next to the fire pit, Blaze's furs were stacked in a neat pile. On top of the pile lay Blaze's woven ankle bracelet. His bundle of weapons, wrapped in a gray pelt, lay beside the stack. A whirlwind licked the ashes in the fire pit and lifted them to create a spinning, gray phantom.

Seeing Blaze's possessions thrilled me, and I looked around for Blaze with hopeful expectation. When I realized that Blaze never abandoned his weapons, my excitement died.

Horror rose within me. "No. Did Blaze. . . ."

"Yes," Creator said. "He set himself on fire. His remains are within those ashes. We're sorry."

"I'm too late."

Crushing grief squeezed my lungs, forcing out all the air in ragged bursts. I couldn't breathe. My eyes pinched shut. Then, after inhaling sharply, I released a long, falling, aching moan. I dropped my head in despair. Tears pushed between my rigid eyelids.

Creator wrapped His arms around me and held me as I sobbed. When I finished weeping, He wiped my tears, gazing at me with a look of compassion and tenderness.

"What happened to Blaze's spirit?" I said.

"Blaze chose separation in life, so his spirit follows that same course."

The weight of sadness poured into me like sand. I leaned against Creator and placed my head against His chest. "Is there no hope for Blaze?"

"Blaze destroyed the only body he was given, and his spirit died ages ago. Now, all that's left is a disabled spirit cut off from everything. It's too late to help Blaze."

"Why can't You help him? You said nothing is impossible for Your love."

"Yes, but We can't override free will. We can only help those who want to be helped. Blaze spurned Us during his life. He chose death, instead. You must accept his choice."

I couldn't accept it. Why could nothing be done? Didn't my love for Blaze count for something? I wanted him to find healing and peace, not this. My grief and tears resumed, and I rubbed my eyes with the back of my hand.

"Don't stop loving Blaze," Creator said. "Love is never wasted. It can create an opening where none existed before."

Those words gave me hope.

"Is there anything of his you wish to take?" Creator said.

"Yes."

While I walked toward the stack of furs, Creator moved toward the fire pit and bent over the ashes. I picked up the woven bracelet and placed it around my left ankle as Blaze used to do. When I turned around, I saw a small tree growing out of the middle of the ashes. The end of each stem had seven pointed leaves.

"In memory of Blaze, I have created a new type of tree," Creator said. "We shall call it an ash tree. Each of the spear-shaped leaves is for the seven weapons that Blaze always carried."

Creator opened His hand and showed me what looked like brown dragonfly wings. "These are ash tree seeds. Take them and plant them near your shelter so you can remember him."

I took the seeds and said, "Thank you, Creator. I won't forget Blaze." After placing the seeds inside my animal-skin pouch, I wrapped my hand around the wooden whistle that still hung around my neck and remembered what Blaze meant to me.

Later, when I was home alone, I planted the ash seeds in the spot where Blaze used to crouch by the fire. I envisioned a small tree taking his place by the fire pit in the evenings. After I watered the patch of dirt, I sat and stared at the wet mound. Life had disappointed me in Blaze's death, but the seeds' promise of new life encouraged me. What cheered me more was Creator's love. I knew one thing to be true and reliable, that if I trusted in Creator, Their love would never disappoint.

Chapter 102

Completion

I was watering my garden when Radiance came rolling toward me along the lakeshore. She sparkled and flashed as her many light beams struck my eyes because of her vigorous bobbing. Overjoyed, I dropped my watering gourd and ran toward her. Placing my hands on her sphere, I said, "Radiance. I'm so glad you're all right."

Radiance wrapped me in two curved beams and lifted me into the air, shaking me in rhythm with her bouncing. "Thanks for your concern. What matters most is that Creator has restored you. I am exceedingly glad that you have a new spirit. I missed our talks." She put me back on the ground.

"I missed you, too. Now we can be friends again."

"I was always your friend."

The movement of Radiance's eyes across the sphere seemed less mechanical than before. They glided with smooth spontaneity. Her light beams now had softer edges.

"You're different," I said.

"You noticed." She glowed brighter. "Do you remember my firefly? It is no longer caged or small, but fills my entire being. I have fully become my firefly, my inner self, my drop of Creator's glory. Inner and outer are the same, now."

"That's wonderful. How did this happen?"

Radiance blinked a few times. "It was you who suggested I divulge every piece of myself to Creator. The result was so profound that I dug ever deeper to claim buried parts of myself, parts I did not know existed. By doing that work, I became more connected to myself, so much so that I became myself, my true self, if that makes any sense."

"It does makes sense. But you said that angels don't change."

"I was wrong. Exceedingly wrong."

"You know what that means?" I said with growing excitement. "Maybe Illuminos can change, too."

She stopped bobbing altogether. "Let us not revisit that topic."

"I'm sorry. I'll let it go."

Radiance paused for a long moment. Then every eye opened at once. With surprising zeal, she blurted, "I value you, Cherished." She wrapped me in warm light beams and shook me again. After putting me down, she said, "I do not know what made me do that. I want to hold you and not let go."

"It's because we're friends."

"It is more than that," she said. "I feel a strong urge that is far bigger than me. I want to give you everything I am."

"I know what that is. It's love."

"That cannot be. I am incapable of love. It is not part of my makeup."

"Maybe you're wrong about that, too, Radiance."

"Just yesterday, I discussed this exact subject with other angels. I have become somewhat popular of late, but that story I must tell you some other time. Anyway, we all agreed that love is beyond the capability of angels. It is impossible I am the only exception."

Something Creator had said came to my remembrance.

"I know what makes you different from the rest," I said. "You have received love. My love. Creator once told me that when we receive love, we are able to give love. Because Creator has loved me, I could love you, and, now, you can love."

"So, it is true. I can love. I did not believe it possible, but I can love." She bounced with elation, her eyes blinking and flashing.

I smiled on seeing her joy and noticing her freedom from the need to scan for eavesdroppers.

Radiance glowed so bright, I had to squint. The brightness had a quality I recognized. Her light radiated love, Creator's love, and I recalled Creator saying that They abide in love itself.

After she dimmed, Radiance said, "Thank you, Cherished, for loving me."

"You haven't heard? Creator changed my name to Companion."

Her eyes became wide. "Too much has happened these last few days. But a name change? That implies a whole new identity."

"I haven't yet given it much thought. Creator said that my destiny is to become a companion to Them for eternity. That's a big deal, I suppose."

"Exceedingly big," she said, wobbling on purpose for effect. "The friendship you and I have, you also have with Creator. I cannot think of anything more wonderful . . . Hold on. I am being summoned. My life has become so busy of late. I have so much to tell you, but it will have to wait until next time. Until then . . . Companion."

Radiance rolled forward in place, simulating a bow, then vanished.

I stood by the lakeshore and pondered Creator's love. What compelled Creator to love me in the first place? I had learned that love, by nature, compels itself to give. But Creator's love always yearns to give more. When we were separated, Creator loved me from afar, but Their love wasn't content to stay at a distance. Their love needed to be up close and interactive, to connect with my soul. To that end, They sacrificed everything to bring me into intimate communion with Them again. Radiance was right. I couldn't think of anything more wonderful.

Chapter 103

Rebirth

When my life had burned down to its last cinder, decrepitude seized my body. I lay confined within my cave, its front wall of tied branches weathered from many years of sun, wind, and rain.

Creator tended to my needs during those last days. They fed and bathed me, and sat with me, holding my hand and retelling my favorite stories. They remembered every one of them. Many I had forgotten.

When death was imminent, Ennoia knelt beside me and placed His hand on my chest. His face hovered over mine, and in His eyes I saw inexhaustible love and compassion. Outside my cave, a mid-day breeze kicked up, causing the mulberry trees to rustle. I felt uneasy about dying, not knowing what was to follow. Creator sensed this and spoke comforting words.

"Be at peace," Manna said. "We'll stay with you as your soul leaves your body and enters Our care. Of course, you know your soul has always been under Our loving care."

I spoke, but my words came out as a hoarse whisper. "I'm not afraid." After everything I had been through, I knew I could trust Creator with my soul.

"Death is a transition," Aable said. "When the transition is complete, you will have a new container for your soul. You will still be you on the inside."

My soul's connection to my body wore thin until it was a fine thread that snapped. Then a strange sensation followed, a peeling away, bit-by-bit, like an eggshell cracking apart as a baby bird pecks its way out. Each crack exposed my soul to increasing light. As each fragment dropped away, my soul unfurled into space.

Buoyant and at peace, I floated like a pine cone in a wide, calm lake. Then a current caught me and pulled me into my umbilicore, the conduit through which Creator's life had flowed into me. Now, the stream reversed, my life flowed toward Creator. Joyous anticipation rose in me as I traveled toward a shimmering pool of the purest light.

Like a drop of water falling into the ocean, my tiny self merged with the vastness of Creator. They embraced me in ecstatic, naked union. Time and space compressed into a single point where everything could be observed at once, the way Creator sees the universe. I saw my entire life in an instant. Unable to take in this panoramic vision, my mind shut down.

After a timeless period of being, free of thought and reason, Creator spoke to my soul. "Companion, We've reserved a new body for you. This body will never decay or die."

I coalesced into a solid form and found myself standing in a meadow. The familiar senses of sight and sound resumed, but were heightened. I could see behind me without turning my head. My breathing had stopped, and I wondered if I still had lungs. I inhaled and smelled a thousand aromas at once. My new body appeared the same as the one I received on my first day of existence. I looked at the back of my hand and realized I had forgotten what brand-new skin looked like. My skin was smooth and lustrous, without blemish.

"The old is gone," Creator said. "Behold, We make all things new."

Like a just-hatched butterfly, I exulted in my new form. I moved my arms and spun around. My joints didn't hurt. I felt light and free and energetic. This new body didn't create a sense of separateness as had my old body. I continued to experience the same euphoria of union with Creator as when I was disembodied. We were now knitted together for eternity, sharing in each other, rejoicing in each other, loving each other.

My soul filled to bursting. I voiced my awe and gratitude. "Creator, you are great in love, perfect in wisdom, awesome in power. To You I give everything I am and everything I have. I empty myself so You can fill me with Your being. Your being is everything to me. You fill me to overflowing with Your fullness. Everything You give, I return to You so as to honor You in all things. I love You, Creator."

"In love, you become complete," Creator said. "Our joy is made full because we are now one in spirit, one in heart, one in mind. Our love is fulfilled because you have learned to reciprocate the love you have received, allowing Us to enjoy the mature fruit of love given. You have learned to reflect Our nature so that in you we clearly see Ourselves. We take great joy in seeing Our image being made perfect in you."

As Creator spoke, I noticed the sky had no sun. Instead, Creator illuminated the world with the light of Their presence.

A new journey stretched out before me. My exploration of love had but skimmed its breadth and depth. I understood, now, why Creator had apportioned an eternity for this endeavor, because no finite span of time was adequate to delve into something so boundless as Their love.

The End

The three leaves of the flourish
at the top of every chapter
represents the triune Creator.

The plain, single stem at the bottom
represents Cherished's connection
to that divine relationship.

Further Steps

Review

If you enjoyed reading *Four in the Garden*,
please post a review at amazon.com or goodreads.com.

Discuss

Discussion questions are printed on the following
pages. For intensive group study spanning
multiple meetings, download free questions at
rickhocker.com/fourinthegarden/questions.html.

Subscribe

Subscribe to receive free inspirational articles at
rickhocker.com/subscribe.html.
Or subscribe to receive author updates at
rickhocker.com/join.html.

Follow

Follow the author at rickhocker.com/weblog
or facebook.com/RickHockerAuthor.

Questions and Topics for Reflection and Discussion

1. The theme of this book is that life can transform us if we trust. How did this book illustrate that theme? How do you define spiritual transformation? Why is it important?

2. This story is told in first person so readers would feel as if they were experiencing it firsthand. In what situations did you relate to Cherished?

3. What scene or section impacted you the most and why?

4. What elements of the Garden of Eden story did you find in this book? In what ways did the stories differ?

5. Although this book is classified as fantasy, the author wrote about spiritual realities he believed to be true. What elements in this story do you believe are true? What elements do you consider fictional?

6. At the beginning of this story, how did Cherished respond to the Teachers? To Creator? What role did each play in Cherished's development?

7. Cherished's misconceptions about Creator were corrected over the course of this story. Identify those misconceptions. Which misconceptions about God do people often have? Why are they common misconceptions?

8. How did Cherished's relationship with Creator change over time? What triggered those changes?

9. Radiance saw herself as unimportant in relation to her service to Creator. In what ways did Radiance change? How did she accomplish those changes? In what situations do you put service ahead of self-nurture? Does self-nurture enhance or hinder spirituality? Explain.

10. Blaze represented those who fail to trust and try to manage life on their own. Did you find it easy or difficult to sympathize with Blaze? In what ways did you identify with Blaze?

11. This story explored the tension between dependence and independence. What conclusions did this story make regarding free will and independence?

12. Creator's love was a constant in Cherished's life, but that love sometimes expressed itself as discipline or withdrawal. Give an example of loving discipline. Give an example of loving withdrawal or separation. Would God ever act this way toward people? Why or why not?

13. When Creator disciplined Cherished, did you view Creator as patient or punishing? Why? Discipline or separation implies pain. Does your view of God allow Him to act in a way that might cause you pain? Can love ever lead to pain? Explain.

14. Cherished's relationship with Creator was damaged multiple times because Cherished's ego often got in the way. How was the relationship healed in these situations? What was Creator's highest priority for Cherished? How did this priority determine Creator's response?

15. How did this story affect your relationship with God or your understanding of God? Which aspect of Creator did you have the hardest time accepting? Why?